# RE-CREATING NEIGHBORHOODS FOR SUCCESSFUL AGING

# RE-CREATING NEIGHBORHOODS FOR SUCCESSFUL AGING

Edited by

**Pauline S. Abbott, Ph.D.**
**Nancy Carman, M.A., C.M.C.**
**Jack Carman, FASLA**
**Bob Scarfo, Ph.D., M.L.A.**

Forewords by

Robert N. Butler, M.D.
Robert H. McNulty, J.D.

*HEALTH*
*PROFESSIONS*
*PRESS*

Baltimore • London • Sydney

**Health Professions Press, Inc.**
Post Office Box 10624
Baltimore, Maryland 21285-0624

www.healthpropress.com

Typeset by Karen Wenk.
Manufactured in the United States of America by Versa Press, Inc.,
East Peoria, Illinois.
Cover and interior designs by Mindy Dunn.

Library of Congress Cataloging-in-Publication Data

Re-creating neighborhoods for successful aging / edited by Pauline S. Abbott . . . [et al.].
    p. ; cm.
  Includes bibliographical references and index.
  ISBN 978-1-932529-24-1 (pbk.)
  1. Aging—Social aspects—United States. 2. Older people—Housing—United States.
3. Neighborhood planning—United States. I. Abbott, Pauline S.
  [DNLM: 1. Housing for the Elderly. 2. Aged. 3. Community Health Planning.
4. Environment Design. WT 30 R311 2009]

HQ1064.U5R372 2009
362.610973—dc22

                                                               2008039262

British Library of Cataloguing-in-Publication data
are available from the British Library.

# CONTENTS

# About the Editors

**Pauline S. Abbott, Ph.D.,** is the Director of the California State University Fullerton Institute of Gerontology and the Ruby Gerontology Center. Her research interests include life-long learning and strategies for teaching older adults; life review and reminiscence; caregiving issues; and spontaneous social networks examining successful strategies that older women are creating to combat loneliness in later age. She has presented this work at major conferences in the United States and internationally. Dr. Abbott is a past president of the California Council of Gerontology and Geriatrics and in that capacity has developed and testified at a number of hearings of the California State Senate and Assembly committees on aging/long-term care. Dr. Abbott was recognized as the Shining Star of Education for 2006 by WomanSage, and by the Red Cross Association in 2003 for her work in aging.

**Nancy Carman, M.A., C.M.C.,** is the Director of Marketing Services for New Life Management & Development, Inc., a national consulting firm that works with a variety of clients to develop, market, and manage continuing care retirement communities throughout the United States. With over 25 years in the field of aging, her wealth of experience includes the creation and promotion of a unique hospital-based geriatric care management program, extensive senior focus group and support group work, successful grant writing, the development of age-sensitive training programs, and consulting in the senior housing industry. She is a frequent speaker at state and national conferences addressing topics related to successful aging. A writer on important aging topics, for four years she wrote a monthly newspaper column, "Aging Well," for the *Courier Post* newspaper, which has a circulation throughout southern New Jersey and Philadelphia. For six years she served as a board member for the Delaware Valley Chapter of the Alzheimer's Association. She has a master's degree in gerontology from the University of South Florida in Tampa and is a certified geriatric care manager.

**Jack Carman, FASLA,** President of Design for Generations, LLC, is a landscape architect specializing in the design and development of therapeutic gardens and landscapes for senior communities and health care facilities. He actively works to promote the design and development of therapeutic gardens through speaking engagements, audio-conferences, and contributing to the publication of technical papers. He is founder of the Professional Practice Committee on Healthcare and Therapeutic Landscapes for the American Society of Landscape Architects.

**Bob Scarfo, Ph.D., M.L.A.,** received both a master of science degree in geography and a doctorate degree in social geography from Clark University in Worcester, Massachusetts. He also has a master's degree in landscape architecture from the University of Massachusetts. Dr. Scarfo is currently an associate professor of landscape architecture at the Interdisciplinary Design Institute at Washington State University–Spokane. He specializes in service learning projects that develop collaborative projects between diverse student and faculty groups and neighborhood organizations. Their focus on infill development aims to increase the potential of successful and productive aging while designing more sustainable, economically vital live, work, play, and learning environments.

# CONTRIBUTORS

Kerry R. Brooks, Ph.D.
Associate Professor, Department of
  Horticulture and Landscape
  Architecture
Interdisciplinary Design Institute
Washington State University
Phase One Building, Room 375
P.O. Box 1495
Spokane WA 99210-1495

Robert N. Butler, M.D.
President
International Longevity Center
60 E. 86th Street
New York, NY 10028

Edward Fox, A.I.C.P.
211 Lakeview Drive
Collingswood, NJ 08108

Laura Bauer Granberry, M.P.A.
Director of National Initiatives
Rosalynn Carter Institute for
  Caregiving
800 GSW University Drive
Americus, GA 31709

P. Annie Kirk, B.S.W., M.L.A.,
  A.S.L.A.
Director, Acer Institute LLC
Principal, Red Bird Design
P.O. Box 83
Aurora, OR 97002

Emi Kiyota, M.S., MArch,
  Ph.D. Candidate
Department of Architecture and
  Urban Planning
University of Wisconsin-Milwaukee
12913 Falling Water Circle, R. 302
Germantown, MD 20874

Frank R. Mandy, M.S.
New Life Management &
  Development, Inc.
20000 Horizon Way, Suite 700
Mount Laurel, NJ 08054

Robert H. McNulty, J.D.
President
Partners for Livable Communities
1429 21st Street N.W.
Washington, DC 20036

Angela C. Pappas, B.S., M.L.A.
AEC, Inc.
40 Sherington Place
Atlanta, GA 30350

# ACKNOWLEDGMENTS

Pauline Abbott captured the character of *Re-creating Neighborhoods for Successful Aging* and the people who made it possible when she said, "I would acknowledge the wisdom of colleagues who recognized the challenges we will all face as we age and who acted upon it with this book." Among those colleagues willing to open their minds to new and diverse collaborations we have to thank Scott A. Bass, Ph.D., Vice President for Research and Dean of the Graduate School at the University of Maryland, Baltimore County. In 2002 he entered into a dialogue with Bob Scarfo, a landscape architect, regarding the extent to which gerontological research on successful and productive aging considers the spatial implications of community and neighborhood character and content. In like fashion, as part of a speaking engagement at the Health Sciences department at Washington State University–Spokane, Dr. Robert Butler, President and CEO of the International Longevity Center, happily discussed with Dr. Scarfo the value of greater collaboration between the spatial professions and gerontological researchers and practitioners. We thank him for contributing one of the forewords for this book. Our gratitude also extends to Robert H. McNulty, President of Partners for Livable Communities, for helping to introduce *Re-creating Neighborhoods for Successful Aging* through his foreword, which presents a balanced introduction to aging in place, specifically the importance of healthy living and health services related to the built environments in which they are located.

In our journey from initial conversations to completed publication we were fortunate to find each other. Pauline Abbott, Jack Carman, Nancy Carman, and Bob Scarfo's willingness to join together was not new to us. Each of us had been working across professions in an effort to provide more comprehensive outcomes in each of our arenas of work. Our wish to extend our awareness of the values derived from gerontological and health care professionals working with environmental design and land planning professionals was accepted by the organizers of the 2004 Gerontological Society of America (GSA) annual conference. Our grateful thanks to those organizers who accepted our proposed educational session, "The Spatial Implications of Successful Aging." Their willingness to allow two landscape architects and two gerontologists to share their collaborative efforts with the GSA membership not only further validated our efforts, but also got us in front of Mary Magnus, Director of Publications at Health Professions Press (HPP).

Many thanks to Mary for questioning us about our ideas and their value to professions that often do not work together. We are also thankful for Mary pushing us to explain and verify the value of a potential publication that would inform a broad audience: gerontologists and health care and public health professionals and practitioners; architects, landscape architects, and land planners; and the faculty and students working in support of and feeding into the futures of each of those professions. HPP also provided us with our Production Manager, Cecilia González. To say she was our guardian angel would be an understatement. Cecilia's eye for detail and for questions not asked and answers not given kept us on track. Without her almost omniscient presence through emails and phone calls, and without her HPP cohorts and staff, we would not have completed this work.

Crossing professional boundaries can be a daunting exercise. Often we had to question the correctness of our thinking and the value of our dabbling in another's area of expertise. But like everyone noted above, our co-contributors were golden discoveries who were willing to allow and facilitate crossover. Our heartfelt thanks to each of the contributors for their hard work in writing insightful chapters that have resulted in a fine body of knowledge.

Our grateful appreciation to all those coworkers, teachers, students, and most of all family members who have supported our work as well as listened to and contributed to our thinking over the years.

And, finally, it must be noted that without Jack Carman's patience and endurance, this publication would not have been completed.

*Pauline Abbott*
*Jack Carman*
*Nancy Carman*
*Bob Scarfo*

# FOREWORD

In 2006, the first members of the cutting edge of the baby boom generation—the largest generation in U.S. history—reached 60, including former president Bill Clinton and President George W. Bush. Yet the baby boomers are not prepared for their own longevity, nor is society prepared for them. The boomers have not saved enough money for their retirement, built skills that might be necessary for the likelihood that they will have to work longer, maintained the best health habits, or carefully considered the kinds of living arrangements that will bring them the highest quality of life and the best ways to maintain their health. Society, meanwhile, has not supported the training of doctors to better care for older adults, provided sustained support to solve the problem of Alzheimer's disease and other forms of dementia, or created the variety of living arrangements that would best offer older persons a better quality of life.

*Re-creating Neighborhoods for Successful Aging* provides a collection of interesting and innovative ideas on how to transform senior living for an aging society. The intersection of the life cycle with the immediate physical environment and the medical perspective (that is, public health and health care) is a topic that is only now beginning to receive the attention required. This topic must be addressed for those who are fortunate enough to maintain robust health well into their later years as well as for those who may require long-term care.

The family in America and in most of the developed world has changed dramatically. More people are living alone and there are more blended families and greater geographic mobility. Thus we need to create an unrelated public family that provides social and physical support as well as networks of care when necessary.

We must focus on more than the finest of newly developed retirement communities, such as continuing care retirement communities, and focus also on better understanding the needs of those who are choosing more and more to "age in place" and whose concentrations in a community may reach a level that creates a new phenomenon called a naturally occurring retirement community or NORC. We must build upon housing and care alternatives in very special ways, including contributing to physical health and to the intellectual life by incorporating new opportunities to learn. Lifetime learning must be tied together with health and quality of life.

Partnerships that involve the entrepreneurial and business communities, nonprofits, and government are needed to carry out this agenda. A new home in the later years necessitates built-in provisions for health care, community life, and leisure. Where aging in place occurs, such necessities and amenities also must be incorporated. Finally, we need new models— new imaginative, entrepreneurially conceived elder housing alternatives that enrich the later years of life.

*Re-creating Neighborhoods for Successful Aging* addresses these and other quality-of-life issues that concern our aging population and the collaboration needed to make successful aging a reality.

*Robert N. Butler, M.D.*
President & CEO
International Longevity Center–USA
New York, NY

# FOREWORD

*Re-creating Neighborhoods for Successful Aging* is a landmark work at a particular time of need in our nation's community development. Partners for
Livable Communities, a nonprofit organization that works to improve the
livability of communities by promoting quality of life, economic development, and social equity, calls this issue "aging in place": the need to retrofit
and rethink community support not only for our growing senior population, but also for all those with special needs or disabilities.

We have a unique opportunity. The White House Conference on
Aging, held every decade, concluded in December 2005 with a banner of
"livable communities for all" held high. In the past, the White House Conference has dealt with special interests of the aging population as it relates
to health legislation. I believe we are entering into a new era where the
word *livability* implies a broader civic agenda. It implies coalition building
and rethinking our planning, housing, and urban strategies to remove the
barriers that inhibit full participation in life within our neighborhoods and
communities.

I believe the issue of caring for the older citizen is no longer a concern
for just the health community, but also for the broader civic community.
Partners for Livable Communities, which has been advancing this issue for
more than a decade, since 1994, is pleased that this publication can gather
together health concerns with community, planning, development, and
housing needs in creating a universal community—one that supports,
employs, and nurtures people of all ages, advantages, and disabilities.

In the last two decades we have seen a revival of "urbanism," a march
toward sustainable development, and a growing concern for "green" energy
and water conservation. Rarely have those "urban strategy" movements

encompassed a more influential ally for their future—the baby boomers, a population that votes with great regularity, is blessed with a great degree of wealth, and has the ability to support foundations and community causes. Boomers began turning 60 in 2006. From *The Wall Street Journal* special sections to reports on the national televised evening news, there is tremendous speculation about how boomers as they age will be different from any other generation in American history. They will work longer, live longer, have greater means, and be more civically and recreationally engaged. As a result, they will demand an entirely different type of "aging" strategy.

There is hope that this anticipated population wave will once and for all move the aging agenda away from the stereotype of a begrudging elder voter who is reluctant to pay taxes for schools to instead building a broader civic movement that combines retirement, work, and public involvement as a natural outcome of continuing to be an active part of the community.

This population will not tolerate being isolated by transportation, segregated by housing style, and marginalized by narrow interest, but instead will serve as a strong new voice for livable communities for all our citizens.

This book will make an important contribution, and I am pleased to be associated with it.

*Robert H. McNulty, J.D.*
President
Partners for Livable Communities
Washington, D.C.

# PREFACE

Senior living as we know it is changing. The new old, which currently comprises the incoming baby boom generation, are calling for a greater understanding of people's health, the behaviors they value, and the built environments that will welcome and support those behaviors. That realization, the blending of health and the built environment, is in its infancy. Yet, the collaboration we call for here, between the health-related and spatial professions of landscape architecture, architecture, and urban and rural town planning, cannot happen too soon. The importance of the interrelationships linking health and the built environment is reflected in the two forewords to this book, written by Robert Butler, M.D., and Robert McNulty, J.D., both highly regarded experts in their respective fields of medicine and architecture.

*Re-creating Neighborhoods for Successful Aging* is an outgrowth of a wish to stimulate greater collaboration among the medical, health, environmental, design, and planning professions. My own journey in this realm began with my father-in-law's stroke in 1999 and a subsequent series of events that led my wife and me to buy the house next door and move my parents-in-law to live there. They came from the rainy Pacific coast where even in the winter months my father-in-law got outdoors to walk every day. Once in Spokane, Washington, however, the snow and ice made him house bound. As a landscape architect and social geographer, I wondered about the pressures he was experiencing. As I shoveled their walkways, I wondered how changes to downtown Spokane's built environment might reduce those pressures and provide him with more readily available and vibrant daily activities.

In an effort to better understand what downtown Spokane might offer older residents, I immersed myself in what I now refer to as the more traditional literature on aging. After a year of reading about aging as it relates to the onset of one's loss of independence, I read two statistics. First, I read that in 2030 there would be about 72 million people 65 years old and older. Second, I found that at the time of my research 5% of the people over 65 were in home care and nursing care facilities. In 2008, that percentage is 4%. I couldn't believe it. I felt I had been tricked by the media. In 2000 the media had yet to recognize older Americans as vibrant, productive resources. The quantity of negative articles on older people left me (and, yes, I admit to displaying my ignorance) believing that 20% to 25% of older Americans were living in health care facilities. Four percent of 72 million? From the perspective of urban, suburban, and rural environments, I immediately asked what was going to happen with and in response to the other 96% (approximately 69 million) relatively healthy and economically and politically powerful people? Were our neighborhoods ready? Were our cities and towns ready? In an effort to answer those questions, I found Rowe and Kahn's *Successful Aging* (1998), then Freedman's *Prime Time: How Baby Boomers Will Revolutionize Retirement and Transform America* (1999), and Morrow-Howell, Hinterlong, and Sherrand's *Productive Aging: Concepts and Challenges* (2001). My awakening to the growing population of new old and the idea of active, productive older residents brought a whole new twist to my students' design work with neighborhoods.

My students and I, with the help of the nursing students under the tutelage of Cindy Corbett, Ph.D., began to explore infill scenarios for downtown Spokane that would lead to a higher quality of life for grandma and grandpa. Applied to urban and suburban settings, infill development makes use of empty spaces. Vacant or seemingly leftover pieces of land can be built upon to enhance a location's available retail shopping opportunities and professional service. Well-designed infill development makes a community more walkable and pedestrian friendly.

Over the next few years, I gathered about me books, national and regional surveys, and hundreds of articles related to healthy, active aging. My landscape architecture, architecture, and interior design students read selected articles. Their challenge was and still is to show how, through infill development, communities can prepare to take (in the best of ways) full advantage of the elder residents who are, to paraphrase Marc Freedman, our only growing natural resource.

Two important side notes need to be mentioned. First, I came to realize that too few successful and productive aging researchers were aware of the spatial form, content, and character of the built environment at the neighborhood level. The reciprocal was also true; too few land planners and designers had any understanding of the growing implications on their work of the baby boomers moving toward retirement. Second, I realized, and this is the greatly condensed version, that the same kind of built environment (pedestrian-friendly, mixed-use, high-density, intergenerational) contributes not only to healthy aging, but also to active living and energy and water conservation. These combined benefits, I realized, provide a basis on which to build a transdisciplinary research and design practice agenda.

With 30 years of landscape architecture behind me and a Ph.D. in social geography, I can't read anything without visualizing how it fits into or responds to the built environment. So when I first encountered the words *available, accessible,* and *environment* in the aging literature, I imagined built environments that dealt with the spatial questions of proximity: *Can I get there from here? Will I be safe? How long will it take? Are sidewalks set back from the street and shaded?* It was two years into my indoctrination into the literature on successful and productive aging, active living, and healthy aging when it dawned on me that the form and content of the *built environment* was not being discussed. I back tracked and reread what I felt were the more informative articles. The built environment was not there. Words like *access* and *available,* though used, meant only that a service or health care delivery system existed somewhere in a community. How one got to it, or even if one could get to it, was not considered. In some articles I even read the word *environment,* but as I worked to construct a gerontologist's definition of *environment,* I came to realize it could mean social environment, political environment, family environment, but almost never the kinds of built environments we know as neighborhood, downtown, village center, or suburbia. The built environments of everyday life were absent.

At that point I emailed Scott Bass. As the founding director of the University of Massachusetts–Boston doctoral program in gerontology, cofounder of the *Journal of Aging and Social Policy,* and author of numerous articles and books on successful aging, I felt sure he could help me. I explained I was a landscape architect with a limited background in the area of successful and productive aging. I told him that although I had read quite a few articles, surveys, and reports, I wondered if (1) I was missing a body of literature or (2) I was correct in realizing that little of the research and resulting literature recognized the character and content of the built environment. In October 2002, his email response read, "The field of productive aging is still in its infancy. Your question about land use and spatial considerations is right on the money. The work on productive aging has primarily involved the social and behavioral sciences, so what you will find will be written by economists, political scientists, sociologists, psychologists. Your suggestion for further inquiry [by the spatial professions] makes a great deal of sense to me."

Bass's response, in combination with my realization that similar built environments contributed to healthy aging, active living, obesity reduction, and energy and water savings, has since contributed to:

1. Workshops that bring together public health, medical, and nutrition experts with city and regional planners, architects, landscape architects, and rural town planners to realize and practice collaborative problem solving.
2. Six years of infill projects in and around Spokane with the assistance of the neighborhoods' residents.
3. A panel presentation at the Gerontological Society of America's Annual Conference in Washington, D.C.

The panel, "The Spatial Implications of Successful Aging," joined four diverse experts: Pauline S. Abbott, Ed.D., Director of the Institute of Gerontology and the Ruby Gerontology Center at California State University Fullerton; Jack Carman, landscape architect and President, Design for Generations, LLC, Medford, New Jersey; Nancy Carman, M.A., C.M.C., Director of Marketing Services with New Life Management & Development, Inc.; and Bob Scarfo, Ph.D., M.L.A., Associate Professor, Interdisciplinary Design Institute, Washington State University–Spokane. These individuals represented the study of gerontology, landscape architecture, care management, and spatial design.

The purpose of the panel, like that of this book, was to introduce the knowledge and practical skills of the spatial professions into the new gerontologists' work. Our goal was to bolster gerontologists' theoretical and conceptual thinking, expand the practical nature of their recommendations, and enhance the interdisciplinary exploration of ways to enrich the daily lives of older people. In other venues we have sought to contribute to environmental designers' and land planners' awareness of society's aging cohort and its emerging attitudes and changing needs. One result of that panel is the publication of *Re-creating Neighborhoods for Successful Aging*. The goal of this book is to demonstrate and encourage more collaborative endeavors that include older residents as well as transportation engineers, architects, land use planners and landscape architects as well as professionals in public health, health services, and medicine, to name a few, who will contribute to creative community-wide solutions that foster a better quality of life for everyone. It is the editors' belief that greater collaboration among health and built environment practitioners will promote increased opportunities for people of all ages to actively engage in their communities, expand their creativity, and develop spiritually.

*Bob Scarfo, Editor*

## REFERENCES

Freedman, M. (1999). *Prime time: How baby boomers will revolutionize retirement and transform America.* New York: Public Affairs.

Morrow-Howell, N., Hinterlong, J., & Sherrand, M. (Eds). (2001). *Productive aging: Concepts and challenges.* Baltimore: Johns Hopkins University Press.

Rowe, J., & Kahn, R. (1998). *Successful aging.* New York: Dell.

# SECTION I

# The World of Senior Living

LIFE IS SYNONYMOUS WITH CHANGE. Sometimes the changes are slow and sometimes they occur in a New York minute. The aging of the United States, and for that matter of the global population, is only one of several emerging trends that will soon influence how many people carry out their daily routines in their neighborhoods. People's routines are already changing. The near-retiree cohort is redefining *retirement*, *retiree*, *retirement community*, and, for that matter, *grandma* and *grandpa*. Preparing for the coming of age of baby boomers cannot be considered nor planned for in isolation. Rising energy costs due to oil depletion are impacting the costs of heating and cooling homes and businesses, commuting routines, as well as food production, processing, and shipping, to name just a few effects. Health issues associated with obesity and Type 2 diabetes are not only influencing individual well-being, community and business health care costs, and employee and student absenteeism, but also community policies and planning practices and their subsequent design outcomes. It has become apparent that suburban sprawl contributes to weight gain, whereas pedestrian-friendly environments contribute to healthier people. Daily life in many neighborhoods is being redefined by a need to downsize. These trends are each first-time-ever events. Each is contributing to what will come to be known as daily life, active living, and healthy aging. Space, in terms of the form, content, and character of neighborhoods, is in need of greater consideration in the research and literature on aging. That research, its interpretation and practical applications, calls for greater collaboration at each stage along the theory–practice spectrum.

The attitudes and activities associated with retirement, retirees, and retirement communities are also being redefined. Shifts in the three are readily seen in Del Webb's *Baby Boomer Survey* throughout the 1990s and the 21st century. People's attitudes, values, and behaviors are changing, as well as the built environments to which they are being drawn. Given the boomers' increased longevity and their sheer numbers, their history of influencing changes in landscapes, architecture, social systems, and institutions as their cohort has aged is not about to slow down. Being idle is no longer their image of a retiree. Decade by decade, the boomers have caused massive changes in schools and schooling, in the numbers and kinds of advanced degrees in higher education, in housing and recreation, and in industries and technologies. Their intellect and innovative spirit have pushed the envelope in communications, space travel, medicine, aeronautics, film making, and more. Their ideologies have challenged presidents and politics. Now, with so many baby boomers at the brink of retirement, society must recognize and acknowledge that boomers will apply the same energy, inquisitiveness, and innovation to their retirement.

Baby boomers' tendency away from idleness and toward action aimed at bettering communities is evident in a growing number of studies. A 2001 study conducted by the Fannie Mae Foundation and the Brookings Institution Center on Urban and Metropolitan Policy Census found that 18 out of 24 downtowns saw increases in their populations. The authors identified one of the contributing factors as the influx of empty nesters, people no longer responsible for dependent children. This growing restlessness is reinforced in the 2003 Del Webb *Baby Boomer Survey,* which reported that 59% of those surveyed said they would move into a new residence in retirement. In the 1999 survey, only 31% of respondents, age 48 to 52 at the time, said that they planned to move to another residence for retirement. The influence of boomers on existing and proposed communities is noted in the MetLife Foundation/Civic Ventures New Face of Work Survey:

> This new survey of Americans aged 50 to 70 finds that they do not expect to, or want to, put their feet up and not work at all in retirement . . . Fully half of all adults age 50 to 70 (50%) say they are interested in taking jobs now or in the future to help improve the quality of life in their

communities. Leading edge baby boomers are especially interested, with 6 in 10 (58%) indicating they would consider taking jobs now or in the future that would serve their communities. (Civic Ventures, 2005, p. 6)

According to Rosabeth Moss Kanter, Professor of Business Administration at the Harvard Business School,

> Someday soon, going to a university at [age] 50 or 60 could be the norm. Someday, every major university will have graduate schools designed specifically for accomplished professionals who want to make the transition from their primary income-earning careers to their years of flexible service. Someday, corporations will include tuition for these schools in retirement packages and will support scholarships through their foundations. Someday, the federal government will offer tuition grants and tax breaks for attending universities after 50, to support new forms of philanthropy and public service that truly solve problems. (Kanter, 2006)

The American Association of Retired Persons is already offering its Loan to Learn program, which allows members to borrow anywhere between $2,000 and $50,000 a year for all education-related expenses up to $250,000.

The ability to age in place is developing a wrinkle. Although over 50% of those approaching retirement say that they wish to age in place, they plan to move one last time. The two main attractors are an urban setting with diverse opportunities or near a university. The communities and campuses to which older adults will relocate will need to change. Communities with good mass transit, readily accessible goods and services, diverse recreational opportunities, and built environments that foster and sustain social connectivity will attract the aging cohort's energy, entrepreneurial and innovative spirit, and financial and political clout.

---

Architects and interior designers have given and continue to give buildings and their interiors the design attention needed for the benefit of older people. Universal design relates to "inclusive" design. Although the goal of universal design is to make goods, services, and environments useable by many people, the principles of universal design are often applied to the interior of houses and stop at the exterior wall when they should extend into the community. Growing old is as much a process of maintaining one's daily activities in the home as throughout the greater community. In Chapter 1, A History of Long-Term Care in the United States, Nancy Carman brings to light the challenges that elders have faced over the centuries in various familial, state, and public and private institutional settings. Early on, multi- and intergenerational care settings were not an issue. Elders often remained with and were cared for by the family. Over time, responsibility for their care shifted, from almshouses to private nursing houses, to rest homes and convalescent homes, and, more recently, to continuing care retirement communities and assisted living residences. Latent in the progression of caregiving settings has been a change in attitudes and perceptions among older adults regarding where and how they will live. Older adults have become increasingly more involved in the planning and design of long-term care settings, which has resulted in the emergence of a variety of retirement-housing options in the United States today.

In Chapter 2, Public Health and the Built Environment, Pauline Abbott discusses the effects of housing and land-use patterns on mental and physical health and the growing impacts on older adults, many of whom would prefer to age in place. The built environment in which boomers have reached adulthood, raised families, and become empty nesters is characterized by automobile-dependent suburban sprawl that soon may not allow boomers to comfortably and safely live out their later years. Older Americans will face serious challenges in the very automobile-dependent suburban environments they so passionately sought and cherished.

Social connectivity is critical to longevity and aging in place. If social interactions are primarily dependent on the use of an automobile, they will be lost to many older adults who can no longer drive. Life in the suburbs, in the homogeneous regions of sprawling houses separated from retail outlets, recreation, health care, and friends and family, will require changes in community and land-use planning and zoning. Denser, mixed-use community settings will contribute to greater social connectivity, provide more opportunities for walking as an integral part of daily life, and lower the cost of living by decreasing or eliminating the use of a car (now costing about $8,600 a year to own and maintain). Abbott asserts in her conclusion that, "City planners, public health departments, architects, designers, builders, elected officials, and all others who are involved in shaping the built environment must realize and understand their roles as guardians of the future" (p. 31). They must consider and plan for long-term livability factors, which can best be achieved by accessing the growing resources at hand on the impacts of community design on the health and quality of life of older adults who want to age in place.

French philosopher Henri Lefebvre's idea that space is a social product gets to the heart of Chapter 3, Geographic Information Systems. Kerry

Brooks and Bob Scarfo focus on the fact that social space, while often ignored, can be made visible and in so doing can illuminate critical aspects of the relationship between health and the built environment. An early example of the visualization of social space was demonstrated in London in 1854 when Dr. John Snow and Reverend Henry Whitehead mapped the incidents of cholera they treated. By making the cholera epidemic visible, Dr. Snow's map reinforced his belief that the deaths were related to the neighborhood's drinking source, its public well (Johnson, 2006). Today geographic information systems software (GIS) makes the mapping of the invisible, visible.

As Graham Rowles aptly demonstrated in *Prisoners of Space* (1978), one's surroundings contribute to the personal and social aspects of aging. It is the diversity of those aspects that can be mapped via GIS technology as a means of "seeing" their interrelationships. GIS technology also provides ways to visualize the social equality that exists or does not exist in a community, specifically the extent to which the built environment supports access to health care systems, goods, services, recreation, and education.

Access and availability are integral to successful and productive aging and both can be made visible through GIS technology. Together, public heath and city and urban planners can use GIS technology to identify the extent to which a community can contribute to successful aging and healthy aging in place.

Landscape architects have for some time promoted the idea that green environments contribute to healthier living. Their argument has gained evidence-based support wtith the growing involvement of the health sciences in discussions about the effects of the built environment on health. To this growing body of information, Angela Pappas contributes a foundation for Nature-Related Contact for Healthy Communities in Chapter 4 that begins "as far back as Paleolithic times" (p. 53). Even with such a long history, the restorative benefits of nature are often overlooked in the design of communities. That may be changing, she argues, with the growing body of research related to health and the built environment. Pappas reviews four theories that each support the recuperative powers of green environments: biophilia; cognitive, content and spatial perception; psycho-evolutionary; and human environmental value. From calming children with attention-deficit/hyperactivity disorder to extending people's lives to supporting the psychological well-being of people, creating restorative and revitalizing properties of green environments will require greater collaboration across the environmental design, health care, and medical health professions for the benefit of the ill, the aging, and the greater general public. Healthy people contribute to healthier communities and vice versa.

## REFERENCES

Civic Ventures. (2005). *New face of work survey.* Retrieved January 2008, from http://www.civicventures.org/publications/surveys/new-face-of-work.cfm.

Del Webb. (2004). *Del Webb baby boomer survey: Empty nester syndrome.* Retrieved June 2007, from http://www.pulte.com/pressroom/2004BabyBoomer/BabyBoomerDetailReport.pdf.

Johnson, S. (2006). *The ghost map: The story of London's most terrifying epidemic—and how it changed science, cities, and the modern world.* New York: Riverhead Books.

Kanter, R. M. (2006). Back to college. *AARP The Magazine.* Retrieved January 2008, from http://www.aarpmagazine.org/lifestyle/back_to_college.html.

Lefebvre, H. (1991). *The production of space.* Cambridge, MA: Blackwell.

Rowles, G. (1978). *Prisoners of space?: Exploring the geographical experience of older people.* Boulder, CO: Westview.

1
_____

# A History of Long-Term
# Care in the United States

*Nancy Carman*

The famous author Pearl S. Buck once very wisely said, "One faces the future with one's past." What we do now in navigating through the existing long-term care system, while at the same time planning ahead to make it better, is greatly influenced by what has been done historically. This chapter puts together the historical pieces in order to have a better understanding of where the long-term care industry has been and where it needs to go in the future.

With the advent of baby boomers reaching retirement age, the need for long-term care will not simply increase but grow significantly. The Centers for Medicare and Medicaid Services has estimated that in 2006 there were approximately 9 million individuals age 65 or older needing long-term care in the United States. Looking forward to 2020, an estimated 12 million seniors will need long-term care (U.S. Department of Health and Human Services, 2007). The 1994 *Columbia Retirement Handbook* defines *long-term care* as

> The medical and social support services needed by people whose capacity for independently performing the activities of daily living is impaired, according to recognized or approved standards, for a prolonged period of time by a chronic illness or deteriorating condition. Long-term care may be provided at home, in the community, or in a nursing home (at the level of custodial, intermediate, or skilled care). (Mering, 1996, p. 259)

Historically, long-term care was neither defined nor provided according to this description. Looking back to the mid-1700s, there were not many individuals age 60 or older in the United States, as very few lived to a ripe old age. In fact, people over the age of 60 made up less than 2% of the general population (Fleming et al., 2003). The average life span at this time was between 30 to 40 years (Sussman, 1995). Moreover, because the journey to America was perilous and life on the new continent was difficult, few elderly people gave thought to making the trip from England or other parts of Europe (ElderWeb, 2006). For those who made the journey successfully or who lived into old age, security in old age meant having many children and/or property. Until the mid-nineteenth century, it was common for a woman to give birth to her last offspring near the age of 40. This and the promise of a larger portion of the estate ensured that an unmarried child would remain in the family home to take care of the elderly parent(s). (Haber & Gratton, 1994). At that time families were large and, because there were no railroads or automobiles to enable them to leave the fold, children stayed near home. Before 1800, less than 5% of the population in America lived in cities. Most resided in rural areas where large, extended families could live inexpensively. Families typically cared for other family members. Able-bodied elderly women with no immediate kin who owned property often became the proprietor of a boarding home for elders (Haber & Gratton, 1994). Those who had no children, such as aging bachelors and spinsters, found themselves at a great disadvantage and had to align themselves with a family to receive long-term care. The only other option was to hire a helper to function as a surrogate family caregiver. Children were expected to care for their aged parents or to pay for others to provide the needed care (ElderWeb, 2006). Some adult children, wishing to avoid the time and cost of providing direct care, chose to board elderly parents in the homes of others (Haber & Gratton, 1994).

Those elderly people who had no family to provide care and who were poor resorted to taking charity or were at the mercy of public welfare. Towns and villages had informal arrangements for the impoverished older adults without family assistance who needed care. Food, care, and fuel were brought to the person's home; however, if hands-on care was required, the elder was taken in by another household and that household was reimbursed by the municipality for the care that was rendered (Kaffenberger, 2000). Recipients of public welfare had to demonstrate that they were not transients and lazy, but rather inhabitants of the community and worthy of assistance (Haber & Gratton, 1994).

Although slave traders did not bring elderly slaves to America, any slaves who lived into old age were dependent on their master's charity for care. Because slave families were routinely separated, care by a family member was the exception rather than the rule. Some slave owners emancipated their slaves when they became old and unable to care for themselves (Fleming et al., 2003). Many states banned the freeing of slaves age 40 or older for fear that the state would have to care for elderly slaves (Fleming et al., 2003).

## ELDERCARE AND PUBLIC AND PRIVATE WELFARE (1700s–1800s)

In eighteenth and nineteenth century America the public welfare system was one that was patterned after the English poor laws (ElderWeb, 2006). Initially the poor were given a cord of wood, an allotment of food, or modest cash payouts called "outdoor relief," which was funded by city or county taxpayers. As more and more money was required, local governments, seeking to come up with a less costly alternative, created a system of generic "indoor relief" that consisted of facilities in which the poor had to reside in order to receive assistance. Funding for these facilities came through community taxation, private fees, and charitable giving (Kane et al., 1998). These impersonal institutional facilities were owned and operated by counties, cities, or states, and each community had one. They were called poorhouses, almshouses, workhouses, poor farms, county infirmaries, asylums, and county homes (ElderWeb, 2006).

Almshouses were only required to care for those residing in their jurisdiction, and the town decided whom they would help and how much help would be provided. As a result, there were bands of homeless, elderly indigent people who went from facility to facility looking for a place to live (ElderWeb, 2006). Boston, Massachusetts, was home to the first almshouse in 1664 (Haber & Gratton, 1994). In 1865, Massachusetts reported that the average age of an almshouse resident was just under 50, indicating that most were elderly (Kaffenberger, 2000). Older adults considering a move to an almshouse had to prove that they were impoverished and that their children were either unwilling or unable to care for them (ElderWeb, 2006). A few states continued to board the poor with local farmers and even pay their own families to care for them. The state of Tennessee actually auctioned care of the impoverished to the lowest bidder (ElderWeb, 2006).

Existence in an almshouse was made as unattractive as possible to prevent the "woodwork effect" (i.e., many people falsely identifying themselves as impoverished in order to get free care at the expense of community taxpayers) and as a way to encourage families to take care of their elder relatives. There was also a deep-seated fear among officials that almshouse residents would become lazy and dependent (Haber & Gratton, 1994). Residents were called inmates and had to wear a uniform. Almshouses were located out of sight in the countryside and residents were not allowed to leave (ElderWeb, 2006). All residents were expected to earn their keep (e.g., older, frail women were required to do sewing), and it was not unusual for the poor elderly to reside in the same room as petty criminals, alcoholics, orphans, unwed mothers, or people with mental illness (Elder-Web, 2006). Poor, frail, and elderly almshouse residents were terrified and often were injured by residents who were criminals and alcoholics. Because of these adverse conditions, the woodwork effect was avoided. Ending up in the abhorred almshouse became the residence of last resort and every older adult's worst nightmare.

A limited alternative was available only to "respectable" elderly women of a certain faith who were residing in specific communities in the form of private rest homes, Charitable Homes for the Aged, and Mutual Aid Societies run by Christian and Jewish denominations along with fraternal orders, benevolent societies, and Scottish and African-American communities (Schulz, 2006). One of the nation's first old-age homes, Philadelphia's Indigent Widows' and Single Women's Society, was founded in 1817 (Haber & Gratton, 1994).

The early American nursing home first appeared in private homes during the beginning of the nineteenth century and typically housed 16 to 18 people. Unlike modern nursing homes, where residents receive around-the-clock skilled nursing care and rehabilitation, these were in reality board-and-care homes. The shelter and services provided were questionable, depending on the charity of the owner, and nursing care was provided by nurses who visited the older adults living in the homes (Schulz, 2006).

Around 1865, after the Civil War, specialized institutions were created to house former almshouse occupants. Orphanages were created to house orphans, mental institutions were established for individuals with mental illness, and special schools were formed for persons with physical disabilities (Schulz, 2006). Elderly people, however, remained in almshouses, which over time were transformed into facilities strictly for the poor elderly (Holstein & Cole, 1996).

The structure of the American family was also changing. At the beginning of the nineteenth century, land in outlying areas saw more settlers and consequently became more valuable. Fathers, who had traditionally subdivided their land to give parcels of it to their children to farm to keep them near the family homestead, were limited as to how many times they could subdivide their property. As a result, there was less and less land to go around. More and more children left home to travel west to find land or to a large city where they could find work. Thus, the geographically scattered American family had its beginning (ElderWeb, 2006).

Adding to the dispersal of younger family members, the 1869 transcontinental railroad was completed, which enabled East Coast dwellers to travel to the West Coast. Land in the West was cheap, sold by the railroads to encourage relocation and by the federal government to encourage development of the western states. The Homestead Act of 1862 was passed and gave American citizens the opportunity to claim 160 acres of unoccupied land in "public dominion states." This included states outside of the original 13 colonies. Few families brought frail elders on the difficult journey west, leaving them in the care of the local government (ElderWeb, 2006).

With families traveling to the West Coast in search of cheap land and prosperity, the almshouse population exploded in the early 1800s. Their conditions continued to be horrific and often they were run by unscrupulous individuals who did as little as possible for the government money they received. Almshouses were also becoming more and more expensive for local governments to finance. With increasingly squalid conditions, nonexistent care, and escalating costs, a number of states in the mid-1800s (Massachusetts, New York, Rhode Island, Pennsylvania, Illinois, Ohio, Michigan, Wisconsin, and Kansas) created state-run "boards of charities" to oversee operations of the almshouses (ElderWeb, 2006). As a result, conditions improved and, as mentioned previously, specialty institutions were created for populations previously lumped together in the almshouse. In fact, in 1845 Congress gave states public land to construct facilities for the indigent insane, many of whom were elderly and had "senile dementia" (ElderWeb, 2006). Almshouses eventually gained improved status as an appropriate place to care for the sick elderly (Holstein & Cole, 1996).

In response to a growing need during the mid-1800s, not-for-profit organizations established old-age homes. Poor elderly people now had an alternative to the dreaded almshouse. Hundreds of benevolent and fraternal organizations that were established by wealthy benefactors, such as the

Irish Benevolent Society, the Hebrew Benevolent Society, Odd Fellows, the Masons, and the Knights of Columbus, created voluntary old-age assistance programs and old-age homes. Other old-age homes were run by religious denominations for the specific purpose of caring for elderly missionaries or poor church members (ElderWeb, 2006). An underlying desire to "rescue" the U.S.–born elderly from the immigrant-filled almshouse also fueled the creation of the private old-age home (Haber & Gratton, 1994). Most of the not-for-profit organizations, however, were concerned with the "worthiness" of the elderly people who were seeking assistance. An individual's work history and record of thrift were considered measures of whether or not he or she was worthy of help (Holstein & Cole, 1996).

In contrast to the lowly almshouse, old-age homes were almost luxurious. Some were newly constructed, while others were converted from old stately mansions. Residents were still called inmates, had to ask permission to leave the property, and were expected to do chores and work to bring in money. Some old-age homes required the resident to pay an up-front fee and to turn over any income, assets, or pension to the facility for the guarantee of lifelong room, board, and care. Many years later this concept evolved into what is now known as "Lifecare" (ElderWeb, 2006).

Like nursing homes, hospitals had their roots in the poorhouse system. The modern hospital structure was created in the mid-1800s. Many poorhouses became poorhouse hospitals and continued to receive state and local funding. Private hospitals emerged where no poorhouse hospitals existed and took the available government funding. At the same time, the federal government built hospitals with attached homes to provide long-term care for disabled soldiers and sailors who were veterans of the Civil War (ElderWeb, 2006).

During the mid-1800s, people who were chronically ill and who had family or other means of support were still cared for at home. In the late nineteenth century, trained nurses were available and were primarily hired by wealthy families as live-in caregivers or as private-duty nurses for their elderly family members. Another alternative to institutionalization in urban areas were early home-care agencies whose visiting nurses would go into the homes of the chronically ill poor. One of the earliest of these agencies was the Visiting Nurse Society of New York, established in 1893. These agencies were supported financially by societies of wealthy women who took an interest in public works. Rest houses and convalescent homes also became part of the long-term care housing mix. Rooms within these privately owned residences were typically rented out to nonindigent elderly individuals (ElderWeb, 2006).

During the nineteenth century, planned retirement communities became a part of the long-term care system in the United States. William Enston Home in Charleston, South Carolina, was one of the earliest planned retirement communities. It featured 24 two-story brick residential cottages, a community building, an infirmary, an engine house, a water tower, an entrance gate, and spacious landscaped grounds. In order to become a resident, seniors had to be "old" (age 45 to 75) and sick, but without any accompanying mental illness. The Sailors' Snug Harbor community for old seamen was another planned retirement community. Built in 1833 in Staten Island, New York, and operated until the late 1960s, the community was situated on a 130-acre campus and featured dormitories, dining rooms, workrooms, barns, a dairy, a hospital and sanitarium, a bakery and snack bar, a laundry, a library, a Vaudeville house, a church and chapel, gardens, and a greenhouse, much like a present-day continuing care retirement community (ElderWeb, 2006).

A few employers provided retirement housing for their employees. One example was the George Lobdell House located in Minquadale, Delaware, which had been a summer estate that was remodeled around 1891 as a retirement home for Lobdell's employees. Later it became known as the Minquadale Home for the Aged (ElderWeb, 2006).

## GOVERNMENT FUNDING OF LONG-TERM CARE (1900s)

During the twentieth century, long-term care underwent tremendous changes. Elders were living longer and there were more of them. After World War I, health officials realized that acute care hospitals were costly and inappropriate for those needing long-term care as a result of chronic illnesses (Shultz, 2006). Although almshouses were becoming more respectable, in the early twentieth century there were over 1,000 private homes for the aged in the United States (Mering, 1996). Aside from almshouses, the private, not-for-profit sector had become the biggest supplier of nursing home facilities (Kaffenberger, 2000).

The growing labor movement's resistance to giving tax support to almshouses, along with the financially crippling effect of the Great Depression beginning with the Wall Street crash of 1929, made affordable long-term care scarce. The first old-age assistance law was passed in 1915 (Kaffenberger, 2000), and even though it took effect throughout many states by the 1930s (approximately 28 states and 2 territories), the funding of long-term care was very restricted and inconsistent. Even benevolent societies and charities, feeling the growing economic burden of providing long-term care for more and more seniors, started looking to the government to pay for care (ElderWeb, 2006).

Enacted by President Franklin Roosevelt, the Social Security Act of 1935 had two major programs. Title I was called Old-Age Assistance (now known as the Medicaid program) and was seen by many as the beginning of the long-term care system (Sultz & Young, 1999). Funding was a 50/50 match by state and federal government. Individual states determined individual eligibility and cash payments or "pensions" were given to poor seniors, regardless of their work history. Title II of the Social Security Act was called Old-Age Insurance (now known as Social Security). A pool of funds, which was established through contributions by workers and employers, became available beginning in 1940 (ElderWeb, 2006).

Title I Old-Age Assistance benefits were designed to encourage poor elderly people to remain in their own or a family member's home for long-term care (a cheaper alternative). This, along with the long-standing issues of almshouses, led the government to decide that cash benefits would be paid to an individual residing in his or her own home or a private home for the elderly but not to a person residing in a public facility such as an almshouse (Schulz, 2006). The provision of the Social Security Act was a direct attempt to eliminate the almshouse institution (Haber & Gratton, 1994). Because of the dramatic decrease in government funding to public institutions, the existence of almshouses declined drastically after 1935 (ElderWeb, 2006).

## THE EVOLUTION OF THE NURSING HOME

The lack of long-term care funding to public institutions enabled the proprietary and voluntary nursing home industry to take hold (Kaffenberger, 2000). Old-age assistance payouts were meager; however, the poor elderly, with cash in hand and unable to live alone, became a desirable commodity. Although cash was scarce, large private homes were not, and a cottage industry emerged of mom-and-pop residences that boarded poor elders in unused rooms (ElderWeb, 2006). Some of these board-and-care homes were run by unemployed nurses who provided basic care. From this care setting came the term *nursing home*. Homes such as these were under the supervision of community physicians, clergymen, and businessmen (Kaffenberger, 2000). Although they met a growing need for long-term care of the poor, these community nursing homes were largely unregulated and uninspected (Schulz, 2006).

After World War II, from 1930 to 1960, public nursing homes fared poorly due to a lack of government funding. Voluntary or not-for-profit homes held their own, but it was the commercial or for-profit nursing homes that proliferated (Holstein & Cole, 1996). This was due in large part to an amendment to the Social Security Act in 1950 that allowed nursing home operators to contract directly with states for payment of long-term care. In addition, the dollar cap on payments to nursing homes was eliminated in 1956; thus, the nursing home business became very attractive to entrepreneurs (Holstein & Cole, 1996). Hundreds of hotels, large private homes, and old buildings were converted into nursing homes (ElderWeb, 2006).

It was largely recognized that the development and construction of long-term care facilities had gone dormant because of World War II. The nation's health care infrastructure was desperately in need of replacement. In 1946 Congress passed the Hospital Survey and Construction Act, commonly known as the Hill-Burton Act, which helped finance not-for-profit hospital expansion. These federal government construction grants were expanded to include public and not-for-profit nursing home participation beginning in 1954 (ElderWeb, 2006). The actual disbursement of these monies was delayed due to the lobbying efforts of the for-profit nursing home industry (Kaffenberger, 2000). Monies were provided for public and not-for-profit hospitals, who repaid the government loan by providing free care to the indigent. Many old hospitals that were replaced by new hospitals became nursing homes. Although in a minority, nursing homes that were recipients of Hill-Burton construction monies were required to become affiliated with an acute care hospital. The federal government, unfamiliar with long-term care, needed construction standards and turned to the hospital model for nursing home design. With the same design standards, construction, and staffing levels as the hospital model, it is no wonder that nursing homes built under the Hill-Burton Act resembled miniature hospitals (Kane et al., 1998).

With the need for nursing home beds still on the rise following World War II, a 1950 amendment to the Social Security Act allowed the few remaining almshouses that housed poor elderly people to receive funds through the Older Americans Act and through Old Age Insurance to become public nursing homes (Holstein & Cole, 1996). In an attempt to regulate a fast-growing industry, the federal government in 1953, under the 1950 Social Security Act, required states that received federal matching monies for long-term care to create systems to license both hospitals and nursing homes. Until then, only hospitals receiving Hill-Burton Act monies had to be state licensed (ElderWeb, 2006). In addition, nursing homes receiving federal monies officially became the stepchild of the hospital system, as they were now required to become affiliated with a hospital (Holstein & Cole, 1996). Although licensing had become required, no standards of enforcement were implemented. Nursing home regulators overlooked licensing noncompliance for fear that the much-needed beds would disappear and that costs would escalate if standards were enforced (Holstein & Cole, 1996).

At the same time, for-profit nursing homes, which were still ineligible for Hill-Burton Act monies, lobbied Congress and received government-sponsored Small Business Administration and Federal Housing Administration construction loans that covered 90% of their construction costs (Kaffenberger, 2000). Not-for-profit organizations were also eligible for the construction loans, but declined the opportunity to behave like for-profit businesses (Kaffenberger, 2000). As a result, for-profit nursing homes proliferated.

The first national inventory of nursing homes was done in 1954. There were four classifications of long-term care homes: nursing care homes, personal care with nursing homes, personal care homes (akin to what is now called assisted living), and domiciliary care homes (board-and-care homes). There were 270,000 residents living in 9,000 homes. Of these, 86% were for-profit, 10% were not-for-profit, and 4% were publicly owned (ElderWeb, 2006).

After the passage of Medicare and Medicaid in 1965, long-term health care increasingly became seen as the proverbial pot of gold, and thousands of nursing homes were built by developers. Along with the growth of an aging population and the need for a higher level of health care, the enactment of Medicare reimbursement became one of the greatest incentives of the private nursing home industry (Haber & Gratton, 1994). One of the nation's largest nursing home chains, Beverly Enterprises, expanded rapidly in the state of California. Even companies alien to the business of health care built nursing homes. Holiday Inn, for example, formed a nursing home subsidiary, Medicenters of America (Kaffenberger, 2000).

With little or no regulation and oversight by the government, nursing home construction quality was poor and profits were high. Medicaid covered all of the owner's capital construction costs, and if the nursing home changed hands, Medicaid would reimburse the new owner's capital costs at the new higher value. Thus, in the 1960s and 1970s it was common for ownership of nursing homes to change several times and for the homes to be built and sold far above construction costs before the first resident moved in (Goldberg, 1995). Federal and state oversight was nonexistent as the nursing home business flourished. There were no federal standards for design or operation, and nursing homes were not required to be licensed. Many buildings were unsafe and potential firetraps (ElderWeb, 2006). With no quality control, actual nursing care was minimal and allegations of abuse and neglect were commonplace.

In 1965, Medicare under Title 18, which reimbursed for short-term rehabilitation care, and Medicaid under Title 19, which reimbursed for long-term care, still had not addressed standards of care in the nursing home setting (Schulz, 2006). Under Medicaid, there was no cap on federal matching payments to states for long-term care. Nursing home benefits were virtually open ended, with no dollar limits or time limits on length of care (Kaffenberger, 2000). As a result, states began to transfer patients from state-supported institutions, such as mental hospitals, to nursing homes in order to take advantage of federal payments (Holstein & Cole, 1996). This added to the need for more nursing home beds, with the number of beds increasing from 460,000 in the early 1960s to 1.1 million by the end of the decade (Fleming et al., 2003).

During the 1980s the federal government gave the Institute of Medicine of the National Academy of Sciences the task of reporting on the condition of the nation's nursing homes and of recommending steps to be taken to improve them (Kaffenberger, 2000). They looked at 14,500 nursing homes with 1.48 million beds across the country and by and large found that the quality of care in most nursing homes was deplorable. As a result of these findings, the Omnibus Budget Reconciliation Act of 1987 (OBRA), also called the Nursing Home Reform Law, was enacted. It required all nursing homes to post and enforce resident rights, to adhere to minimum nursing staffing ratios, to institute an interdisciplinary care team approach, to use a Resident Assessment Instrument, and to complete a Minimum Data Set (MDS) on each resident. The MDS, which is still in use, required comprehensive care planning and outcome norms. As a uniform resident assessment tool, the MDS was to be used as an initial baseline for care planning and thereafter at designated intervals for resident reassessment. In addition, OBRA required the monitoring of physical and chemical restraints, the compulsory training and certification of nurse assistants, and a resident-centered quality-of-care survey (Schulz, 2006).

By 1999 there were approximately 18,000 nursing homes with 1.9 million Medicare- or Medicaid-certified beds (Schulz, 2006). By then the 1991 federal Patient Self-Determination Act (PSDA) had been instituted within the nursing home setting. The PSDA gives nursing home residents the right to create an advance directive identifying what type of medical care they do or do not want in the event they are not able to communicate their wishes to staff. Special care units also emerged in the nursing home setting. These could take the form of subacute care units that provided Medicare-covered skilled rehabilitation, dementia care units, ventilator units, traumatic brain injury units, hospice units, oncology units, and AIDS/HIV units (Schulz, 2006).

The Balanced Budget Act of 1997 imposed an overall financial cap on Medicare payments to nursing homes as well as on payments for physical therapy and other paid services that up to that point had assured the profitability of the nursing home industry. These changes in government reimbursement had a severe negative economic impact on the nursing home industry. As the cost of long-term care continued to rise and the public continued to observe problems with quality care, there was an accelerated demand for an alternative to the unsatisfactory, welfare-driven system (Smith, 2003).

## MODERN HOUSING ALTERNATIVES

Even in the heyday of nursing homes, care of older adults by family members in their homes has been the norm. However, consumer awareness, rising need, and other factors have been leading elders who need long-term care to seek options other than care by a family member. In just one generation, lower birth rates in the United States have led to smaller families and hence to fewer caregiving children. Increased life expectancy has led to more living generations, and aging adult children need care themselves, in addition to their aging parents. Additionally, increasing numbers of women have entered the workforce, leaving a gap in in-home caregiving (Montgomery, 1999). Consumers seeking care services, however, are questioning the value of nursing home care and its high cost and are demanding privacy, choice, control, and autonomy in the long-term care setting (Goldberg, 1995).

Today, the most familiar formal long-term care settings, other than the nursing home, are what are known as continuing care retirement communities (CCRC) and assisted living residences. A CCRC is defined by the American Association of Homes and Services for the Aging (AAHSA) as

> A habitat that offers a full range of housing, residential services, and health care to serve its older residents as their needs change over time. This continuum consists of housing where residents live independently and receive certain residential services, such as meals, activities, house-keeping, and maintenance; support services for disabled residents who require assistance with activities of daily living; and health care service for those who become temporarily ill or who require long-term care. (Mering, 1996, p. 259)

As an integrated long-term care network, a CCRC is the most complete model of long-term care in America (Schulz, 2006). Located on one campus, a CCRC offers the services and amenities of a fine hotel, the care of an assisted living residence and nursing home, the social and recreational activities of a club, the benefits of long-term care insurance coverage, and the convenience of a small town (Schulz, 2006). Although the CCRC concept has been around since the 1970's, 80% of all CCRCs are said to have been built in the 1980s. In 1990 there were an estimated 800 CCRCs in the United States, housing around 230,000 elderly residents. In 2000, it was estimated that the number of CCRCs had increased to 1,500, housing roughly 450,000 seniors (Holstein & Cole, 1996). As of 2007, the American Association of Homes and Services for the Aging (AAHSA) estimates that there are 2,240 CCRCs in the United States housing approximately 745,000 older adults (AAHSA, 2008).

The assisted living residence initially evolved in the late 1970s and early 1980s as a sophisticated board-and-care setting. Initially these residences were a product of studies of European elderly housing, and care models and construction was privately financed. Typically a rental product, assisted living has been and continues to be primarily for the private-paying resident (Brummett, 1997). The Assisted Living Federation of America defines *assisted living* as the long-term care option that combines housing, support services, and health care, as needed. Seniors who choose assisted living enjoy an independent lifestyle with assistance customized to meet their needs as well as benefits that enrich their lives and promote well-being and family connectedness. Communities typically offer dining as well as social and wellness activities designed to support a well-rounded lifestyle (Assisted Living Federation of America, 2006). A 2000 national survey of assisted living residences by Hawes, Phillips, and Rose found that the average resident was age 85 and that 79% were women. Of those, 99% were Caucasian and their average length of stay was 2.5 to 3 years (Wright, 2004). One of the big differences from CCRCs is that a resident may have to move from an assisted living residence if the individual's health and independence decline to the point that his or her needs exceed the services of the facility.

There is no federal government oversight, and each state handles assisted living differently. Not all states require assisted living licensing, and enforcement varies from state to state even in those that do. By 2006, 41 states and the District of Columbia had adopted the term *assisted living*, defining it very narrowly (Oregon and New Jersey) or very broadly (Florida and North Carolina), and only 29 states and the District of Columbia had incorporated assisted living licensing (Hernandez, 2006).

According to the American Association of Retired Persons, most assisted living settings include the following: 24-hour supervision, house-keeping, meal preparation, and assistance with activities of daily living, while also meeting the resident's scheduled and unscheduled needs in a home-like environment (Wright, 2004).

One of the best-known assisted living residence for-profit chains is Sunrise Senior Living. Headquartered in Reston, Virginia, Sunrise was founded by Paul and Terri Klaussen. The assisted living concept was familiar to Paul Klaussen, as both his maternal and paternal grandmothers had resided in assisted living–like homes in Holland. As of 2006, responding to consumer need and demand, Sunrise Senior Living operated more than 420 senior communities in the United States, Canada, Germany, and the United Kingdom (Sunrise Senior Living, 2006).

The growth of assisted living residences has been unprecedented since the late 1970s. In 2004 there were 36,000 licensed assisted living facilities in the United States caring for more than 9 million residents (Hernandez, 2006). Occupancy in 2006 was at about 95%, and demand for this style of supportive living is on the increase (McKnight's, 2006). Typically assisted living is paid for privately, but on a limited basis about 41 states and the District of Columbia use Medicaid dollars to purchase assisted living care for qualified individuals needing long-term care in an assisted living setting (Hernandez, 2006).

During the early 1990s the building frenzy of long-term care retirement communities slowed. Irresponsible practices of banks and other lending institutions, coupled with the fact that many people who entered the senior-housing industry did not understand it, created huge problems. Large nursing home chains sold off portions of their holdings, and major retirement community developers were forced to file for bankruptcy (Keslosky & Stevens, 1999). Once again, the sheer number of frail older adults saved the day. The senior-housing industry rebounded in the mid-1990s as a result of increasing consumer need, and assisted living soon became the "darling" of investors and developers (Gordon, 1998).

Today there are a variety of long-term retirement-housing options in the United States. From age-restricted, active-adult retirement communities, to senior living communities, to assisted living residences, to nursing homes, to CCRCs, we can be assured that the senior-living marketplace will continue to evolve to meet the needs of future savvy senior consumers.

## REFERENCES

American Association of Homes and Services for the Aging. (2008). Aging services: The facts. Retrieved January 2008, from www.aahsa.org/aging_services.

Assisted Living Federation of America. (2006). About assisted living. Retrieved June 2006, from http://alfa.org/i4a/pages/index.cfm?pageid=3285.

Brummett, W. (1997). *The essence of home: Design solutions for assisted living housing.* New York: Van Nostrand Reinhold.

ElderWeb. (2006). History of long-term care. Retrieved December 2006, from www.elderweb.com/history.

Fleming, K. C., Evans, J. M., & Chutka, D. S. (2003). A cultural and economic history of old age in america. *Mayo Clinic Proceedings*, Symposium on Geriatrics. Available at http://www.mayoclinicproceedings.com/inside.asp?AID=384& UID=6388, 200678:914–921.

Goldberg, S. L. (1995). Where *have* nursing homes been: Where are they going? *Generations: Journal of the American Society on Aging*, Winter 1995/1996 [Supportive Housing for an Aging Society], 79.

Gordon, P. A. (1998). *Seniors' housing and care facilities: Development, business and operations* (3rd ed.). Washington, DC: Urban Land Institute.

Haber, C., & Gratton, B. (1994). Old age and the search for security: An American social history. Bloomington: Indiana University Press.

Hernandez, M. (2006). Assisted living in all of its guises. *Generations: Journal of the American Society on Aging*, Winter 2005/2006 [Supportive Housing for an Aging Society], 18–19.

Holstein, M., & Cole, T. R. (1996). The evolution of long-term care in America. In R. H. Binstock, L. E. Cluff, & O. von Mering (Eds.), *The future of long-term care: Social and policy issues* (chapter 2). Baltimore: John Hopkins University Press.

Kaffenberger, K. R. (2000). Nursing home ownership: An historical analysis. *Journal of Aging and Social Policy, 12*(1), 35–48.

Kane, R., Kane, R., & Ladd, R. (1998). *The heart of long-term care.* New York: Oxford University Press.

Keslosky, M. A., & Stevens, G. L. (1999). *Assisted living industry: An industry overview and performance analysis of public firms.* Lancaster, PA: Franklin and Marshall College.

McKnight's. (2006). Long-term care news (daily update). Retrieved June, 2006, from http://www.mcKnightsonline.com.

Mering, O. von. (1996). The evolution of long-term care in america. In R. H. Binstock, L. E. Cluff, & O. von Mering (Eds.), *The future of long-term care: Social and policy issues* (chapter 12). Baltimore: John Hopkins University Press.

Montgomery, R. J. V. (1999). Family role in the context of long-term care. *Journal of Aging and Health, 11*(3), 402–403.

Regnier, V. (2002). *Design for assisted living: Guidelines for housing the physically and mentally frail.* Indianapolis, IN: Wiley.

Schulz, R. (2006). *The encyclopedia of aging* (4th ed.). New York: Springer.

Schwarz, B., & Brent, R. (1999). *Aging, autonomy and architecture: Advances in assisted living.* Baltimore: Johns Hopkins University Press.

Smith, D. B. (2003). *Reinventing care: Assisted living in New York City.* Nashville, TN: Vanderbilt University Press.

Sultz, H. A., & Young, K. M. (1999). *Health care USA: Understanding its organization and delivery* (2nd ed.). New York: Aspen.

Sunrise Senior Living. (2006). About Sunrise Senior Living. Retrieved December, 2006, from www.sunriseseniorliving.com/about/AboutSunrise.do.

Sussman, S. W. (1995). *The encyclopedia of aging* (2nd ed.). New York: Springer.

U.S. Department of Health and Human Services. (2007). Retrieved December, 2007, from www.medicare.gov/LongTermCare.Static/Home.asp.

Wright, B. (2004). Assisted living in the United States. Retrieved October 2006, from http://www.aarp.org/research/housing-mobility/assistedliving/.

# 2

# PUBLIC HEALTH AND THE BUILT ENVIRONMENT

*Pauline Abbott*

IN 2030, 72 MILLION BABY BOOMERS will be age 65 or older, twice the number in 2000. It is well known that most people would prefer to age in place in their community (Lawler, 2001). However, some will voluntarily decide to relocate, while others will need additional support services and require a move to a more sheltered environment. Wherever life takes them, the impact on society, the environment, and daily existence will be significant. It is important to take a serious look at the environment that has been created during the last century. Is it adequate to support this aging cohort? Is it what is needed? And is it the best it can be?

## BACKGROUND

The *built environment* is all around—homes, stores, roads, and businesses. Where one lives can significantly impact one's physical and mental health. At the turn of the 20th century, communities were designed with business centers that were within walking distance from housing, an arrangement that is fondly looked back on as the "village" concept.

As cities began to fill up with the demand for manpower in industries, inventions in transportation provided alternatives to walking, and paved roads began to crisscross towns. This allowed more access to areas in the outer environments of the built area, and so began the seeds of urban sprawl. Towns and villages became so closely linked that it was hard to determine where one ended and the other began, which resulted in new living environments that were designed at the farthest outskirts. Convenience centers with mini-malls were created, but by then it was far easier to use the car to access them than to walk. At the same time, cities continued to grow to heights never before imagined, and, like the canopy of the rain forest, another world developed within this skyward reach that differed from the ground below, which became the domain of the not so fortunate. While daytime at street level contained the bustle of workers, automobiles, and eateries, the scene changed as night fell and became the domain of the poor, out of work, disenfranchised, and addicted. In contrast, the corporate world expanded and thrived in this upward environment, with the development of penthouses and high-end living milieus.

A serious price has been paid for expansion, invention, and development, however. Land-use changes have created losses in the natural environment, and water resources and quality have declined (Dearry, 2004; U.S. Environmental Protection Agency, 1992). The changing landscape has been scarred and water-runoff patterns have been seriously affected, creating the need for concrete drainage channels and other artificial methods to divert and protect the built environment. To compensate, parks and recreational areas have been fashioned to appeal to the human need for light, space, and natural surroundings (Evans, 2003). People then bring with them into those environs inventions and toys. Anywhere the road goes, people go too, and beyond, further expanding the changes to the natural landscape.

Not all changes are negative, and the manner in which society has improved the quality of life for the masses is a tremendous feat. Indoor plumbing alone and the treatment of human waste have significantly contributed to improved health factors. Drinking water purification systems have made major impacts on quality of life, as have improved hygiene and concerns for the public health and welfare. The built environment has facilitated growth from the industrial age to the technological age, producing the greatest changes in both human activity and the physical environment over the shortest time in history. These factors, in combination with groundbreaking medical research, have added significantly to human longevity, allowing more children to reach adulthood and more adults to survive longer. The post–World War II boom of children born between 1946 and 1964 poses a unique phenomenon as these "boomers" now evolve into their late-life years. Having had the luxury of being born in an era that nurtured survival, the baby boom generation will come of age in 2011 as they begin to turn 65 at the rate of one every three minutes over 18 years.

## IMPACT OF THE BUILT ENVIRONMENT

Today there are large numbers of future older adults who are living in an environment that has been handcrafted to meet their current live, work, and play desires and needs. In other words, individuals live, work, and play differently and at various times in their lives, and what functions well for youthful endeavors may not appeal equally to older abilities. The choice of automobile, for example, is determined partially by life stage and by economic feasibility; the choice of living space depends on the size of a family unit or single dwelling and whether the choice is based on expansion or downsizing; and the choice of play site depends on access and interest (e.g., park playgrounds, water recreation with boats, snow-related venues, golf courses, arboreta, cyber cafés, mega-shopping complexes). These choices are further segmented by gender, age, ethnicity, economics, physical and cognitive ability, and culture. For example, with respect to individuals with disabilities, special amenities have been incorporated into many facilities to accommodate disability access.

Research into the impact that changes to the built environment have made on public health has come from many sectors, and there is no shortage of concern about the negative impacts that continue to bombard society as the unintended consequences of the quest to maximize various lifestyles. While more studies are needed to establish definite cause and effect, it is recognized that poor designs of the built environment that increase traffic and cause air and water pollution have also been associated with a rise in chronic diseases, such as asthma, obesity, diabetes, and depression (American Institute of Architects, 2003). Traffic congestion patterns increase commute times and impact behavior, creating new phenomena, such as road rage. The poor and disenfranchised segments of the population are more vulnerable in circumstances in which environmental justice and the built environment intersect (Frumkin, 2005). Disparities in the built environment for the privileged versus the underprivileged can be seen in access to housing, health care, education, transportation, food, parks, and green space. For example, fewer resources and food choice options are available in lower-income neighborhoods, where members of minority groups disproportionately live. Junk food, soda, alcohol, and cigarettes are readily available in small, local inner-city markets, but fresh foods are expensive and limited, which ultimately impacts diet and health (Frumkin, 2005). In contrast, the opportunities for healthy food choices increase measurably in higher income neighborhoods, which traditionally have larger supermarkets as well as gourmet food markets (Dearry, 2004).

One of the most widely addressed issues has been the link between the built environment and obesity. Frank and Pivo (1995) found that communities that are less densely developed have more vehicle travel and less walking and biking than more densely developed communities (Dearry, 2004). Frank, Andresen, and Schmid (2004) reported that the likelihood of obesity increases with the time spent per day in a car. Trinidad (2005) found that from 1982 to 2000 the hours spent in traffic annually per person in urban areas increased from 16 to 62. In contrast, it was found that obesity declines with increases in mixed land use (Frank et al., 2004), suggesting that when people have an opportunity to live, work, and play in a closer proximity, they are more likely to walk or take the time to participate in activities that facilitate movement. This supports the trend toward the live–work concepts that are currently being integrated into many inner-city redevelopment projects, with retail on the ground level, offices above, and residences on the top floors.

There is also a balancing effort that must be considered regarding mixed-use communities. The type and quality of a neighborhood and of housing have been linked to mental health concerns (Evans, 2003). The Centers for Disease Control (CDC) in May 2004 called for changes to building and planning codes to favor environments that would allow people to connect with others and that would encourage exercise. "We need sidewalks, bike routes, and a variety of housing types," according to Richard Jackson CDC advisor. The Web site Medical News Today in 2004 noted that state and federal funding have not matched the rhetoric. However, on April 4, 2006, U.S. Senator Barack Obama and Representative Hilda L. Solis introduced a bill in Congress to address the built environment's health effects, such as diabetes, obesity, and asthma, on the nation's children (U.S. Newswire, 2006). The announcement coincided with National Public Health Week (April 3–9), which is organized by the American Public Health Association. The bill would be implemented through the Healthy Places Act and would help states and local communities by establishing health impact assessments, interagency work groups that would focus on environmental health, and a grant program that would address environmental health hazards as well as provide additional support for research. The bill, however, never became law.

Concern for the public good is well founded and responses are widespread. The Society for Medical Anthropology created a Web site that includes research tools, discussion, and publications that address the complex and multiple issues of health disparities and the built environment (Society for Medical Anthropology, 2006).

Eggleston (2003) called for further research into the health effects of the built environment and suggested that community planning should include public health professionals, the community, and civic leaders. The National Association of County and City Health Officials (NACCHO) and the American Planning Association provide a variety of fact sheets on public health with respect to land use planning and community design. The importance of communication is underscored and addressed through a "jargon fact sheet," which demonstrates that for progress to be made, a universal understanding of terminology must exist across all agencies and personnel.

NACCHO also has created and made available a useful Land Use Public Health Collaborations Flowchart that outlines recommended planning steps and strategies that take public health issues into consideration. There is also a Walkability Resource List that includes a worksheet that can be used to determine community walkability, or how easy it is to walk in a community, and that offers recommendations to improve walkability (Robert Wood Johnson Foundation, 2006).

The National Institute of Environmental Health Sciences, Division of Research Coordination, Planning, and Translation notes on its Web site that education outreach is a key mechanism for increasing awareness of the link between the environment and human health. The site provides suggestions and resources for enhancing public awareness (Schmidt, 1998, 2004).

## THE SENIOR ISSUE

The older one gets, the greater the likelihood of developing a health-related condition that is chronic in nature. He et al. (2005) found that half of all older adults have at least two or more chronic health problems and that up to 80% have at least one. In dealing with the challenges of disability, functional or cognitive, significant limitations are placed on the capacity of the older adult to negotiate the environment. There is some optimism that the boomer cohort, which is better educated, healthier, and generally wealthier than prior generations, may remain independent and engaged over a longer period of time. Comparison data show, however, that this is not true for all, particularly for African-American women living alone, as well as for their Hispanic counterparts (He et al., 2005).

Historical records show that environmental changes are made according to opportunities, particularly where there is an economic incentive. Howe (2001) points out that "through land use planning and regulations, public investments, private financing, and dominant societal values, we have created communities that present significant obstacles to the continued independence of older adults," noting in particular that the housing stock of single-family homes favors healthy households with higher incomes. Affordable housing alternatives are being pushed toward less desirable environments that are even more transportation dependent. Even those who felt secure in their homes are being threatened with new liberal interpretations of eminent domain, in which local jurisdictions are authorizing higher tax-based, multiple-occupancy buildings to replace single residences in order to reap increased community income.

Mobile home community parks have filled a significant housing and social network role, but are continuously challenged by the economic pressure of alternative land use. The recreational vehicle, once the domain of the wealthier retiree for leisure travel, is being adapted by some as a primary dwelling for the "full-timer" as an economic alternative to home ownership or renting, and as a means to stretch the retirement income to accommodate an anticipated longer life.

Economic conditions may require many boomers to remain in the workforce longer. The built environment will have a significant impact on the ability of elders to maintain independent function with respect to such factors as transportation, home-to-work distance, and individual mobility in both the home and at work. Those for whom the challenges of independent function are too great will be forced to make alternative choices. Hence the development of retirement living communities where the leisure lifestyle is promoted, and the senior-care industry for assisted and protected living, and home modifications to secure residences for aging in place.

The concept of universal design has been promoted as a best practice for new construction to adapt home use throughout the various stages of life. Universal design is barrier-free, accessible design that helps everyone, not just people with disabilities, and takes appearance as well as function into consideration. Examples of universal design include doorways that are wide enough for wheelchairs as well as strollers, designer-styled bathtub grab bars that can help older adults as well as children and expectant mothers, and level entry ways or ramps for walkers, wheelchairs, and strollers. Some cities, such as Brea, California, have developed preferred building strategies that require elements of universal design to be incorporated by developers in new construction as well as senior-friendly considerations in new home developments. In 2004, however, the National Institute on Disability and Rehabilitation Research examined whether to discontinue granting research funds for universal design development.

Concern for the independent functioning of future seniors has been growing. The bias toward the automobile in the United States has contributed to environments that are especially unsafe for pedestrians (Howe, 2001). Once seniors lose the ability to drive, alternative transportation options open to them are limited, particularly if they are physically unable to meet current public transportation expectations. Even if they are able to find bus routes or voluntary driver programs, there are reservation limitations and time constraints. If a senior needs to walk to work, a business, or to a health care facility, most likely it will not be possible or safe to do so.

The American Public Health Association's 131st Annual Meeting in 2003 followed the Environmental Protection Agency's national agenda on the environment and aging. The goals of the agenda are to (1) prioritize and study environmental health threats to older persons; (2) examine the effect that a rapidly growing aging population might have on the environment; (3) encourage older persons to volunteer in their own communities to reduce hazards and protect the environment. Michael and Cunningham (2003) presented their work in measuring the impact of the built environment on physical activity among seniors. They developed an audit instrument to comprehensively assess the built environment in ten communities in Portland, Oregon. The Senior Walking Environmental Assessment Tool (SWEAT) measured each community's walkability factor. Several studies have shown that physical activity is essential for older adults in maintaining overall well-being and independence. A pedestrian-unfriendly environment significantly deters the quality of life of an older adult and can have a negative impact on health factors.

This is particularly relevant when looking at the senior housing demographic. According to data from the 1999 American Housing Survey, homeownership for Americans over the age of 65 was close to 80% nationally, with the majority of seniors living in suburban areas. The majority of renters were found in central cities. Differences arise, however, when regions are compared around the country. The survey found that boomers (those between the ages of 45 and 54) overall had nearly a 75% owner rate and a 25% renter rate, again with regional differences (Lawler, 2001). It is difficult to project what the boomers will actually do. It can be surmised, however, that some will elect to age in place, which will require home-modification alternatives and services, as at least half of the current disabled senior population has already done. Some will decide to move to other locations, some will downsize, and some will move in with family. Those who have used their homes as a retirement investment strategy are likely to seek an alternative lower-cost accommodation or innovative financing restructures, such as a reverse mortgage annuity. Government-funded housing options, which are predicated on income, already have waiting lists that will continue to grow in the future. What can be assured is that the existent built environment will require adaptations to be safe and user-friendly for tomorrow's seniors.

City planners, developers, public health officials, and architects must consider long-term livability factors. One significant resource contribution has been developed by the Gerontology Research Centre at Simon Fraser University. A compendium of Activities in the Built Environment includes books; reports; journal articles; book chapters; conference proceedings; newspaper, newsletter, and magazine articles; book reviews; conference papers and posters; and materials in electronic format (Gerontology Research Centre, 2007).

## CONCLUSION

The built environment has a significant impact on physical and mental public health. The ramifications of life choices for where one lives, works, and plays directly affect one's immediate environment, the expanded environment, and the health of fellow and surrounding community members. Research clearly demonstrates a link between lifestyle and health. A strong argument is developing that links the built environment and its unanticipated consequences on the public health. Of special concern are the impacts on disenfranchised populations, including those with special needs and those of disadvantaged socioeconomic status.

There are warning signs that should be heeded as boomers age. There is a growing body of knowledge and information about how one ages, what physical and social support is needed as one ages, and how to optimize the resources at hand for the best use. Terms such as *universal design*, *best practices*, and *model programs* are touted as the right way, but they are often not necessarily the most economical, cost-effective, or profit-enhancing options in a specific area.

City planners, public health departments, architects, designers, builders, elected officials, and all others who are involved in shaping the built environment must realize and understand their roles as guardians of the future. It is a charge not to be taken lightly. The built environment must be closely examined. Is what currently exists adequate to support the aging cohort? Is what exists what is needed? And is what exists the best it can be?

## REFERENCES

American Institute of Architects. (2003). Public health and the built environment. Retrieved July 2006, from http://www.aia.org/liv_TP_health.

Dearry, A. (2004). Impacts of our built environment on public health. *Environmental Health Perspectives, 112*(11), A600–A601.

Dorfman, S. (2004). Exploring the built environment. Retrieved June 2006, from www.medscape.com/viewarticle/489023.

Eggleston, M. (2003, Winter). Built environments. *The practice connection,* University of Pittsburgh Graduate School of Public Health, Center for Public Health Practice.

Evans, G. W. (2003). A multimethodological analysis of cumulative risk and allostatic load among rural children. *Developmental Psychology, 39,* 924–933.

Frank, L., Andresen, M., & Schmid, T. (2004). Obesity relationships with community design, physical activity, and time spent in cars. *American Journal of Preventive Medicine, 27*(2), 87–96. Available at www.act-trans.ubc.ca/documents/ajpm-aug04.pdf.

Frank, L., & Pivo, G. (1995). Impacts of mixed use and density on utilization of three modes of travel: Single-occupant vehicle, transit, and walking. Transportation Research Record no. 1466, Issues in Land Use and Transportation Planning, Models, and Applications.

Frumkin, H. (2005). Health, equity, and the built environment. *Environmental Health Perspectives, 113*(5), A290–291.

Gerontology Research Centre. (2007, July). Aging and the built environment. Vancouver, British Columbia: Simon Fraser University at Harbour Centre.

He, W., Sengupta, M., Velkoff, V. A., & DeBarros, K. A. (2005). *65+ in the United States: 2005.* Current Population Reports, pp. 23–209. Washington, DC: U.S. Government Printing Office.

Howe, D. (2001, December). Aging and smart growth: Building aging-sensitive communities. Funders' Network for Smart Growth and Livable Communities and Grantmakers in Aging, Translation Paper no. 7.

Lawler, K. (2001, October). Aging in place: Coordinating housing and health care provision for America's growing elderly population. Joint Center for Housing Studies of Harvard University, Neighborhood Reinvestment Corporation.

Medical News Today. (2004, May 17). Designing our environment to improve our health. Retrieved July 2006, from http://www.medical newstoday.com/medicalnews.php?newsid=8371.

Michael, Y., & Cunningham, G. (2003). Measuring the impact of the built environment on physical activity among seniors. American Public Health Association 131st Annual Meeting, November 15–19, abstract no. 59788.

Robert Wood Johnson Foundation. (2006). How walkable is your community? Retrieved July 2006, from http://www.rwjf.org/files/newsroom/ interactives/walkability/walk_app.html.

Schmidt, C. (1998). The specter of sprawl. *Environmental Health Perspectives, 106*(6), A274–A279. Available at ehponline.org/docs/1998/106-6/ focus-abs.htm.

Schmidt, C. (2004). Sprawl: The new manifest destiny? *Environmental Health Perspectives, 112*(11), A620–A627. Available at ehponline .org/docs/2004/112-11/focus-abs.htm.

Trinidad, S. (2005). The built environment and public health. The Congressional Hispanic Caucus Institute Fact Sheet.

Society for Medical Anthropology. (2006). Academic Resources: topical resources: health disparities and the built environment. Retrieved July 2006, from http://www.medanthro.net/academic/topical/built.html.

U.S. Environmental Protection Agency. (1992). Environmental impacts of storm water discharges: A national profile. EPA 841-R-92-001. Washington, DC: U.S. Environmental Protection Agency.

U.S. Newswire. (2006). American public health association: Bill introduced to address health effects of built environment as part of agenda to improve children's health. Retrieved July 2006, from http://www .redorbit.com/news/health/457443/apha_bill_introduced_to_address_ health_effects_of_built_environment/index.html.

3

# GEOGRAPHIC INFORMATION SYSTEMS
## Health and Aging as a Spatial Construct

*Kerry R. Brooks and Bob Scarfo*

KNOWING THE DEMOGRAPHIC COMPOSITION of a clinic or exercise facility (such as the YWCA) is one thing. Mapping and seeing where the user population lives in relationship to the clinic or exercise facility is another. Thinking spatially brings a new understanding of access to health care systems and the degree to which they are available to potential user groups. The geographic aspects of location, the distance from point A to point B, and the modes and quality of travel between locations contribute valuable insights to understanding access to or the availability of goods or services. When a greater comprehension of an issue or problem is achieved through considering its spatial aspects (e.g., a disabled population's ability to access and use a community's mass transportation system), it highlights the value of having health care, land planning, and design professionals working together. Before a discussion on building such collaborations, the following sections will define what geographic information systems (GIS) are and identify their potential for contributing to understanding and solving issues related to aging.

## WHAT ARE GEOGRAPHIC INFORMATION SYSTEMS?

Any textbook on the subject of GIS will invariably include several definitions of GIS. Kennedy (2006) defines GIS as a computer software program designed to make a computer think it is a map. In its emphasis on function, this definition subsumes some of the more typical ones that emphasize the capabilities that a GIS must have in order to make a computer act like a map. A typical definition (c.f., Aronoff, 1989) characterizes GIS as a "toolkit" of hardware and software capabilities for manipulating spatial data (e.g., locations, distances between locations, area coverage of a cohort, land use). To the spatial data, other data referred to as *attributes* can be added (e.g., density of cohort, geographic orientation, physical characteristics, character of larger setting). The generic GIS toolkit includes hardware and software tools that support data input, data management and query, data analysis and manipulation, and data output. In software implementations there typically exist many tools in each of these generic categories, such that the total number of tools can range from hundreds to thousands.

Another defining characteristic of GIS subsumed under Kennedy's functional emphasis is that GIS can represent and use spatial relationships (e.g., the location of a health care facility in relation to the people it serves, which may in turn be in relation to local bus routes) (Cowen, 1988). The capability of GIS to function like a map is a key feature lacking in other types of software that may graphically display map data but not allow manipulation or use of spatial relationships. An equally important aspect of GIS is a supporting infrastructure of knowledgeable users. As in any other technological endeavor, having the tools at hand is not enough. Successful and correct use of the tools requires knowledgeable analysts, who in turn depend on supportive organizations.

### GIS SOFTWARE

The first mention of GIS occurred in the literature in the mid-1960s (Foresman, 1998), but massive growth in GIS technology began only in 1980 with the introduction of super-minicomputers (Johnston et al., 2000). Today, GIS is applied in many markets, including business, natural resources, human services, and defense. This is not surprising, considering that 80% of all data have a spatial component.

GIS software tools underlie all of these applications. GIS software often includes large sets of tools, and developers may select, enhance, and bundle certain tools to serve a particular application need or vertical market. Large, often complex GIS toolsets are available as commercial software. The latest innovations are capitalizing on new data sources from Web mapping services, such as MapQuest and Google Earth, and from the instantaneous locating capabilities supported by the GPS (Global Positioning System) satellite network, available even in cell phones. Several low-cost or free GIS software packages also exist.

## GIS DATA: REPRESENTING THE REAL WORLD

On paper maps, the real world is represented by a consistent set of features that are symbolized in ways denoted in a legend. As with any model of reality, a level of abstraction has taken place. In digital GIS, the archetypical paper map is further abstracted or deconstructed. That is, in comparison to the same features on a paper map, each feature is individually entered into the computer (or *digitized*) as a feature class (see Figure 3.1). Each feature is typically referred to as a *layer* or *theme*. In fact, to re-create the look of an original paper map on the computer screen, themes are usually *stacked* so that the point or linear features are layered over the more continuous or area-extensive features.

As with paper maps, all GIS data represent real-world features as one of the following generic feature types:

- Points in space (e.g., home addresses, bus stops, doctors' offices, city and county offices, spas, entertainment)
- Lines (e.g., roads, sidewalks, paths through parks, walkways in courtyards, hallways in healthcare buildings)
- Polygons or areas (e.g., neighborhoods, census tracts, parks and park systems)
- Surfaces or volumes (land elevations, accessibility surfaces).

Note that a single real-world feature may be represented by more than one data type. For example, even the largest city is likely to be represented on a global map as a point, but its boundaries may also be represented as an area for more localized applications. In GIS, the locations of these features are recorded in real-world coordinates and are coregistered with one another in their correct spatial relation to each other. Locations of objects, areas of activities, or grouped attributes may be interrelated and those interrelations may be measured.

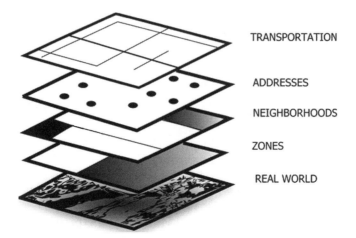

TRANSPORTATION

ADDRESSES

NEIGHBORHOODS

ZONES

REAL WORLD

**Figure 3.1.** Thematic map layers abstracted from the "real world" with features represented as points, lines, or areas. (*Source:* Adapted from http://www.fpa.nifc.gov/Library/Documentation/FPA_PM_ Reference_Information/Output/images/gis_layers.jpg)

## GIS DATA TYPES

GIS data are one of two major types: raster and vector. *Raster data* is also referred to as *grid data* or *cell data*. The data consist of a matrix of cells that are referenced by row and column location and stored in the computer as an array. In this data model, the cells represent a given area on the ground (e.g., 10 square meters). The number in each cell represents that area's value on the subject or theme being mapped (e.g., soil type). A type of raster data commonly employed is digital elevation data (see Figure 3.2). Aerial and satellite imagery are also raster data. With regard to active living, areas may be coded to portray a landscape's percent of slope or social-interaction potential.

*Vector data* represent points, lines, and areas by tracing and recording locations or boundaries as X and Y coordinates. Figure 3.3 illustrates the strings of vertices that make up one polygon in a GIS map feature. Innovations in modern GIS technology allow any one vector feature (e.g., a single road segment) to be linked to an integrated database table so that the non-spatial world of data tables can be applied to geographic representations of real-world features to create useful *data attributes*. For example, a point representation of a town might contain several attributes that describe the town as a whole—the state in which the town is located, the town's population, the number of housing units, and so forth. This example is illus-

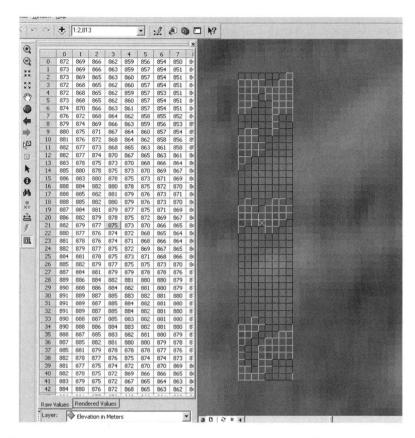

**Figure 3.2.** Raster data. In raster data ground phenomenon are represented by a matrix of numbers where the values stored in cells represent a characteristic of interest for a specific area. Grid size (or resolution) describes how much ground is covered by each cell (e.g., 30 meters). In this example, a grid of 10-m cells represents elevation above sea level. On the right, a graphic displays outlines of the cells, which are also displayed using a color scheme that represents the underlying values. The actual data stored in the outlined cells is shown in the matrix on the left of the figure.

trated in Figure 3.4, where the attribute for one of several towns on the map is highlighted.

## USING GIS TO VISUALIZE SPATIAL DATA AND EXPAND HUMAN CAPABILITIES

Modern GIS employ computers. Therefore, all of the features that in general make computers useful apply as well to GIS. Many of the advances in computing, from faster processors, to inexpensive large storage devices, to

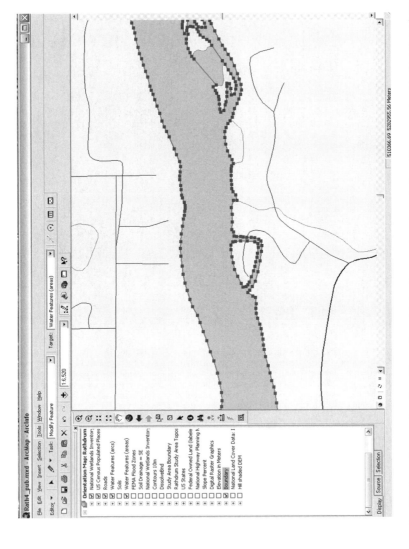

**Figure 3.3.** Vector data. This figure shows vertices (X and Y coordinates) that make up vector polygon features. The area enclosed by the polygon boundary represents uniformly distributed phenomena of interest, in this case a river.

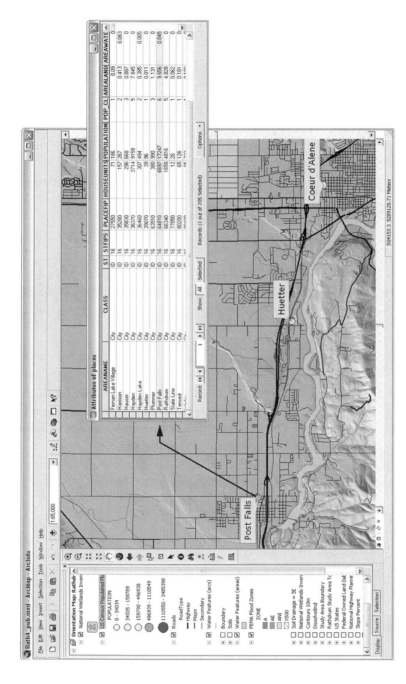

**Figure 3.4.** Attributes stored in the geographic feature's data table. In this example, the town of Post Falls, Idaho, is represented as a point feature. The shaded area in the table shows the attributes for the selected feature (Post Falls).

high-resolution displays, have made desktop viewing and analysis of large geospatial datasets quite possible. Also, computers can repeat the same computation on any number of features. In fact, they do this well and much more rapidly than a human ever could.

GIS software duplicates and expands how persons use maps, changing the traditional static paper map into a dynamic digital map that can be viewed on a computer screen. GIS expands human capabilities by allowing dynamic changes to what is displayed and how it is displayed, as well as by allowing essentially infinite expansion of the areas displayed. GIS can process large amounts of spatial data and can create new data through various spatial manipulations (e.g., overlay). Human capabilities lag when asked to quickly measure distances between hundreds or thousands of features. A GIS properly configured and operated can do this easily.

## EXPLORING SPATIAL QUESTIONS

In addition to dynamically handling potentially massive amounts of spatial data, GIS can help answer spatial questions similar to those people ask when looking at an analog map. David Rhind (1989) categorized these spatial questions in the following manner:

*What is at?* This query is concerned with the attributes of a location that is known.

*Where is?* This query is the inverse of the first. In this case, the query is about a characteristic or phenomenon for which the location is not known. For example, a geospatial query on housing prices can result in a display of the locations of affordable housing.

*What has changed?* This question concerns the dynamic aspects of data. It relies on the existence of time-series data from long-term data collection efforts, for which there is growing demand.

*What spatial pattern exists?* This type of query focuses on understanding spatial patterns or relationships (simple or complex). In GIS applications, this may well be the main question pursued. For example, in gerontology, analysts are interested in the patterning of a particular cohort's residences as related to the location of clinics, educational facilities, or other services.

*What if?* This spatial question is concerned with prediction, and again may well be the major focus of a GIS application. To a large degree, the ability to ask and analyze this question depends on the ability to support the other questions posed above. That is, some *what if* queries may depend on the availability of time-series data as well as on a spatial pattern analysis at each time interval.

Answering these questions calls for incremental, sequential application of various tools and for operators skilled in GIS software. The expert analyst is capable of, first, structuring problems in spatial terms and, second, organizing the flow of analysis to achieve the desired result. The ability to think spatially is critical.

## GIS, ACTIVE LIVING, AND HEALTHY AGING

Two overarching concepts describe the potential of GIS in relation to environments for active living and healthy aging. The first is as a means of research to better understand the relationships that link aging and the built environment. The second is as a means for illuminating design intervention or the interpretation of research findings into specific community, or built environment, recommendations. The working definition of *built environment* applied here reflects that of the U.S. Department of Health and Human Services. Built environment encompasses all buildings, spaces, and products created, or modified, by people. It includes homes, schools, workplaces, parks/recreation areas, greenways, business areas, and transportation systems. The built environment extends overhead in the form of electric transmission lines, underground in the form of waste disposal sites and subway trains, and across the country in the form of highways. It includes land-use planning and policies that impact communities in urban, rural, and suburban areas. The built environment should also include interiors and the interconnectivity or flow of people's movement from inside to outside and back again (Benzel, 1998).

Geographers know all too well that research that questions the spatial aspects of daily life helps establish certain life–environment relationships (Ley, 1983; Mitchell, 2005; Rowles, 1978; Tuan, 1977). This relates to Tobler's First Law of Geography, which states, "everything is related to everything else, but near things are more related than distant things" (Tobler, 1970, p. 236). The formal term for this phenomenon is *spatial autocorrelation*. Studies of spatial relationships may seek to establish, refute, or perhaps employ this relationship.

GIS software is used to identify and measure spatial variables. Spatial researchers use GIS to collect, combine, and analyze spatial data against other data sets. Mapping the location of a clinic and the clients it serves and then overlaying local bus routes would show the extent to which the patients may access and take advantage of the clinic. One outcome may be to relocate the clinic or to improve alternative transportation routes, sidewalks, and crosswalks. Another outcome may be a more formal analysis of the extent to which bus route locations might predict clinic locations.

The use of GIS brings into play spatially referenced observational variables that can improve traditional social scientific research methods aimed at proving or disproving a hypothesis. An extensive review of successful and productive aging literature finds little to no inclusion of built environment factors. Terms such as *access* and *availability* are found, but they refer only to the fact that a health care delivery system exists somewhere in a community. Factors such as locations relative to client groups; pedestrian, bicycle, and transit routes; and required time in transit (number of bus transfers) are not considered in the narrow definitions of *access* or *availability*.

While predating most GIS software, Graham Rowles's *Prisoners of Space?* (1978) provides excellent insight into the myriad environmental variables confronting an elder trying to access goods and services. With a geographer's view of the spatial world of daily life, Rowles provided an answer to the question, "to what extent is an elderly person involved with the spaces and places around him or her?" Through participant observation, Rowles showed that gerontologists' common explanation of gradual geographical contraction as people age is an oversimplification (Rowles, 1978).

Hughes et al. (2006) examined several thousand physical activity program centers (e.g., commercial gyms, senior centers, YMCAs, YWCAs) in three areas of the United States. The goal was to assess the supply and use of physical activity programs. One finding was that "facilities reported 69,634 individuals as current weekly program participants, equaling about 6% of the sites' total older-adult population" (p. 667). One question that the study did not answer is to what extent the physical environment played a role in the percentage of people who took advantage of the physical activity sites. In other words, how many more people 65 and older would have used the activity sites and programs if the built environment had allowed them to easily get there? Another question, specific to the character of a neighborhood, might be what number of people 65 and older live in surroundings that readily allow them to bicycle, walk, roller blade, or jog as part of their daily routines and, as a result, to feel little need to use the activity sites?

Another significant example of an application of GIS that can be used to better understand the relationship between successful and productive aging (SPA) and the built environment correlates active living elders, their primary living environments, and a mapping of their daily routines (Rowe

& Kahn, 1998). The hypothesis is that older people who display SPA attributes live in high-density, mixed-use, and pedestrian-friendly built environments. Wonderful descriptions of such environments, as well as of the social and health benefits they provide, are found in *The Death and Life of Great American Cities*, by Jane Jacobs (1961). The rationale is that older people who do not display SPA attributes most likely live in automobile-dependent, homogeneous land-use, low-density settings. Applying GIS technology would make possible the exploration and quantification of relationships between location, activities of daily living or everyday tasks, hobbies, interests, resources, and so forth, all of which contribute to successful and productive aging.

Using GIS in this way would allow for the development of objective measures of SPA environments. Such measures would provide a template by which to assess the SPA potential of most any existing or proposed environment. Some communities would be deemed excellent retirement destinations for people who want to live active lives and contribute to the betterment of the community. Half of Americans ages 50 to 70 want jobs that contribute to the greater good now as well as in retirement, according to the 2005 MetLife Foundation/Civic Ventures New Face of Work Survey (Met Life Foundation/Civic Ventures, 2005). The SPA potential of other communities with less dense and less pedestrian-friendly, mixed-use environments would be identified as needing improvements. The template would aid in recommending which improvements should be made in the community to increase its attractiveness to retirees. Some other communities would likely be found so lacking that they could do little to become vibrant and economically stable retirement destinations.

The Robert Wood Johnson Foundation funded the development of environmental evaluation matrices and checklists aimed at identifying the built character of city blocks. These "audit tools" were records of observed conditions (see http://www.activelivingresearch.org/resourcesearch/tools andmeasures). While mapped to some degree, they were limited in terms of the specific (actual) neighborhood locations and of the aerial views of the progression of a person's movement to and from a location. In that the degree of identified and located land uses was limited, the studies missed an opportunity to provide a more refined association between health and the built environment.

These research projects provided detailed assessments of block faces. Absent from the descriptions, however, were the dispersion and sequencing of the identified land uses. As a result, there was no way to tell whether all of the identified land uses were located in one multi-story structure at the end of a block, were spread evenly throughout, were mixed along the street level, or were mixed horizontally and vertically throughout a block. To identify only the land uses within a city block misses the opportunity to see the true character of a place as a public setting that provides accessibility and contributes to healthy, active living. Visual identification is needed. The visually diverse use of space, the spatial organization of land uses along the street level and its upper stories, and their specific locations, frequency, and density would provide land planners and public health officials a clearer understanding of the health and built environment quality of a community on a block-by-block matrix. This more precise and accurate degree of detail, including access points to each building, can easily be provided with the help of GIS mapping.

Architects, urban designers, landscape architects, and land use designers and planners have for years called for denser, more diversified mixed-use environments that contribute to healthy active living (Bacon, 1974; Calthorpe, 1993; Jacobs, 1961; Katz, 1994; Lynch, 1960). Only recently have studies been funded that show the link between health and built form (e.g., many smaller store fronts, varied goods and services, diverse interests, and walking routes). The vibrancy of built environments called for by designers and planners is found in the urban fiction of 1900 Chicago, Montreal, and New York in *Sister Carrie* (Dreiser, 1969) and again in 1930 New York in *Manhattan Transfer* (Dos Passos, 1925). Science, with the help of GIS, is now providing evidence-based facts in support of what has been known for more than a century by fiction writers and environmental designers. Dreiser and Dos Pasos describe urban environments that invited people on foot, that attracted the flaneur (an urban invention; one who stands back and watches life), and that contributed to the development and spread of changing social and cultural values. This is the detail needed to differentiate between city blocks that attract people throughout the day and night (Jacobs, 1961) and those blocks made up of a single mega-structure that concentrates goods and services, often requires the use of an automobile to get to, and contributes to limited social interaction, thus reducing the probability of successful and productive aging.

## SPOKANE PEDESTRIAN PROJECT

The following is a description of a project that illustrates how GIS can support both research and intervention in gerontology. In Spokane, Washington, GIS information is broken down by individual parcels of land along each street, as is common with many other major cities. In this way one can represent each parcel in terms of what its specific characteristics of interest are, and not have to aggregate all of the information to a block face. This is the data collection research mode.

Until recently, and also in common with many other communities, Spokane lacked detailed sidewalk and street-crossing (pedestrian network) data. With fine-scale GIS data, however, researchers can determine whether there are particular relationships between people and locations and can construct a more refined definition of *access* and *availability*. Such visual data sets, made available through the Word Wide Web to the general public, might also enhance a community's degree of social justice and equity. When environmental assets and liabilities can be seen (measured), then a transition to an intervention mode can begin and strategic recommendations for changes that foster and sustain active living can be developed. More detailed decisions related to the built environment within the greater urban and regional contexts can also be developed.

Beginning in 2004, a project in the Spokane region has been developing just such a data set. With the help of graduate students Michael Wilhelm and Lynne Gearhart, Dr. Kerry Brooks has gathered environmental data on the quality of sidewalks and the specific locations of Americans with Disabilities Act (ADA; PL-101-336) curb ramps, their materials and conditions, their running and cross slope, and other attributes that can be measured against the criteria associated with active living and successful aging. The Spokane pedestrian project has contributed to greater social equity and social justice by giving more people the ability to identify routes to selected destinations.

Thus far, the study data covers the entire Spokane Transit Authority (STA) service area, including most municipalities in Spokane County and the areas in between. Work on the project began with digitizing features from the highest resolution aerial photographs available. A review of similar studies helped to identify the particular kinds of data that they would collect. The result was a long list of sidewalk attributes: side of the street, next to the street, or separated from the street by a planting strip or traffic barriers; length; materials (dirt, concrete, asphalt); surface quality (smooth, rough, broken up); and street, alley, or driveway crossings. Also mapped were various barriers and aids to mobility, such as locations and attributes of ADA curb ramps. The research was guided by the question of what features enhance or restrict physical use of the pedestrian network, particularly for those with disabilities. Eventually it will be possible to map and analyze the most accessible route from one point to another through the transit service area. This is of concern for users if transit and transit stops are accessible, but the final destination for the trip is not. For an example of this data, see Figure 3.5.

In his master's thesis, Mike Wilhelm (2007) used the data to model the differential accessibility to parks as experienced by local residents. He located a route between a park and a point a quarter mile from the park to see the degree of ease or difficulty in a direct route (most efficient) versus the most accommodating or feasible route (see Figures 3.6 and 3.7). Objective measures of the accessibility of the parks as well as of the capacities of GIS were supported by the data described above. Using the measures refined in the thesis, the goal eventually is to identify the extent to which people can use the transit infrastructure.

While local residents may use the data to enable them to plan pedestrian trips, the project is using it to look for gaps in the transportation infrastructure, primarily around each bus stop and particularly for people with disabilities. The gap analysis focuses on where the breaks are and what needs to be done to repair them, or to help clients to access the system, including para-transit opportunities. In addition, there is great interest on the part of city neighborhood organizations in using these data to inform pedestrian planning aspects of their community development plans. These data may also be employed in a Spokane-focused research project aimed at understanding and reducing childhood obesity. These additional uses illustrate how GIS can be used to support various built form interventions.

In similar projects in other locales, children are mapping their routes to school so that planners can see what the children are walking past (e.g., fast food shops, types of billboards, unsafe neighborhoods), and older citizens can map routes to goods, services, recreation, education, entertainment, and so forth that they would like to access (Casey & Pederson, 2007; Dicken, 2007). Seeing what can and cannot be carried out as part of one's daily activities contributes to the fostering and sustainability of a community's social capital.

The Spokane pedestrian data may also be used to identify or create potential for active living in other ways. Spokane's promotional identity ("Near Nature. Near Perfect") led Dr. Brooks to consider whether that branding would derive even more support if pedestrians and bicyclists were provided with sufficient Web-based data to plan (map) their routes ahead of time. People with health concerns who were planning to move to Spokane could see where a house they want to buy is located as well as the extent to which they would be able to access goods and services and potential jobs and resources as pedestrians.

At a more macro level, GIS mapping of a community's entire transportation infrastructure enhances environmental justice and equity. How

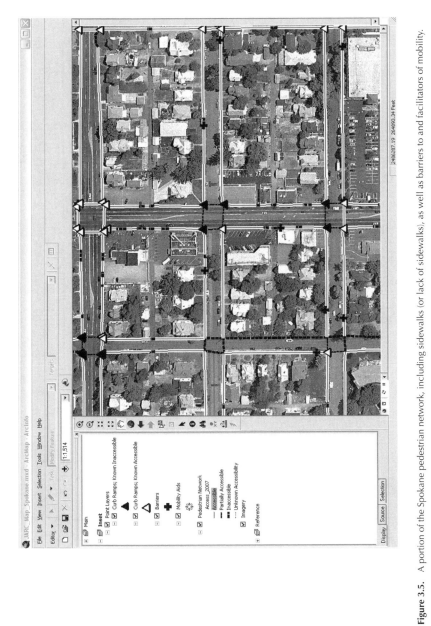

**Figure 3.5.** A portion of the Spokane pedestrian network, including sidewalks (or lack of sidewalks), as well as barriers to and facilitators of mobility.

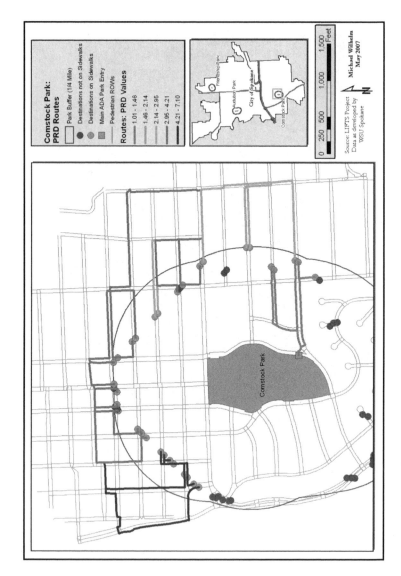

**Figure 3.6.** Pedestrian routes based on difficulty (or possibility) of travel using sidewalks. The polygon represents the boundary of a hypothetical 15-minute walk from the park under the assumption that sidewalks are present. The lines represent the shortest possible route that uses existing sidewalks. Pedestrian relative distance (PRD) values are the ratio between the "actual" route that accounts for difficulty and the shortest potential route. (*Source:* Wilhelm, 2007)

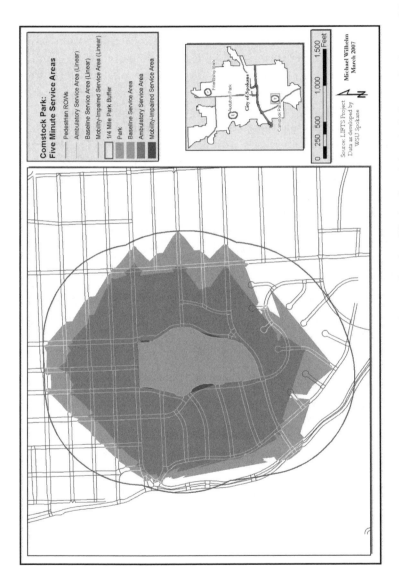

**Figure 3.7.** Comstock Park pedestrian service areas (15-minute walk in any direction), based on difficulty of travel along the Spokane pedestrian network in relation to a hypothetical unimpeded walk (outer polygon). The ADA accessible areas are barely visible near the park itself, which means that this park is minimally accessible. (*Source:* Wilhelm, 2007)

just is it when an able-bodied person can travel from origin A to destination B in 5,000 feet and a person in a wheelchair requires 21,000 feet? The Spokane Transit project offers its residents (current and future) the ability to measure how accessible the community is. This is a step forward from concepts such as *accessible* and *available* in much of the literature on successful aging. The GIS data sets used in the Spokane Transit project have helped to answer whether there is equitable access for everyone. If communities wish to move to a more pedestrian-friendly state to become less automobile dependent, then people can answer ahead of time, "How far can I get in the time I have or do I need to find an alternative mode of transit?"

In asking the last question, a community resident would plug in his or her personal abilities and likely see a polygon on the map. The shape of the bounded area would display the geographical extent to which he or she could travel through the surrounding neighborhood(s) in a given amount of time (e.g., refer to the thesis discussion above and Figure 3.6). A circular-shaped service area around an origin is the most equitable alternative, signifying equal travel distances all around. However, as the uniformity of an environment varies outward from a point of travel, the shape changes. A boundary drawn closer to the center (the individual's home) represents a walking environment of greater difficulty, and a boundary drawn further out from the center represents a pedestrian environment of less difficulty in terms of the friction of travel and, therefore, the distance able to be covered within a certain amount of time. These polygons, or spheres of travel, provide objective measures that allow people to compare their situation to what an equitable situation would be.

The idea of a shaped area of travel is not new. An excellent review of such systems can be found in Buttimer and Seamon's *The Human Experience of Space and Place* (1980). The big difference, as noted earlier, is that today computers can make numerous calculations and visually display the interrelationships between people and their environments. In combination, how geographers and built environment professionals think about lived space is of tremendous value to understanding the needs and aims of health care professionals, and vice versa.

## CONCLUSION

Geographic information systems software makes the mapping of the invisible, visible. As Graham Rowles aptly demonstrated in *Prisoners of Space?*, one's surroundings affect the personal and social aspects of aging as well as a person's access to health care systems and other goods and services. Access and availability are so often a part of successful and productive aging, and both can be made visible and measured through GIS.

GIS may be just one tool in mapping and measuring the accessibility and availability of goods and services, but it is a powerful tool. Gerontologists and built environment professionals can be brought together through collaborative research projects that use GIS to measure and define access in terms of walkability or travel time on a bus, a bicycle, and so forth. These collaborations can enable residents and city planners to identify the extent to which one environment over another may contribute to successful aging, aging in place, and more.

## REFERENCES

Aronoff, S. (1989). *Geographic information systems: A management perspective.* Ottawa, Canada: WDL Publications.

Bacon, E. (1974). *Design of cities.* New York: Viking.

Benzel, K. (1998). *The room in context: Design beyond boundaries.* New York: McGraw-Hill.

Buttimer, A., & Seamon, D. (Eds.) (1980). *The human experience of space and place.* London: Croom Helm.

Casey, L., & Pederson, T. (2007). Urbanizing GIS: Philadelphia's strategy to bring GIS to neighborhood planning. Retrieved September 2007, from http://gis.esri .com/library/userconf/proc95/to150/p107.html.

Calthorpe, P. (1993). *The next American metropolis: Ecology, community, and the American dream.* New York: Princeton Architectural.

Cowen, D. (1988). GIS versus CAD versus DBMS: What are the differences? *Photogrammetric Engineering and Remote Sensing, 54,* 1551.

Dicken, C. (2007). Using interactive maps to analyze USDA food assistance programs. Retrieved September 2007, from http://gis.esri.com/library/userconf/ proc04/docs/pap1787.pdf.

Dos Passos, J. (1925). *Manhattan transfer.* New York: London, Harper & Brothers.

Dreiser, T. (1969). *Sister Carrie.* Columbus, OH: C. E. Merrill.

Environmental Systems Research Institute. (2007). Model builder. Retrieved October 2007, from http://www.esri.com/software/arcview/extensions/spatial analyst/about/model.html.

Foresman, T. W. (1998). GIS: Early years and the threads of evolution. In T. W. Foresman (Ed.), *The history of geographic information systems: Perspectives from the pioneers* (pp. 3–7). Saddle River, NJ: Prentice Hall.

Hughes, S., Williams, B., Molina, L., & Bayles, C. (2006). Characteristics of physical activity programs for older adults: Results of a multisite survey. *The Gerontologist, 45*(5), 667–675.

Jacobs, J. (1961). *The death and life of great American cities.* New York: Vintage.

Johnston, R. J., Gregory, D., Pratt, G., & Watts, M. (2000). *The dictionary of human geography.* Malden, MA: Blackwell.

Katz, P. (1994). *The new urbanism: Toward an architecture of community.* New York: McGraw-Hill.

Kennedy, M. (2006). *Introducing geographic information systems with ArcGIS.* New York: Wiley.

Ley, D. (1983). *A social geography of the city.* New York: Harper & Row.

Lynch, K. (1960). *The image of the city.* Cambridge, MA: Technology Press.

MetLife Foundation/Civic Ventures. (2005). New face of work survey. Retrieved November 2007, from http://www.civicventures.org/publications/surveys/new-face-of-work.cfm.

Mitchell, A. (2005). *The ESRI guide to GIS analysis: Spatial measurements and statistics* (vol. 2). Redlands, CA: ESRI Press.

Rhind, D. (1989, Summer). Why GIS? *Arc News, 11*(3), 28–29.

Rowe, J., & Kahn, R. (1999). *Successful aging.* New York: Dell.

Rowles, G. (1978). *Prisoners of space?: Exploring the geographical experience of older people.* Boulder, CO: Westview.

Sambells, J., Turner, C., & Purvis, M. (2006). *Beginning Google maps applications with PHP and Ajax: From novice to professional.* New York: Apress.

Tobler, W. (1970). A computer movie simulating urban growth in the Detroit region. *Economic Geography, 46* (June), 234–240.

Tuan, Y-F. (1977). *Space and place.* London: Edward Arnold.

Wilhelm, M. (2007). *Analysis of pedestrian accessibility as applied to Spokane city parks.* Unpublished master's thesis, Washington State University, Spokane.

4

# NATURE-RELATED CONTACT FOR HEALTHY COMMUNITIES

## From Hunter–Gatherer to Horticultural Therapy

*Angela C. Pappas*

THE FIRST HUMANS DEPENDED on botanical knowledge for their daily existence. Plants contributed to sustenance and well-being. Early humans had no cultivated or domesticated tree or plant, yet they knew where to find and how to use the abundant surrounding vegetation. Few cave paintings chronicle this knowledge. However, as far back as Paleolithic times there is evidence of the importance of plants to humans. Dating back to ancient times, burial customs included floral offerings to the dead. Pollen found in burial tombs shows that plants held significance and symbolism in the everyday life cycle, even during the early phases of the development of humankind (Janick, 1992).

Relationships to the earth and nature make up some of humankind's deepest memories and have fostered a close bond to the earth and to living things. Plant life is fundamental to life on Earth. Contact with plants and nature offers humans a glimpse of the significance of life processes, whether it is simply a view of flora and fauna or the act of growing and nurturing a plant. This response to nature may be genetically based. As E. O. Wilson wrote in his book *Biophilia*, "humans have an innate [genetic] tendency to focus on life and life-like processes" (1984, p. 85). The emotional affiliations and physical attractions [or aversions] to other living things "are too consistent to be dismissed as the result of purely historical events working on a mental blank slate. This implies an hereditary development" (1993, p. 85).

The rise of humanity is the story of the human struggle to dominate and overcome the environment. Agriculture and gardening, the controlled or managed growth of plants, contributed to the course of humankind. Ten thousand to twelve thousand years ago a universal, diffuse pattern of humans functioning in harmony with nature stopped, and humans began the effort of making nature work for humankind. Horticulture arose as a science, skill, and occupation (Gerlach-Spriggs et al., 1998).

Successive waves of war and disease often kept humans separate from nature and there was discovery, loss, and rediscovery of gardens, primarily through monastic institutions during the Dark Ages. Religious symbolism in gardens grew over time with the incorporation of significant elements, ideals, and rituals of early cultures. Creating *paradise* (a term that originated in Persia) has been referenced as the ideal in Genesis. Middle Eastern literature talked of a garden being desirable and life sustaining. A vine and water were considered the minimum for a blessed life. A single river (water source) with four river heads (four sections of the garden) is common in Eastern and Western cultures, as is the symbolic "tree of life." Fertility, economy, and peace are also symbols related to a healthy garden. Many monastic gardens in Europe became places that provided health care for the sick and poor, and from this the term *hotel-Dieu* or "hostel of God" was coined. Thus came the first hospitals, which incorporated a garden for the provision of health care and well-being (Gerlach-Spriggs et al., 1998). By the late 15th and early 16th centuries, Christian care evolved into secular care and patient access to gardens was periodically restricted. Spanish hospitals built at this time followed Arabic architecture and traditions, which included arcades, courtyards, and windows that allowed air and light to stream in to patients.

The idea of sun and fresh air for patients made its way to England through the prison and hospital reformer John Howard. His reports of European hospital gardens, along with new scientific ideas on hygiene, brought about experimentation with new hospital architecture and design that included the incorporation of sunlight, breezes, and gardens. The success with patient welfare in this setting led to the continued use of gardens, and this type of design dominated 19th-century hospital construction. Unfortunately, no one drew the direct parallel between what gardens offered and the benefits that could be derived for patient welfare.

Pavilion hospitals, where several related buildings formed a complex with gardens and patio spaces, blossomed at the end of the 19th century. The war wounded who were not confined to the hospital had a lower mortality rate, while traditionally hospitalized patients experienced an alarming rise in nosocomial infections. Outdoor bridges, gardens, roof walkways, and sun porches became de rigueur for hospital construction, reaching a peak during World War I (see Figure 4.1). Physicians, nurses, and architects realized that outdoor treatments benefited patients, but still no one drew any direct conclusions on exactly how and why they were beneficial. Florence Nightingale (1820–1910) came closest:

> Second only to the [patients'] need of fresh air is their need of light. It is not only daylight, but direct sunlight they want. People think the effect is upon the spirits only. This is by no means the case. We must admit that light has a real and tangible effect on the human body (Nightingale, 1860, p. 120).

> I mention from experience, as quite perceptible in promoting recovery, *the being able to see out of a window, instead of looking against a dead wall*; the bright colors of flowers; the being able to read in bed by the light of the window. While we can generate warmth, we cannot generate daylight. (Nightingale, 1863, pp. 19–20) [Emphasis added by author.]

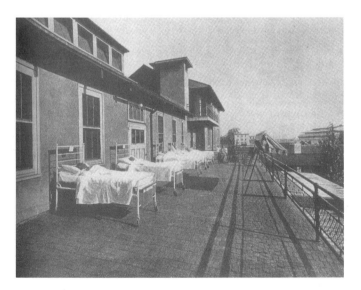

**Figure 4.1.** Peter Bent Brigham Hospital, circa 1913. Patients on the terrace. (*Source:* Brigham & Woman's Hospital Archives)

Powerful scientific advances occurred as a result of the research and development that took place during World War I. Germ theory was proven, followed by vaccines and antibiotics. Physician specialization, as well as patient separation based on disease state or social standing, became popular and even expeditious. Industrialization was adopted by the hospital market. Mass treatment of similar diseases involving the same body system contributed to the implementation of wards to facilitate speed of treatment and patient rounds for doctors. Enclosed, single-building facilities enabled many different diagnostic departments to be housed under one roof, which increased the speed at which patients could be attended. Ever-growing building height saved money and expedited treatment, but eroded the patient's environment. Elevators and air-conditioning as well as growing scientific knowledge of contagious diseases created even more patient isolation and insulation, and the garden was pushed out. The garden became a feature of the entrance or even a thing of the past. Only occupational therapy held on to the garden's palliative and curative benefits.

Occupational therapy came into its own as an allied health field following World War I. It was a field devoted to the rehabilitation of life skills of returning veterans as well as to the redevelopment of small motor skills. Garden therapy, farming, or agricultural skills were found to be motivational and beneficial for veterans. The positive outcomes from these treatments drove the need for more therapeutic environments, which subsequently gave rise to horticultural therapy as a subset specialty of occupational therapy (Gerlach-Spriggs, 1998).

Occupational therapy was incorporated into the curriculum of psychology and social work programs at various colleges as psychologists and social workers began working with military and veterans hospitals. This new allied health science, occupational therapy, provided a means to develop methods for patients to return to working with plants in the garden. By the 1960s, Dr. Donald Watson and Alice Burlingame of Michigan State University published the first horticultural therapy textbook (Gerlach-Spriggs et al., 1998). The mid-1970s saw the integration of hospital and garden poised for tremendous growth opportunities. Unfortunately, scientific data was slim, and management and insurance companies valued health differently. Horticultural therapy remains a subset of occupational therapy and is practiced primarily with the elderly, persons with mental illness, and wounded veterans. Patients with specialized injuries (e.g., spinal damage, stroke, or other brain injuries), with multiple trauma, and even individuals with AIDS can benefit from horticultural therapy rehabilitation, which can heighten confidence and assist in maintaining fine or gross motor skills (Westphal, 2005, personal communication).

All of this aside, hospital architecture continues to look increasingly like office or commercial ventures that do nothing to alleviate the anxiety, fear, and disorientation felt by most patients and even by visitors (Gerlach-Spriggs et al., 1998). Incidental information from patients' and employees' enhanced emotional states when outdoor environments are available are too often rebuffed. The long history of human need for and even genetically based affiliation with restorative nature is often overlooked in the design of hospitals and their spaces. Hospital garden spaces need to reflect human-kind's deep, rich past of being tied to the natural world.

## THEORIES ON NATURE:
## VISUAL PREFERENCE OR GENETIC PREDILECTION?

Researcher Rachel Kaplan wrote of her study results (completed in the 1980s) that

> Nature matters to people. Big trees and small trees, glistening water, chirping birds, budding bushes, colorful flowers—these are the important ingredients in a good life. (1983, p. 155)

Civilization covers several thousand years, and urbanization only a generation or two. It is hard to believe that within this short time span all that humans innately know regarding nature could be erased (Frumkin, 2004). People are bonded to nature emotionally and genetically as a result of the many millennia that humans have been in tune with and worked with nature (Wilson, 1984; 1993). Environmental preference studies show people's distinct inclination for green views as well as for natural objects within those views that cut across gender, age, and cultural lines. Green nature is preferred over urban and random outdoor worldviews (Kaplan & Kaplan, 1989; Kaplan & Talbot, 1983; Lewis, 1979; Ulrich, 1993).

Over 100 years ago, Frederick Law Olmsted, the venerated father of landscape architecture, discussed how space, light, and pastoral views had recuperative powers for all people through healthy recreation in accessible nature (Olmsted & Kimball, 1922). Various similar theories have since been put forth and researchers are testing and investigating why nature plays such an important role in people's psychological well-being (Gerlach-Spriggs et al., 1998). Seminal scientific studies advancing these theories have been performed by Rachel Kaplan and Stephen Kaplan and colleagues (1983, 1989, 1990, 1992, 1998); Edward O. Wilson (1984, 1993); Stephen Kellert and E. O. Wilson (1993, 2005); and Roger Ulrich and colleagues (1983, 1984, 1991, 1992, 1993, 1999). They each found that natural restorative environments do indeed positively influence one's psychological and physiologic responses. Each has tested and advanced his or her own theory explaining why exposure to nature provides benefits for human health and well-being.

## BIOPHILIA THEORY

Biologist and naturalist Edward O. Wilson introduced and popularized his biophilia theory in his 1984 book *Biophilia*. *Biophilia* literally means "love of life" and has been used to describe a productive psychological orientation or state of being. Wilson redefined the term as "the connections that human beings subconsciously seek with the rest of life" (1984, 1985). It is this type of instinct that has been ingrained in humans over millennial time. Biophilia is profound and relevant to how people respond emotionally to nature and landscape (Wilson, 1993). Humans respond positively to high-depth, spatially open views. They also respond with avoidance to certain natural spaces. Biophobic reactions occurred in studies evaluating nature views when blocked-view settings were observed (imagine a forest with a tangle of vines and trees) as well as settings that would present traditional evolutionary survival risks (imagine the survival difficulties experienced living in an open desert environment) (Heerwagen & Orians, 1993; Kaplan, 1983; Kellert, 1993; Ulrich, 1993; Wilson, 1993). This lends credence to the theory of humans being tied to natural living things and the emotional phenomenon created by human interpretation of natural areas as an opportunity to conserve nature (Wilson, 1984) and to create livable spaces that reflect natural and healthful environments (Kellert, 2005).

## COGNITIVE, CONTENT, AND SPATIAL PERCEPTION THEORY

Since the mid-1960s, conservation psychologists Rachel Kaplan and Stephen Kaplan have studied people's perception of the natural environment. They define *nature* as "any place where plants grow" (Kaplan & Kaplan, 1989, p. 2). Through their work the Kaplans found that blocked views or vistas that were too open and that provided no opportunity for cover or safety were less preferred by research participants (Kaplan & Kaplan, 1990). The ability to obtain information quickly, remain oriented, and feel a sense of orderliness were all recurring themes in the participants' preferred views (Kaplan & Kaplan, 1989). Water, paths, light, accessibility, and understandable direction were important features. People seemed to have deep-seated preferences for certain natural settings, which led the Kaplans to predict nature preferences along a matrix. They postulated that humans need immediate visual understanding of their surroundings. People look for patterns within the landscape that provide orientation, safety, and information about the environment. The Preference Matrix can be used to predict characteristics of natural or designed areas that would provide positive or therapeutic benefits to the observer (see Figure 4.2) (Kaplan & Kaplan, 1989). The Kaplans identified the preferred characteristics as coherence, legibility, complexity, and mystery. *Coherence* is found within the landscape as visually recognizable patterns that provide a sense of order necessary for survival. Such patterns of order might be noted in plant material or color repetition at predictable intervals. *Legibility* provides orientation within the environment, such as recognizable landmarks that trigger memories of orientation or location within the landscape. Groupings of trees or significant plants offer legibility. *Complexity* refers to diversity, visual richness, variability, depth, or spatially opened views to a scene. An example of complexity would be a variation in plant material, texture, or color. Visual richness can add elements that encourage one to examine or investigate a space. Elements such as a path bending out of site, a sheltered trail that opens into a spacious setting, or portions of plants peaking out without being fully revealed are examples of *mystery*. These elements appeal to the human need for continued information, exploration, and knowledge about a scene. Coherence is required to prevent mystery from becoming a surprise and creating a less inviting space. Legibility goes hand in hand with coherence in providing an understanding of the

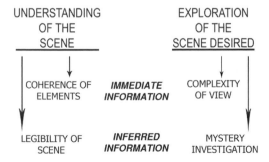

**Figure 4.2.** Visual comprehension of nature views.

landscape. Legibility is also needed with elements of mystery so that one can understand the area as well as imagine the space. Legibility is needed to keep complexity from becoming chaos. Complexity is required to fully realize mystery. Complexity and coherence work together to provide a place that allows creativity and problem solving for understanding and safety (Kaplan & Kaplan, 1989; Kellert, 2005). The Kaplans' research shows that there are definite themes and predictable characteristics involved in human inherent choices of natural environments. One can use this matrix to elucidate the preferred elements of a landscape that benefit one's long-term well-being. These elements may occur naturally or may be designed into environments for healthy contact with nature.

The Kaplans also examined the way in which the restorative effect of preferred nature is achieved and what properties make it possible. They found that people tend to search for restoration when mental fatigue sets in as a result of worry, anxiety, illness, or intense mental effort. The Kaplans defined *mental fatigue* as prolonged directed attention. Directed attention requires a great deal of effort to be sustained and may involve inhibiting other stimuli and distractions. Examples of directed attention include deep concentration, work activities, or testing. Mental fatigue can be manifested in an individual as aberrant behavior, increased irritability, aggression, and a tendency toward being accident-prone. The Kaplans noted that directed attention that causes mental fatigue was relieved by the engagement of involuntary attention, which requires little or no sustained effort (Kaplan & Kaplan, 1989).

Frederick Law Olmsted instinctively knew that viewing nature could "arouse the attention and occupy the mind without purpose," thereby refreshing and invigorating the body (Ranney, 1990). In order to recover from the fatigue of directed attention, an environment must engage involuntary attention and allow directed attention to rest. Positive distraction defines involuntary attention. Watching clouds or changing light patterns or being attracted to brightly colored objects are examples of using involuntary attention. The Kaplans identified the following four components that engage involuntary attention, provide mental restoration, reduce stress, and allow the body to be recharged to a healthy state.

1.  *Being Away:* Environments that contribute to a sense of escape from ordinary distractions and that allow one to get away from the details that require deep concentration or mental escape. Examples of this environment are nature preserves, botanical gardens, or outdoor recreation areas.

2. *Extent:* Environments that enable one to feel that he or she is in a whole other world. The experience must be complete enough to allow one to become immersed in a suspension of reality, such as walking in the forest, viewing interesting or unusual plants, or visiting Disney World, yet still allow the person to remain connected to the world.

3. *Fascination:* Typically triggered by the attributes of places that capture the involuntary attention. No data exists to define what constitutes fascination. Bright, shiny, moving objects or wild things as well as learning puzzles or sequencing information into a larger, connected pattern are examples of fascination. Color patterns, shadows, reflections, breeze motion, or sound are examples of outdoor characteristics that produce fascination.

4. *Compatibility:* A match between an environment and one's purposes or inclinations, such that one's directed attention is not needed and is allowed to rest. Such environments are easily understood, clearly articulated, and provide no surprises that would produce concern for personal safety. This is a sort of form-follows-function approach to experiencing a space (Kaplan & Kaplan, 1989). Nearby nature can offer all of these components and allow for restorative benefits to people through such activities as walking or hiking, gardening, watching wildlife, or participating in survival skills (e.g., hunting or building shelter) (Kaplan & Talbot, 1983). Familiar vegetation in a spatially open setting with enchanting wildlife that allows one to wander among elements such as light pattern, motion, or sound can provide stimulation for involuntary attention, pleasure, and stress recovery (Kaplan & Talbot, 1983). Pleasure can control pain and reduce the pressures of directed attention. This type of environment can be designed and allows one to achieve what he or she desires—a preferred, natural space with healthful, restorative effects.

## PSYCHO-EVOLUTIONARY THEORY

Environmental psychologist Roger S. Ulrich studied psychological arousal and overload theories. He determined that environments high in visual obstruction, noise, intensity, and chaotic movement can overwhelm and fatigue normal human coping systems and lead to high levels of stress responses that create negative psychological and physiological effects.

Prolonged or chronic stress can have deleterious effects on human health. It can alter the body's normal responses and immune systems in such a way that typical "aging" conditions are more likely to occur (Ulrich, 1999). *Stress*, as defined by Ulrich, is the response to events or elements of the environment that are threatening to well-being (Ulrich, 1999). Studies show that stress conditions are common to people experiencing illness, bereavement, prolonged concentration, or even pollution. These factors can create a resultant reduction in cognitive function or physiologic performance (Ulrich 1983, 1993; Ulrich & Addoms, 1981).

Ulrich theorized that a quick, positive response to the natural environment is central to one's thoughts about nature and stress relief. A positive reaction to nature may be dictated by learned memories from childhood that involve meaning and behavior or may be from a genetically adaptive need for restoration. Humans are biologically prepared to find areas where they feel safe and comfortable (Ulrich 1983, 1991; Ulrich & Addoms, 1981). Biological preparedness can offer positive responses to natural content not offered by urban stimuli (Ulrich, 1991). Ulrich proposed that clear and spacious views of the landscape provide risk information that people need, on a biologic level, in order to ascertain safety and subsequently to build the capacity for restorative responses (Ulrich, 1991). Three necessary characteristics provide the information needed for restoration when viewing nature: aesthetic liking, stress recovery, and high-order cognitive enhancement (Abbott et al., 2004; Hartig et al., 1991; Ulrich, 1993; Weuve et al., 2004).

## AESTHETIC LIKING

Ulrich wrote that "consistent cross-cultural patterns in aesthetic preferences for natural scenes provide circumstantial support for the hypothesis that biophilia is at least partly genetic" (Ulrich, 1993, p. 87). He found that people have a high preference for outdoor environments that integrate water, vegetation, mountains, and light. People's strong tendency across cultures to respond consistently to natural scenes and to prefer natural elements even in the absence of recognition supports the perception that aesthetic liking is both genetic and learned (Ulrich, 1991, 1993).

## STRESS RECOVERY

Life for early humans was no "walk in the park." Physically and mentally exhausting, each day was a test of survival. From an evolutionary perspective, a physiologic response to a stressor or threat followed by a rapid return to baseline physical functioning and restoration would be required of prehistoric humans to maintain cognitive functioning for survival (Hartig et al., 1991; Heerwagen & Orians, 1993; Ulrich, 1991). This change of state would be expected to occur at a rapid rate in early humans for them to be prepared to successfully face the next danger. A number of studies have found that individuals who viewed unthreatening nature scenes showed quick positive responses and recovered more completely from stress symptoms than those who viewed other content (Ohman et al., 1989; Schriffin & Schneider, 1977; Zajonic, 1980). The participants in a study conducted by Ulrich expressed a reduction in fear, anxiety, and aggression (Ulrich, 1983).

## COGNITIVE FUNCTIONING

Exposure to nature can reduce stress and can improve cognitive performance. As noted earlier, Olmsted espoused the curative power of natural scenery (Ranney, 1990). Positive emotional states created by aesthetically pleasing natural surroundings can elicit cues for positive associations, making information recall easier. The ability to integrate remote associations, to think creatively, and to retrieve interrelated information occurs more readily with a positive emotional state (Kellert, 2005).

This body of scientific evidence reveals that most types of nature exposure are better than none at all and are clearly better than monotonous views that are often seen in urban environments. Ulrich theorized that the information and subconscious learning that views of nature can provide allow the body to recover from the effects of persistent, chronic stress. A loss of control, lack of exercise, decrease in social support, and inability to be in contact with nature all contribute to chronic, persistent stress (Ulrich, 1999). Exposure to nature can provide feelings of safety and comfort and allow the body to recover from the protective flight or fight posture, thereby reducing stress and its related negative physiological and psychological effects. Individuals who view unthreatening nature scenes show more complete recovery from stress symptoms than those viewing urban or built environments (Honeyman, 1992; Sheets & Manzer, 1991; Ulrich, 1993).

Ulrich's work centered on hospital patients and the psychological and physical improvements they experienced through exposure to nature within the hospital setting. The study group provided measurable medical outcomes that support and validate the subjective reports of stress reduction from nature contact. Hospitalization is filled with physical settings that are counterproductive to health and healing. Ulrich noted that the inability to maintain control over one's situation, the loss of social support

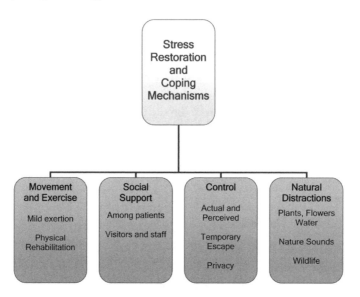

**Figure 4.3.** Ulrich's stress restoration and coping mechanisms.

while being hospitalized, a marked reduction in physical exercise and freedom of movement, and the loss of access to nature and other positive distractions are primary contributors to stress-related effects (Ulrich, 1999). Anxiety about surgery or fear of an impending life-changing procedure can exacerbate a patient's ill health. People need the coping mechanisms of situational control, social support, physical exercise, and mental distraction to reduce and manage stress-related effects.

A wide variety of studies have found that the phenomena of temporary escape or of being away, where a park or garden user daydreams or has "another world" feeling, can offer restoration and relief from stress (Cooper-Marcus & Barnes, 1995; Kaplan & Talbot, 1983; Ulrich & Addoms, 1981). Nature contact benefited the individual whether he or she was an active or passive participant. The ability to escape in either form offered "perceived or actual control" of the individual's situation. Benefit was gleaned by just knowing that if one needed to get away, nature was nearby and accessible (Ulrich & Addoms, 1981). The Kaplans' studies support the same response of being away in that one can distance him- or herself from negative surroundings or situations (Kaplan & Kaplan, 1989; 1998; Kaplan & Talbot, 1983). Nearby nature allows a patient visual and mental restoration when he or she perceives a sense of control that is all but lost to most hospitalized patients. If nature contact is easily accessible to a patient in the form of a garden or natural space, the individual can achieve some actual control during his or her stay by going out when he or she wishes. An unobstructed view or paintings representative of nature can provide some perceived control. Many patients experience a reduction in stress by way of these control-related benefits.

Hospitalized patients often lose direct contact with their social support system. The more social ties and interactions a patient has, the more likely he or she will have increased healthful responses. In a 1995 study of California health-care gardens, Cooper-Marcus and Barnes noted that 73% of garden users engaged in visiting and talking while in the space and 36% of users were in the garden to visit with a patient. Whether used as an area for private reflection or a space to visit with friends or family, evidence exists that gardens provide increased emotional and social support for patients.

A lack of opportunities for physical movement and exercise is another aspect of hospitalization that contributes to stress and negative health outcomes. Increased exercise has been linked to a reduction of depression, heart disease, and mortality (Ulrich, 1999). The ability to move about increases a patient's perception of control, and aerobic and even nonaerobic exercise offer measurable health benefits. With the change of scenery that ambulation can provide, restoration may come in the form of improved circulation and muscle strength as well as physical and mental stimulation.

Finally, the lack of access to nature and to the positive distractions in nature has been identified as a stressor for hospitalized patients. Worrisome thoughts can increase stress, blood pressure, respiration, and depression (Ulrich, 1999). Temporary distraction from a stressful situation can engage a person's involuntary attention, allowing directed attention to restore itself and to improve cognitive functioning. These results concur with Ulrich's assertion that nature views provide therapeutic influences and benefits. This knowledge of the health benefits of nature views should be taken into consideration in deciding where to build a hospital or medical facility as well as which environmental design elements would make nature and nature views more accessible to patients and create more healthful spaces.

## HUMAN ENVIRONMENTAL VALUE THEORY

The work of social ecologist Stephen R. Kellert focuses on understanding the connection between human and natural systems. His interest is in the value and conservation of nature as well as in ways to harmonize natural and built environments. Kellert identified nine theoretical values in nature in which humans derive meaning and benefit from their relationship with nature. These values have been learned, have persisted over time, and signify that a diminution of human dependence on nature will lead to the degradation of the environment and of human existence (Kellert, 2005).

*Aesthetic:* Physical appeal of and attraction to nature

*Dominionistic:* Mastery and control of nature

*Humanistic:* Emotional attachment to nature

*Moralistic:* Moral and spiritual relation to nature

*Naturalistic:* Direct contact with and experience of nature

*Negativistic:* Fear and aversion to certain nature views

*Scientific:* Study and empirical observation of nature

*Symbolic:* Nature as source of metaphorical and communicative thought

*Utilitarian:* Nature as source of physical and material benefit

Natural landscape features that are valued and appreciated foster social and psychological benefits that encourage positive identification with nature as well as a sense of place. Natural landscapes of poor environmental quality produce the opposite effect—people feel a lack of connection with their surroundings as well as a poor quality of life. Even in increasingly urban times, direct contact with healthy nature promotes physical and mental well-being (Kellert, 2005). A lack of adequate exposure to nature may result in the degeneration of these values or the values may not develop at all, resulting in deficits to the human intellectual and emotional mind. The extent to which individuals value nature reflects the benefit each person derives from contact with nature (Kellert, 2005).

Aesthetic values are universal in human associations with nature. The impact that nature's beauty exerts on daily life is unparalleled by any other force (Kellert, 2005). Individuals who hold aesthetic values recognize order, symmetry, harmony, and balance in the natural world (Lynch, 1971). The concepts of order, symmetry, harmony, and balance along with a genetic predisposition for universal aesthetic traits can lead a person to feel safe and secure and can support and encourage one's ability to endure and thrive. The human desire to control and influence natural processes is reflected in dominionistic values. People achieve physical and mental fitness when working with nature, thereby creating feelings of safety and security as well as heightened self-esteem and increased coping skills. The world viewed through humanistic values is a place of emotional bonding and physical support. The nonjudgmental responses of plants and animals enhance human self-esteem and self-confidence. Also, nurturing or caring for another can increase capacities for cooperation and sociability. Nature as a moral and spiritual inspiration gives rise to moralistic values. An underlying unity of all lifeforms cultivates faith and confidence. A moralistic experience of nature encompasses strong feelings of affinity and ethical responsibility for the natural world. A connection with creation increases an understanding of and respect for nature and fosters a universal connection to all living things as well as an acceptance of the cycle of life. The immersion of oneself in nature arises from naturalistic values. Akin to the fascination and "being away" tenets of the Kaplan theory, naturalistic values foster mental stimulation and imagination as well as feelings of calm and peacefulness, thereby evoking involuntary attention, release of tension, and mitigation of stress. Negativistic values are similar to the human genetic biophobic responses identified by Wilson. Aversion to some natural forms or scenes implies awareness of surroundings and control of risk-taking behavior. The ability to observe and measure the environment reflects the scientific value of nature. It involves knowledge of the surroundings and evaluation of risk and safety, and also provides stimulation, improved cognitive ability, and competence. Symbolic values of natural elements are probably the most common associations humans have with nature. People use nature as a method for developing language and for communicating imagery and metaphor. Symbolism using universally recognized components within nature provides language for envisioning and explaining complex thought through the ability to define identity (e.g., "strong as an ox") and to describe issues (e.g., "can't see the forest for the trees"). Nature perceived through the physical and material benefits it provides as resources to be used is a reflection of utilitarian values. Nature may offer a craft or a skill that a person can derive emotional and intellectual benefits from, even in the absence of need. Utilitarian values can produce feelings of safety, predictability, and connectedness to nature that can then lead to feelings of independence, security, and confidence.

Benefits from nature come as a result of upholding the quality of nature and the realization that the nature one experiences and its benefits are only as good as the environment that one encounters. A sense or spirit of place reinforces a person's connection to the land and helps to maintain the secure and satisfying feeling that one derives from being connected with a safe and accessible setting. Poor environmental quality, lack of exposure, or poor design that inhibits access or use can diminish the nature experience. Spirit or sense of place can be viewed as the fusion of social and environmental forces that combine stability and heritage as well as the shared relationships that create harmony and intimacy with the land.

---

The four theories (biophilia; cognitive, content, and spatial; psycho-evolutionary; environmental value) tie together to support one another. Nature views that produce a sense of protection in the form of hiding places or cover and spatially open vistas that allow clear views for assessment of danger and the promise of water and food are universally preferred. All of these preferences and theories point to the ability of nature to reduce stress and provide mental recovery, thereby improving quality of life, whether for the active or passive user of nature or for the healthy or hospitalized individual.

## FROM SUBJECTIVE PERCEPTION TO SCIENTIFIC SUPPORT FOR THERAPEUTIC NATURE

If tranquility and rest for the mind are the goals of all humans, they can be achieved through a relationship with nature, as seen in data that shows the benefits of nature for all people. Nature is a critical component in how people perceive their environment. Whether it is a deep, bio-cultural subconscious knowledge of environmental connections or a sense of place determined by inherent value systems, an association with nature or preferred views can affect coping systems. The availability of and ease of access to nearby nature can influence one's perceptions of well-being and satisfaction with one's surroundings. A review of studies concerning the human–nature connection finds that stimulus, refuge, and symbol are the most common benefits of nature experiences. For example, the results of a people–plant survey logged 4,000 responses regarding how nature and plants were beneficial to people's lives. Sixty percent of respondents cited characteristics of refuge, such as feelings of "peacefulness" or a "source of quiet and tranquility" (Lewis, 1992). Seventy-one percent of a group of university students who were polled regarding places of refuge or healing from mental or emotional stress preferred nature and outdoor settings (Cooper-Marcus & Barnes, 1999). A questionnaire pertaining to a visit to the Morton Arboretum revealed that 90% of respondents chose attractive nature views that incorporated flowers (symbols of healthy nature) as their most positive memories. Visual contact with nature helps to increase positive feelings (Ulrich & Parsons, 1992). Ninety-nine percent of respondents to a retirement community survey indicated that "living in pleasantly landscaped grounds" was essential or important (Browne, 1992). Pleasantly landscaped grounds could be refuge or stimuli. Home gardeners indicated that stimuli from gardening activities provided creative outlets, exercise, and increased confidence, and the reduction in stress provided respite and tranquility. The benefits were complex and included health and well-being (Catanzaro & Ekanem, 2004). Circumstantial evidence exists that shows park users achieve psychological benefits not only from direct contact with nature, but also through social interaction with peers (Hartig et al., 1991; Tinsley & Kass, 1979; Ulrich, 1999; Ulrich & Addoms, 1981). Even passive contact with nature can be enough to trigger a chain of positive mental and physical responses (Ulrich, 1983; Ulrich & Addoms, 1981). Low users or nonusers of natural space report a feeling of comfort just knowing the space is easily accessible (Ulrich, 1999; Ulrich & Addoms, 1981). Nature becomes a place of stimulation, peace, memory, and tranquility (Lewis, 1992).

Exposure to nature can provide a person with a persistence of mental arousal or stimuli, hold one's interest, and maintain one's emotional states. Healthy individuals may achieve a benefit from the stimuli of nonthreatening nature, companionship, or ephemeral views. This generates an affective reaction of fascination, which leads to a thoughtful evaluation of a scene and elicits a preference for and remembrance of the sight. In times of stress, a lengthy cognition (as involuntary attention) and recall can allow one the time to modify emotions and can produce changes in physical and mental arousal.

## THERAPEUTIC RESULTS FOR STRESSED PEOPLE

If a person's psychological state is one of stress, excessive arousal, or mental overload, then visual or physical contact with nature can induce feelings of pleasantness and fascination, thereby holding one's interest and suspending stressful thoughts (Ulrich, 1983). Additional benefits may come from physical exertion, social interaction, discovery, and nurturing. Simple aesthetics, fascination, or evolutionary response also may be the genesis for a positive reaction (Thompson, 2006). Hartig et al. (1991) studied subjects who were stressed with a difficult cognitive task then asked to relax by listening to music or walking in either an urban or nature setting. Those who walked in a nature setting reported more subjective positive feelings than either of the other two groups (Hartig et al., 1991; Ulrich, 1993; Ulrich &

Parsons, 1992). A similar study by Honeyman (1992) yielded analogous results. The data showed that participant stress levels were more effectively reduced with the presence of vegetation than during urban walks or through other forms of relaxation. Stress reduction occurred rather quickly, in a matter of just a few minutes. The findings were supported by Ulrich's 1991 study of stress recovery, which showed that stress reduction can occur in as little as 3 to 5 minutes. Determinant measurable medical outcomes included, but were not limited to, decreases in blood pressure, heart rate, and muscle tension, as well as a reduction in electrical impulse conductance of the skin and subjective reports by participants of reduced pain (Figures 4.4, 4.5, 4.6, and 4.7). The results of these studies and others were confirmed by Ulrich's review of a wide variety of studies. The findings are in accordance with the need to reduce stress responses in order for the body to return to normal baseline functioning. Cumulative data reveals that stressed individuals receive an even greater benefit from exposure to nature than those not currently experiencing heightened stress.

## NATURE BENEFITS FOR COMMUNITIES

Considering the health benefits of exposure to nature for all people, steps should be taken to incorporate preventative measures for stress reduction and restoration into neighborhoods and communities. While a person might not consider him- or herself to be stressed in a truly medical way, everyone experiences stressful events through work, traffic, deadlines, family issues, physical inactivity, and so forth. Restoration of mind and body might be a more accurate description of what people need to obtain from nature. The most effective restoration benefits are derived from exposure to natural surroundings when certain configurations and elements are present (Ulrich, 1993; Ulrich & Addoms, 1981; Ulrich & Parsons, 1992). Savanna-like environments (scattered trees, open spaces, grass land) and those that incorporate water are the most visually preferred and result in reported feelings of tranquility (Ulrich & Addoms, 1981). Being outside is apparently not enough. Sheets and Manzer (1991) studied the emotional response of individuals who viewed urban scenes. Their results suggest that the presence of vegetation and street trees markedly increased positive responses to the scenes (Ulrich, 1993). Additional studies that measured mental restoration revealed that participants who viewed urban or built environments did not have a thorough recovery from stress (Hartig et al, 1991; Honeyman, 1992; Ulrich, 1993). This concept is not new. Frederick

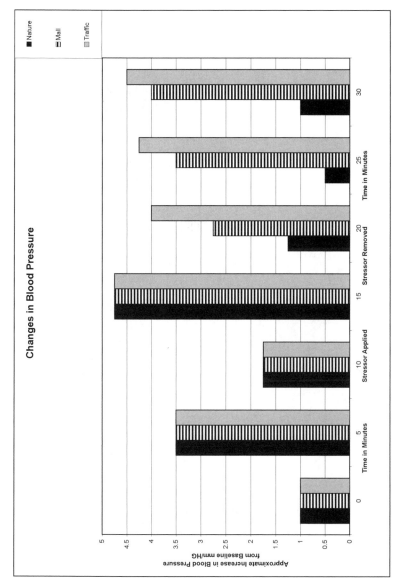

**Figure 4.4.** Environmental influences on blood pressure.

71

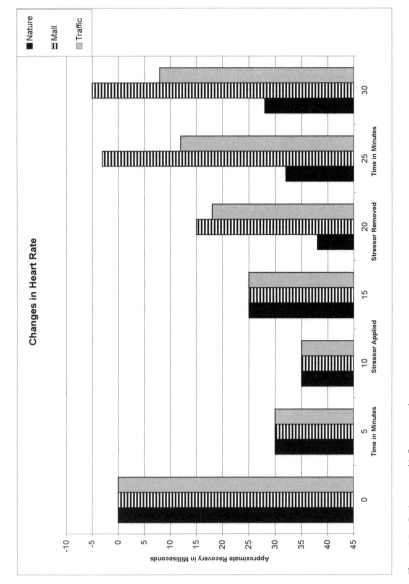

**Figure 4.5.** Environmental influences on heart rate.

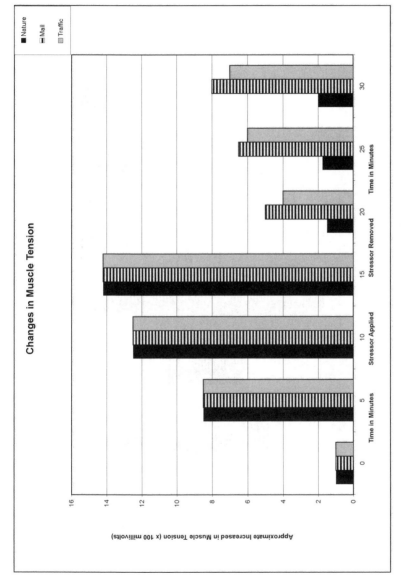

**Figure 4.6.** Environmental influences on muscle tension.

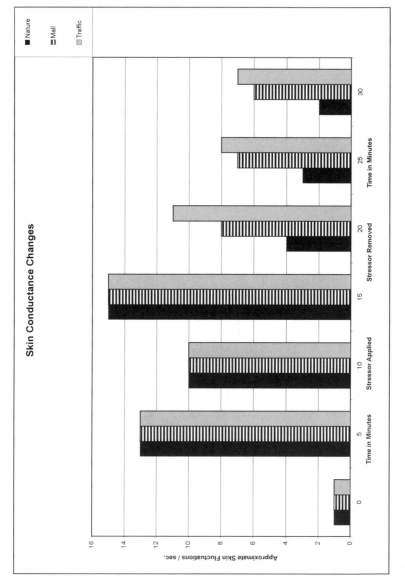

**Figure 4.7.** Environmental influences on skin conductance.

Law Olmsted knew this when he designed Central Park for New York and wrote about the curative power of nature and its need within an urban area (Olmsted & Kimball, 1922). With appropriate views of nature, restorative effects can be felt in offices, schools, work environments, and even prisons (Ulrich, 1993).

The important message remains that not all views to the outdoors are created equal. Research and study data discussed earlier confirm this. Certain characteristics must be met in order to obtain the benefits of nature. For example, including vegetation in a planned urban area can increase the area's appeal as well as its ability to create a positive response (Honeyman, 1992; Ulrich & Addoms, 1981). Institutional venues should be designed and constructed to include direct and visual contact with nature. Easy access to parks, recreation areas, and walking and biking trails can aid all people in the community by increasing exercise opportunities and by creating active and passive contact with nature. Even planned housing for seniors should include exercise spaces as well as passive access to nature views and non-threatening wildlife. Signage and wayfinding are important in assisting all community members in locating a nature setting. A park with no indication of its location, a hospital garden without directional signs, or exercise trails with no pathmarkers would be inadequately used and of little benefit. A review of public health documents found that accessibility to facilities, ease of access to nature, and aesthetics were the most significant factors determining adult physical activities (Humpel et al., 2002). Perceived long distances and topographical barriers negatively affected use of facilities (Troped et al., 2001). The conclusion that can be drawn from these studies is that accessibility, proximity, connectivity, and walkability to nature should be examined when choosing to relocate to a new area (Leslie et al., 2005).

With higher life expectancies and an ever-increasing number of baby boomers retiring but remaining active, communities and housing markets will have to keep up with the demand for change. A *New York Times* article reviewed popular retirement locations chosen by baby boomers (Lee, 2004). Retirees are looking for one-story residences within easy access to exercise and recreation opportunities, national parks, and seashores— essentially one big playground. Active adult neighborhoods tied into a larger community are popular because they include a younger population with which to interact (Lee, 2004). A number of Americans 50 years of age or older are training for the Boston Marathon. In 2006, 20% of its finishers were over the age of 50 (Kadlec, 2006). Meanwhile, many are recovering from orthopedic surgeries due to injuries sustained from long-term or inappropriate physical activity (Demont, 2003). A group this large, diverse, and active must be considered in a community environmental pre-scriptive. From 2003 to 2005, 46.4 million Americans (21.6% of the national adult population) developed some form of arthritis. Activity limi-tation was reported by 17.4 million, or 8.3% of adults. This number is expected to rise to 67 million by the year 2030 (Centers for Disease Con-trol, 2006). Exercise can control the severity of some forms of arthritis and lessen the stress created by pain and inactivity (Centers for Disease Control, 2006). Strength training and resistance training can be accomplished in the garden (Thompson, 2006), and cardiovascular benefits can be obtained from a brisk walk (National Institutes of Health/National Institute on Aging, 2006). In a 2006 National Institutes of Health study, Emma King, age 75, replied "Definitely not!" when asked if she intends to stop walking. She walks 4 to 5 miles per week. Arthur Canfield, age 83, stated "I hate the thought of exercise for exercise's sake. I've never done that" (NIH/NIA, 2006). Outdoor activities of lifelong pursuit can be more interesting to some members of a community. Participants in these activities can main-tain endurance, strength, balance, and flexibility as well as have direct con-tact with nature, which will aid in reducing stress (NIH/NIA, 2006). A 1984 study showed that a 4-month aerobic training program improved IQ scores (Dustman et al., 1984). A 2006 study of participants ages 70 to 82 found that higher levels of activity spent on any daily action lowered the mortality rate by 69% (Manini et al., 2006).

Baby boomers may be aging actively, but some will eventually deal with chronic disease. While these conditions cannot be cured, they can be better tolerated. A landmark study published in the *Journal of the American Medical Association* showed that exercise lowered the rate of reoccurrence of breast cancer, regardless of the size of the tumor (Holmes et al., 2005). A study relating incidence of dementia to amount of exercise noted that peo-ple engaging in leisure activities at least three times per week had a 32% reduction in the possibility of developing dementia and a 59% lower chance of developing Alzheimer's disease (Larson et al., 2006). As stated previously, exercise and contact with nature can reduce stress and improve cognitive ability, which are beneficial to an individual as well as to society.

An additional consideration in creating healthy communities is data showing that baby boomers may cause stagnation in the housing market. In a report published in the *New York Times*, baby boomers living in the suburbs will be less mobile and will prefer to age in place (Tedeschi, 2006). Homeowners over the age of 50 are less likely to move, fewer than 10% move at all, and of those only 5% move out of state. Approximately 80% of baby boomers own their own single-family suburban home and have lived there for over 10 years. Migration is not really a consideration (American Association of Retired Persons, 2006; Wylde, 2002). Suburban homeowners may not downsize or move to urban areas, which will create an older nonworking population with fewer tax dollars supporting services. Seventy four percent of households age 65 and older live outside central cities (AARP, 2006). This will put a strain on health services, transportation, and infrastructure used by this older, suburban demographic (AARP, 2006). Aging in place will involve changing the place and housing, not the person. Current housing may be inappropriate for successful aging in place. Residences may require modifications, such as wider doors, ramps, handrails, raised planting beds, and improved walking surfaces, to maintain barrier-free daily domestic activities (AARP, 2006), or a single, local move to more supportive communities (Frank, 2002). Promoting accessible housing with walkable neighborhoods can enhance residents' abilities to remain active and independent (AARP, 2006). Livable communities must provide a safe, healthful environment on a sustainable basis. Trees, plants, shade, and clean water all contribute to a salubrious outdoor setting. Particularly notable as we age is intolerance for heat and pollution, which can be mitigated with vegetation. Clean, healthy surroundings allow the community residents to be safe and independent and to enjoy life (AARP, 2006).

The psychological well-being obtained from an environment comes from feelings of sameness, dependable stimulation, social structure, autonomy, and achievement (Lawton, 1998). Negative psychological effects and stress occur when moving is required due to illness, fear, and the inability to continue daily activities. The speed and intensity of a move can create negative mental and physical responses, which can be ameliorated when choosing a new living arrangement by incorporating familiar landscape forms, sounds, and symbols and by maintaining some forms of control and privacy over the new environment (Frank, 2002; Golant, 1998). Forward-looking communities are preparing for the Silver Tsunami by instituting best practices for preventative health benefits for individuals who are experiencing lifestyle changes and choices, including age-appropriate fitness programs and adaptable fitness equipment. Convenient public transportation to nature exercise and other fitness sites, easy-to-read signs at these facilities, and even large-print signs for older drivers should be considered in planning a community. Most adults in the baby boomer generation (82%) consider outdoor features when choosing a home. Fifty-five percent want accessible park areas, 52% want walk or jog trails, and 46% want undeveloped open space (Wylde, 2002).

The importance of healthy aging is gaining ground everyday. The three leading causes of death (cancer, heart disease, and stroke) all respond well to regular exercise. The psychological and physical benefits of exercise and exposure to nature can be obtained at any time during a person's life. The cycle of mental and physical disability from chronic disease and aging can be checked by developing environments that allow people to remain physically active or to begin some degree of physical activity. Barriers to physical activity can include climate, walking surface, safety, and proximity. In one study, older people who still lived in their community and who undertook an exercise program experienced a decrease in depression, and their functional decline was slowed after 6 months of activity (Phelan et al., 2002). "Just getting them out of their homes was a helpful step," reported Susan Snyder, a researcher in a fitness pilot study program (Rolden, 2005). The original study, called the Health Enhancement Program at the University of Washington, Seattle, is an example of how communities can offer the benefits of exercise and nature to individuals and receive reciprocal benefits in the form of healthy neighbors.

To improve physical activity, community designs and master planning should not overlook the need for privacy, safety, control, social interaction, and natural distraction. These characteristics are just as important to the aging baby boomer generation as to those who are hospitalized (Proshansky, 1972). Land-use patterns as well as good design and planning for the use of public transportation can create communities that support outdoor exercise, thereby making the community more livable (Handy et al., 2002). A healthy natural environment will offer community health, a reduction of stress-related illnesses, and a sense of place that creates strong connections between memories and surroundings, as well as aid in the ability to exercise (Frank, 2002).

## CONCLUSION

In being a part of the larger living earth, humans need to experience the physical and psychological benefits of nature directly and daily as a preventative measure for reducing stress, illness, and crisis. The lives of individuals resemble the struggle of patients in some ways. People are trying to maintain balance, control, and mental relief in the face of stress, aging, increased speed of change, urbanization, and illness. Therapeutic nature in its broadest sense can be seen as living healthy and buffering the invasive forces of the world.

Contact with nature provides the very things most adults are missing in their lives—exercise, control, privacy, social contact, and natural distractions for stress relief. Appreciation of nature and the ability to access it are essential aspects of healthy lives and should be respected and protected. No ideal landscape exists. It is a combination of necessary characteristics, views, and experiences that are pertinent to each individual or group with shared needs. One feels better in the presence of nature because one is less subject to stress and its negative effects. In the complex network of stress response, the experience of nature enables the various components of the human body to find repose. It is inconceivable that nature is not beneficial for the mind and body as well as for health and healing.

The research data from Rachel Kaplan and Steven Kaplan reveal that in order to have a healthy response to the environment, people must have an area where they can find order, function with ease, assess safety, and disengage direct, focused attention to allow for stress relief. Ulrich notes that without aesthetic appeal, such as water, open views, savanna-type space, and ease of access to nature, individuals will not experience the restoration they need and desire. Wilson and Kellert assert that humans are genetically a part of nature and that positive experiences and benefits lie in the ability to preserve and be in contact with healthy nature with regularity. This subconscious, emotional bond with nature, and the feeling of a sense of place within it, provide mental restoration and improved health.

It is clear from an extensive body of evidence that nature provides a benefit not only of generalized stress reduction for individuals, but also of healing that extends into the arena of measurable medical outcomes. While it is difficult to control a study on nature exposure, evidence-based health outcomes are conclusive—passive and active contact with nature can provide mental and physical benefits to individuals and to the community. Fewer stress-related complications of the body and improved psychological well-being through accessible nature are therapeutic for all people, for each community, and for the earth.

## REFERENCES

Abbott, R. D., White, L. R., Ross, G. W., Masaki, K. H., Curb, J. D., & Petrovitch, H. (2004). Walking and dementia in physically capable elderly men. *Journal of the American Medical Association, 292*(12), 1447–1453.

American Association of Retired Persons. (2006). *The policy book: AARP public policies for 2006.* Washington, DC: AARP Publications.

Browne, C. A. (1992). The role of nature for the promotion of well-being of the elderly. In D. Relf (Ed.), *The Role of Horticulture in Human Well-Being and Social Development: A National Symposium* (section 2, pp. 75–80). Portland, OR: Timber Press.

Catanzaro, C., & Ekanem, E. (2004). Home gardeners value stress reduction and interaction with nature in roles for horticulture. In D. Relf & B. H. Kwack (Eds.), *XXVI International Horticultural Congress: Expanding Roles for Horticulture in Improving Human Well-Being and Life Quality, 639* (pp. 269–275). Belgium: Peeters-Leuven. Available at http://www.actahort.org/books/639/639_35.htm.

Centers for Disease Control. (2006). Prevalence of doctor diagnosed arthritis and arthritis attributable activity limitation, U.S. (2003–2005). *Morbidity and Mortality Weekly Report, 55*(40), 1089–1092.

Cooper-Marcus, C., & Barnes, M. (1995). *Gardens in healthcare facilities: Uses, therapeutic benefits, and design recommendations.* Berkeley, CA: University of California at Berkeley, The Center for Health Design.

Cooper-Marcus, C., & Barnes, M. (1999). Historical and cultural perspectives on healing gardens. In Cooper-Marcus, C., & Barnes, M. (Eds.), *Healing gardens: Therapeutic benefits and design recommendations* (pp. 1–26). New York: Wiley.

Demont, J. (2003). When the body complains. *Macleans, 116*(33), 42–45.

Dustman, R. E., Ruhling, R. O., Russell, E. M., Shearer, D. E., Bonekat, H. W., Shigeoka, J. W., Wood, J. S., & Bradford, D. C. (1984). Aerobic exercise training and improved neuropsychological function of older adults. *Neurobiology of Aging, 5*(1), 35–42.

Frank, J. B. (2002). *The paradox of aging in place in assisted living.* Westport, CT: Bergen and Garvey.

Frumkin, H. (2004). White coats, green plants: Clinical epidemiology meets horticulture. In D. Relf & B. H. Kwack (Eds.), *XXVI International Horticultural Congress: Expanding Roles for Horticulture in Improving Human Well-Being and Life Quality, 639* (pp. 15–25). Belgium: Peeters- Leuven. Available at http://www.actahort.org/books/639/639_1.htm.

Gerlach-Spriggs, N., Kaufman, R. E., & Warner, S. B., Jr. (1998). *Restorative gardens: The healing landscape.* New Haven, CT: Yale University Press.

Golant, S. M. (1998). Changing an older person's shelter and care settings: A model to explain personal and environmental outcomes. In R. J. Scheidt & P. G. Windley (Eds.), *Environment and aging theory: A focus on housing* (pp. 33–62). Westport, CT: Greenwood Press.

Handy, S. L., Boarnet, M. G., Ewing, R., & Killingworth, R. (2002). How the built environment affects physical activity: Views from urban planning. *American Journal of Preventive Medicine, 23*(2), 64–73.

Hartig, T., Mang, M., & Evans, G. W. (1991). Restorative effects of natural environment and exercise. *Environment and Behavior, 23*, 3–36.

Heerwagen, J. H., & Orians, G. H. (1993). Humans, habitats, and aesthetics. In S. R. Kellert & E. O. Wilson (Eds.), *The Biophilia Hypothesis* (pp. 138–172). Washington, DC: Island Press.

Holmes, M. D., Chen, W. Y., Feskanich, D, Kroenke, C. H., & Colditz, G. A. (2005). Physical activity and survival after breast cancer diagnosis. *Journal of the American Medical Association, 293,* 2479–2486.

Honeyman, M. K. (1992). Vegetation and stress: A comparison study of varying amounts of vegetation in countryside and urban scenes, developing a conceptual framework. In D. Relf (Ed.), *The role of horticulture in human well-being and social development: A national symposium* (section 4, pp. 143–145). Portland, OR: Timber Press.

Humpel, N., Owen, N., & Leslie, E. (2002). Environmental factors associated with adults' participation in physical activity. *American Journal of Preventive Medicine, 22* (3), 188–199.

Janick, J. (1992). Horticulture and the human culture. In D. Relf (Ed.), *The Role of Horticulture in Human Well-Being and Social Development: A National Symposium* (section 1, pp. 19–28). Portland, OR: Timber Press.

Kadlec, D. (2006, June 26). The marathon generation. *Time Magazine, 167(26).*

Kaplan, R. (1983). The role of nature. In I. Altman & J. Wohlwill (Eds.), *The urban context in behavior and natural environment* (pp. 127–163). New York: Plenum Press.

Kaplan, R., & Kaplan, S. (1989). *The experience of nature: A psychological perspective.* Cambridge, England: Cambridge University Press.

Kaplan, R., & Kaplan, S. (1990). Restorative experience: The healing power of nearby nature. In M. Francis & R. T. Hester Jr. (Eds), *The meaning of gardens, idea, place, and action* (pp. 238–243). Cambridge, MA: MIT Press.

Kaplan, R., Kaplan, S., & Ryan, R. L. (1998). *With people in mind: Design and management of everyday nature.* Washington, DC: Island Press.

Kaplan, S. (1992). The restorative environment: Nature and human experience, developing a conceptual framework. In D. Relf (Ed.), *The Role of Horticulture in Human Well-Being and Social Development: A National Symposium* (section 4, pp. 134–142). Portland, OR: Timber Press.

Kaplan, S., & Talbot, J. F. (1983). Psychological benefits of a wilderness experience. In I. Altman & J. F. Wohlwill (Eds.), *Behavior and the natural environment* (pp. 163–201). New York: Plenum Press.

Kellert, S. R. (1993). The biological basis for human values of nature. In S. R. Kellert & E. O. Wilson (Eds.), *The Biophilia Hypothesis* (pp. 42–69). Washington, DC: Island Press.

Kellert, S. R. (2005). *Building for life.* Washington, DC: Island Press.

Kellert, S. R., & Wilson, E. O. (Eds.). (1993). *The biophilia hypothesis.* Washington, DC: Island Press.

Larson, E. B., Wang, L., Bowen, J. D., McCormick, W. C., Teri, L., Crane, P., & Kukull, W. (2006). Exercise is associated with reduced risk for incident dementia among persons 65 years of age and older. *Annals of Internal Medicine, 144*, 73–81.

Lawton, P. W. (1998) Environment and aging: Theory revisited. In R. J. Scheidt & P. G. Windley (Eds.), *Environment and aging theory: A focus on housing* (pp. 1–32). Westport, CT: Greenwood Press.

Lee, D. (2004, September 24). Retired? Yes. Retiring? No. *New York Times*, p. 11. Available at http://www.nytimes.com/2004/09/24/realestate/24RETI.html.

Leslie, E., Coffee, N., Frank, L., Owen, N., Bauman, A., & Hugo, G. (2005). Walkability of local communities: Using geographic information systems to objectively assess relevant environmental attributes. *Journal of Health and Place, 13*, 111–122.

Lewis, C. A. (1979). Healing in the urban environment: A person/plant viewpoint. *Journal of the American Planning Association, 45* (Winter), 330–338.

Lewis, C. A. (1990a). People—plant relationships—past and future. In M. Francis & R. T. Hester Jr. (Eds.), *The meaning of gardens, idea, place and action* (pp. 13–25). Cambridge, MA: MIT Press.

Lewis, C. A. (1990b). Gardening as healing process. In M. Francis & R. T. Hester Jr. (Eds.), *The meaning of gardens, idea, place and action* (pp. 244–251). Cambridge, MA: MIT Press.

Lewis, C. A. (1992). Effects of plants and gardening in creating interpersonal and community well-being. In D. Reff (Ed.), *The Role of Horticulture in Human Well-Being and Social Development: A National Symposium* (pp. 55–66). Portland, OR: Timber Press.

Lynch, K. (1971). *The image of the city* (2nd ed.). Cambridge, MA: MIT Press.

Manini, T. M., Everhart, J. E., Patel, K., Schoeller, D. A., Colbert, L. H., Visser, M., Tylavsky, F., Bauer, D. C., Goodpaster, B. H., & Harris, T. B. (2006). Daily activity energy expenditure and mortality among older adults. *Journal of the American Medical Association, 296*(2), 171–179.

National Institutes of Health/National Institute on Aging. (2006). Exercise: A guide from the National Institute on Aging. Public Health Publication, #1 – 4258 (pp. 1–32). U.S. Department of Health and Human Resources. Bethesda, MD: National Institute on Aging.

Nightingale, F. (1860). *Notes on nursing: What it is and what it is not.* London: Harrison and Sons.

Nightingale, F. (1863). *Notes on hospitals.* London: Savill & Edwards.

Ohman, A., Dimberg, U., & Esteves, F. (1989). Preattentive activation of aversive emotions. In T. Archer & L.-G. Nilsson (Eds.), *Aversion, avoidance, and anxiety* (pp. 169–193). Hillsdale, NJ: Erlbaum.

Olmsted, F. L., Jr., & Kimball, T. (Eds.). (1922). *Frederick Law Olmsted, landscape architect, 1822–1903.* New York: G. P. Putnam's Sons. (Reprinted 1970, New York, Benjamin Blom.)

Phelan, E. A., Williams, B., Leveille, S., Snyder, S., Wagner, E. H., & LoGerfo, J. P., (2002). Outcomes of community-based dissemination of the health enhancement program. *Journal of American Geriatric Society, 50*(9), 1519–1524.

Proshansky, H. M. (1972). The environmental crisis in housing: Human needs in housing. In B. M. Morrison & K. Nattrass (Eds.), *Journal of Social Issues* (pp. 24, 29, and 33). Washington, DC: University Press of America.

Ranney, V. P. (Ed.). (1990). *The papers of Frederick Law Olmsted: The California frontier, 1863–1865* (vol. 5). Baltimore: Johns Hopkins University Press.

Rolden, E. (Ed.). (2005). Living longer, stronger in later years. *The Nation's Health, 35*(2), 1–14. American Public Health Associations newsletter.

Schriffin, R. M., & Schneider, W. (1977). Controlled and automatic human information processing: Perpetual learning, automatic attending, and a general theory. *Psychological Review, 84*, 127–190.

Sheets, V. L., & Manzer, C. D. (1991). Affect cognition and urban vegetation: Some effects of adding trees along city streets. *Environment and Behavior, 23*, 285–304.

Tedeschi, B. (2006, December 3). The graying of the housing market. *New York Times*, p. 11. Available at http://homefinance.nytimes.com/nyt/article/mortgage-column-by-bob-tedeschi/2006.12.03.the-graying-of-the-housing-market/?ref=realestate.

Thompson, A. (2006). Why getting down and dirty feels so good. Retrieved May 2006, from http://healthinformation.centracare.com/healthyliving/fitness/apr07gardening.htm.

Tinsley, H. E. A, & Kass, R. A. (1979). The latent structure of need—satisfying properties of leisure activities. *Journal of Leisure Research, 11*, 278–291.

Troped, P. J., Saunders, R. P., Pate, R. R., Reininger, B., Ureda, J. R., & Thompson, S. J. (2001). Associations between self-reported and objective physical environmental factors and use of a community rail-trail. *Preventive Medicine, 32*(2), 191–200.

Ulrich, R. S. (1983). Aesthetic and affective response to natural environment. In I. Altman & J. Wohlwill (Eds.), *Behavior and natural environment* (pp. 85–125). New York: Plenum Press.

Ulrich, R. S. (1984). View through a window may influence recovery from surgery. *Science, 224*(4647), 420–421.

Ulrich, R. S. (1993). Biophilia, biophobia, and natural landscapes. In S. R. Kellert & E. O. Wilson (Eds.), *The biophilia hypothesis* (pp. 73–137). Washington, DC: Island Press.

Ulrich, R. S. (1999). Effects of gardens on health outcomes: Theory and research in healing gardens. In C. Cooper-Marcus & M. Barnes (Eds.), *Therapeutic benefits and design recommendations* (pp. 27–89). New York: Wiley.

Ulrich, R. S., & Addoms, D. (1981). Psychological and recreational benefits of a residential park. *Journal of Leisure Research, 13*, 43–65.

Ulrich, R. S., & Parsons, R. (1992). Influences of passive experiences with plants on individual well-being and health. In D. Relf (Ed.), *The Role of Horticulture in Human Well-Being and Social Development: A National Symposium* (section 3, pp. 93–106). Portland, OR: Timber Press.

Ulrich, R. S., Simons, R. F., Losito, B. D., Fiorito, E., Miles, M. A., & Zelson, M.

(1991). Stress recovery during exposure to natural and urban environments. *Journal of Environmental Psychology, 11*, 201–230.

Warner, S. B. Jr. (1994). The periodic rediscoveries of restorative gardens: 1100 to the present. In M. Francis, P. Lindsey, & J. S. Rice (Eds.), *Proceedings of the Healing Dimensions of People–Plant Relations: A Research Symposium* (pp. 4–13). Davis, CA: Center for Design Research, University of California–Davis.

Weuve, J., Kang, J. H., Manson, J. E., Breteler, M. M. B., Ware, J. H., & Grodstein, F. (2004). Physical activity, including walking and cognitive function in older women. *Journal of the American Medical Association, 292*(12), 1454–1461.

Wilson, E. O. (1984). *Biophilia.* Cambridge, MA: Harvard University Press.

Wilson, E. O. (1993). Biophilia and the conservation ethic. In S. R. Kellert & E. O. Wilson (Eds.), *The biophilia hypothesis* (pp. 31–41). Washington, DC: Island Press.

Wylde, M. (2002). *Boomers on the horizon: Housing preferences of the 55 plus market.* Atlanta, GA: BuilderBooks.com.

Zajonic, R. B. (1980). Feeling and thinking: Preference needs and influences. *American Psychologist, 35*, 151–175.

# Supportive Environments in the Community, the Neighborhood, and at Home

RETIREMENT COMMUNITIES HAVE BEEN EVOLVING over the past 50 years, as documented in scientific, trade, and popular literature. Has it prepared them for the "massive generational age wave that is about to affect all of American society" (p. 92)? Despite the "social imperative" created by the pending onslaught of aging Americans, little has been prepared to meet the needs of the baby boom generation as the window of opportunity closes.

In Chapter 5, The Evolution of Continuing Care Retirement Communities, Frank Mandy follows the transition from elder care provided by others to elder self-care and, specifically, the rise of continuing care retirement communities (CCRCs). The growing role of longevity in making family members face new and hard decisions is becoming increasingly apparent. As parents live longer, they must consider their younger family members' professional pursuits when considering the inevitable development of infirmities. CCRCs are providing one solution to the difficult question of how and where older adults will be cared for. By providing progressively higher levels of care as needed, they allow many older adults to live independently for longer. The establishment of CCRCs has been a challenge because of resistance from communities that impose restrictive zoning or regulatory hurdles, and from neighborhood residents who cry, "Not in my backyard." For CCRCs to overcome such resistance, first they need to be designed to fit architecturally more readily into their surroundings while offering the types of living spaces, programs, and services that older adults desire. Second, CCRC campuses need to break away from the single cohort population and be open to a more multi- and intergenerational population. To address these requirements Mandy describes the benefits that a well-designed and well-located CCRC can bring to a community: architectural and landscape design, daily routines that benefit the residents, and integrated programs with local schools and community organizations. CCRC residents want to be active participants in and contributors to the character and quality of their community. In that same way, community members want to be active contributors to the design and planning of the CCRC that enters their community.

In Chapter 6, Naturally Occurring Retirement Communities, or NORCs, Annie Kirk discusses older residents' growing wish to be actively involved in their communities, which comes as a result of their long-term residency in a location and their affinity for the place they call home. She describes the mounting impact of NORCs as a quietly growing, geographically focused sociologic and demographic phenomenon. Unlike the planned retirement and assisted living communities discussed in Chapter 2, NORCs are emerging as a result of the natural aging in place of a community's residents. While often touted as a nation on the go, a considerable number of Americans have chosen to remain in their communities. There are more than 5,000 urban NORCs nationwide, with a total population greater than 10 million. The number of NORCs is likely to continue to grow, which warrants considerable public health policy attention, particularly at the municipal level (Masotti et al., 2006). NORCs "were not constructed with an eye to the physical and psychological effects of aging" (p. 119) and will likely need retrofitting to enable people to age in place more successfully. Given that the geographic concentration of seniors in such communities varies from mere neighborhoods to entire communities, changes to zoning, property tax structures, and building codes will be a challenge. If dealt with in a positive way, meeting those challenges will not only extend the comfort of a growing aging cohort, but also attract other seniors who may be looking to move one last time at or near retirement (Del Webb, 2004). Kirk's review of demonstration projects considers geographic scale and uniqueness of place and people. Enabling older adults' independence empowers their participation in a community and fosters alliances that benefit no one population, but rather a majority of people throughout a community. Building neighborhoods that perpetuate an intergenerational living environment and that invite people to go outside and remain active also contributes to building social capital and benefits the entire community.

The age wave has brought to the forefront a series of first-time-ever events—so-called third agers living out a quarter to a third of their life in retirement, geographically dispersed families, and the financial pressures of aging in place. In Chapter 7, Cohousing and Shared Housing, Laura Bauer Granberry discusses how cohousing and shared-living arrangements can become "workable, long-term alternatives to nursing homes or other institutional settings" (p. 145). The qualities of cohousing echo the interdependency previously found in the social proximity of people living a century ago in village and town centers. More recently, as Bauer Granberry states, "Akin to the communes of the 1960s, today's cohousing options often feature older adults and help promote connection, independence, and dignity" (p. 145). Sprawling suburbs of homogeneous land uses that require an automobile for the simplest of chores have become such an accepted way of life that for many Americans cohousing and shared housing seem very new. Both are, in fact, not new at all. The historic examples from around the world that Bauer Granberry presents are a wonderful starting point for land-use planners, architects of the built environment, and landscape architects to mine case studies and to bring the goodness of the old ways into the present. Although cohousing is a form of intentional neighborhood, intentionality is not new. Cohousing is a shift from the intentionality manifest of zoning and building codes that are often imposed on communities by developers, planners, and designers to residents who "actively participate in the design and operation of their own community" (p. 146). New Towns, Garden Cities, and Greenbelt Towns were the planned communities of 30 to 75 years ago. Cohousing is the new planned community. The revived emphasis on social connectivity and social capital building to make stronger communities and to support aging in place is in reaction to the manufactured "American Dream" of suburban living that requires the average family to make 11 car trips a day. Cohousing as the new planned community is a shift from seeking autonomous living to seeking the benefits derived from sharing, giving, and receiving that come from acknowledging, and not denying, the growing needs associated with aging.

Shared housing is another alternative for aging well and extending one's opportunity to live independently. A number or organizations can assist individuals who are considering a shared housing arrangement. As discussed in Chapter 7, the National Shared Housing Resource Center is one such organization. Shared housing, as with cohousing, will require institutional shifts in order for one to age with dignity and as an active member of a larger community. One innovative example that Bauer Granberry identifies is the Housing Options for Seniors program through Tompkins County New York's Office for the Aging. Through an extensive Internet directory, the program enables older citizens to locate available forms of cohousing, senior housing, and more. Implicit in Tompkins County's efforts is the realization that community health is more than housing starts and air and water quality measures—a healthy community can support and be supported by a belief in the benefits of interdependence over the automobile.

In Chapter 8, Outdoor Environments Supportive of Independence and Aging Well, Jack Carman and Edward Fox discuss boomers' reformulated views regarding aging and aging in place. Mobility is more than freedom; it is independence. In an automobile-dependent environment, independence is the ability to acquire goods and services, to say nothing of going the distances needed to be with family and friends. But what happens when aging independent boomers can no longer drive? Will the community in which they wish to remain adapt to their changing physical, social, and emotional needs? Carman and Fox explore these questions by discussing the need to create built and natural environments that maintain residents' health, independence, and well-being. They recommend the following goals in the design and development of housing and outdoor environments: maintaining a connection with nature; creating walkable neighborhoods; building and redeveloping housing and communities for older residents that offer a diversity of living options, either shared or independent; and providing personal transportation options as well as adequate local and regional paratransit and public transportation systems. Boomers are reinventing how they will age in place, as evidenced in the development of CCRCs, NORCs, cohousing and shared housing, as well as other models. As these communities take shape, outdoor environments must be designed to be sensitive to and respond to the aging process.

Providing older adults with in-home technologies and services can help those in need, but to a great extent can also contribute to isolation. In Chapter 9, Technology and Aging, Emi Kiyota examines the role of technological interventions in relation to the task of shopping, which is an essential function for an older adult to be able to live independently in his or her home. Kiyota discusses how assistive technologies can enable an older adult with age-related impairments to live independently and maintain community socialization by maximizing his or her capabilities and by reducing the challenges and barriers presented by the surrounding environment. Assistive technologies may maximize an older adult's functional abilities, but cannot fully compensate for them. The limitations of assistive technologies can be enhanced only through help from family members, neighbors, and community social services. Age-friendly built and natural environments and technological aids that improve accessibility to stores need to be developed and integrated into a community. Supportive outdoor environments encourage elders to get out of their homes as well as increase their opportunities to socialize and to be more stimulated by surroundings shown to benefit their health and well-being.

## REFERENCES

Del Webb. (2004). Del Webb baby boomer survey: Empty nester syndrome. Retrieved June 2007, from http://www.pulte.com/pressroom/2004Baby Boomer/BabyBoomerDetailReport.pdf.

Masotti, P., Fick, R., Johnson-Masotti, A., & MacLeod, S. (2006). Healthy naturally occurring retirement communities: A low-cost approach to facilitating healthy aging. *American Journal of Public Health, 96*(7), 1164–1170.

5
———

# THE EVOLUTION OF CONTINUING CARE RETIREMENT COMMUNITIES

## Not Your Grandmother's Retirement Community

*Frank R. Mandy*

THE EVOLUTION OF RETIREMENT COMMUNITIES found across the United States, from the familiar rest home or old age home common in the 1940s and '50s to the modern continuing care retirement community (CCRC), is a story of more than modernization and growth. It is a reflection of the changing needs and demands of the different generations that are moving inexorably through their life cycles. As the familial support systems for older adults have changed during the 20th century, so, too, have the institutions that have been developed to offer residential care and services to older adults.

In 2006, the first wave of baby boomers reached age 60, and each year since they are inching closer to age 65. The CCRC continues to evolve to meet the changing desires of these older adults. Many long-standing retirement communities are exploring ways to redevelop their physical plants, amenities, and services as well as to reposition themselves to address competitive forces in their marketplaces. Meanwhile, despite the prevalence of increasing regulatory barriers and antidevelopment sentiments that impact all types of growth activities, the senior-living field continues to produce a small number of new communities each year. The new CCRCs are embracing modern building systems and technology, innovative amenities, and services that are desired by today's older adults. Given the massive generational age wave that is about to affect all of American society, the creation of new CCRCs would seem to be a social imperative that, so far, has not been widely embraced.

## THE HISTORY OF CONTINUING CARE RETIREMENT COMMUNITIES

The roots of retirement communities in the United States were based first in the public sector and then, eventually, in the voluntary or not-for-profit sector. The public workhouses, poorhouses, and almshouses of the 18th and 19th centuries that were often the only place where needy elders without family caregivers might find assistance gave way to a more charitable group of facilities, most of which were sponsored by religious organizations or community-based not-for-profit organizations. These early rest homes, or old-age homes, were often parts of larger organizations that provided services to orphaned children or other needy segments of society. With the passage of time, as improvements in medical care helped society to address many of the health and social problems that created the need for large institutions to serve children and other needy groups, the primary focus of many of these organizations became the elderly.

### EARLY RETIREMENT COMMUNITIES

The earliest institutions that could be considered CCRCs were created to provide modest but secure living for retired clergy, missionaries, and other members of religious organizations. The pooling of the often-limited resources of these retirees was supplemented by charitable contributions. The sponsoring religious organizations sometimes used outdated church buildings, converted schools, hospital buildings, or donated private homes as the setting for residential living. The contract or legal arrangement for care and services was often nothing more than a verbal agreement to provide needed services (American Association of Homes and Services for the Aging & American Association of Retired Persons, 1988).

At the dawn of the 20th century, with the average life span of most Americans still estimated at less than 47 years, the demand for large numbers of institutions for elderly people simply did not exist. The rest homes sponsored by religious organizations and other not-for-profits were not the societal focal point of care for elders. Indeed, along with the prevailing demographic factors related to mortality and morbidity that reduced the number of older adults who might otherwise need care, there were also social factors emphasizing familial responsibility to care for older family members in need. It was a simple fact of life that most care for seniors was provided at home, and most often it was a daughter or daughter-in-law who acted as caregiver. It was only in the latter half of the 20th century, after World War II had brought large numbers of women into the workforce, that the need for institutional caregivers began to grow measurably. While the return of WWII soldiers caused many of the Rosie the Riveters who had worked in the wartime factories to give up their jobs and return to the more traditional role of homemakers and housewives, a small but growing percentage of women opted to stay in the workforce. In many ways, this change marked the beginning of a reshuffling and redefinition of roles and responsibilities for adults and their aging parents and grandparents, which continues to this day.

As the 1940s gave way to the '50s and '60s and beyond, more and more American families began to rely on a second income to achieve a desired higher standard of living. As women became the secondary breadwinners or, in some cases, the primary ones, the changing dynamics of the American family became more permanent. Caring for elderly parents or grandparents, often in the family home as the most common place for such care to be provided, became less and less of a priority or a duty for adult children. Indeed, not only were younger family members otherwise engaged in professional pursuits, but also a shift occurred in the attitudes of older adults themselves, many of whom did not want to "become a burden" to their children or grandchildren.

Over these same decades of social change came significant improvements in sanitation practices and in the living conditions of great numbers of Americans, advances that began to reduce or even eliminate many of the infectious diseases that had contributed significantly to the mortality and morbidity rates among elders. Hand in hand with the improvements in sanitation came exponential leaps forward in medical care, pharmacology, and health care technology. The results have been staggering both in terms of demographics and improvements in the quality of life for older adults. In a little over a century, the average life span increased from about 47 years to more than 78 years—a 30-year advance that has changed the face of America. Not only has it become more common for

Americans to reach retirement age, but also they have done so in better health.

When these changes are examined in the context of the creation of the Social Security System in the 1930s and, in subsequent years, the creation of a large number of other federal and state programs designed to reduce poverty among the older population, a confluence of governmental, social, medical, health, sanitation, and business factors were combining to fundamentally alter life for America's growing elderly population. As the years passed, not only were older adults living longer and better, but also the pressure increased for them to find ways to receive long-term care and other services from sources outside of the traditional family structure.

## SPONSORSHIP OF RETIREMENT COMMUNITIES

As noted earlier, the roots of CCRCs are in the not-for-profit sector, with many of the earliest communities having religious sponsorship. These include the campuses that evolved over time from freestanding rest homes (or early nursing homes) to sites with expanded independent-living components. A great leap forward in the history of senior living in the United States was the creation of completely new campuses that focused on offering a continuum of care and services.

The unique characteristic of the CCRC is that when a senior resident of the community who is living independently in an apartment or cottage has the need for additional residential care for reasons usually associated with age or frailty, he or she is able to transfer within the campus to a higher level of care, in most cases either assisted living or skilled nursing. In many ways, the lifetime access to these long-term care services causes the CCRC to function like a long-term care insurance policy, with the financing provided by the pooled resources of the community's residents, which is a combination of entrance fees and monthly service fees (Mills, 1996).

In looking back at the history of planned CCRCs, the Society of Friends (i.e., the Quakers) was among the earliest of the developers to focus on a fully integrated continuum of care on campuses designed to allow older adults to live as independently as possible while guaranteeing the availability of long-term care services should they be needed. The earliest of the modern CCRCs offered contracts that required either the turnover of all assets in exchange for "life care" or the payment of a nonrefundable entrance fee, no matter how long a person resided in the community. Over time, variations on the contracts evolved so that, today, older consumers have a wide range of contract choices.

There are three types of contracts. The so-called Type A or life-care contract provides unlimited long-term care services once a resident has paid a predetermined entrance fee (most often based on the size of the independent living unit) and continues to pay a monthly maintenance fee (used to pay for a range of amenities and services). The Type B contract offers a more limited package of long-term care services for a smaller entrance fee and monthly fee. The Type C contract operates mainly using an á la carte, fee-for-service package of services that are paid on an as-needed basis. Examples of all three contracts can be found in CCRCs across the country; however, the Type A and B contracts tend to be more common in the Midwest and eastern United States, while Type C contracts are found more often on the West Coast.

No matter the specific contract type, these new CCRCs focused on providing retirees with a place to enjoy their retirement years secure in the knowledge that should their health care needs change for reasons of illness or age-related disabilities, there were high-quality long-term care services available on the same campus. The care and services were more commonly a mix of domiciliary care (the predecessor of modern assisted living) and skilled nursing care. Also, the earliest campuses generally included some type of dining program and other services, including activities programs.

Many of these early campuses were developed in suburban or rural areas that were near large cities, but that had a decidedly "green" look, with lots of open spaces for lawns, trees, gardens, and other outdoor spaces that the residents could enjoy. This image of the modern CCRC on a parcel of land big enough to include a reasonable amount of green space still dominates today. Unless there are site restrictions, or the development site is urban, most new retirement communities seek to combine the comforts of modern buildings with access to natural surroundings.

## A PERIOD OF GROWTH FOR CCRCS (1970–1995)

The 1970s marked the beginning of an era that, in many ways, changed the face of retirement living for most of the United States. From 1970 to 1995, there was sustained growth as the development of new CCRCs and/or the expansion of existing long-term care campuses increased the number of communities from about 250 to just under 1,700. This growth was seen across the country and in every region. Although higher rates of growth occurred in areas with warm climates—such as the West Coast, southwest, and southeast—there was also notable development around many of the largest suburban and urban areas. This trend reflects that, while some older adults prefer to retire to Florida, Arizona, or other places with warm climates, many others prefer to stay near family and friends. The states with the largest numbers of CCRCs in 2007, therefore, were not only California and Florida, but also Pennsylvania, Ohio, and Illinois.

After the boom period lasting 25 years, an inevitable slowdown in new development or expansion of existing campuses took place. Many markets had absorbed large numbers of new independent-living units offered by the new CCRCs and/or the expansions of existing long-term care campuses. The number of CCRCs nationally has continued to grow since 1995, although at a slower pace. The average since 1996 has been about 40 new CCRCs developed each year, although that number has been slipping in recent years. According to statistics compiled by Ziegler Capital Markets Group, one of the leading underwriters to the senior-living industry, there were approximately 2,400 CCRCs in the United States in 2007 (American Association of Homes and Services for the Aging & Ziegler Capital Markets Group, 2004). Again, this number reflects new development plus a more limited growth in the number of multi-facility long-term care campuses that subsequently added missing levels of care and/or independent living units to achieve a full continuum of care.

## CCRC DEVELOPMENT SLOWS
## AND ASSISTED LIVING BOOMS (1990s)

By the mid-1990s a significant change in the marketplace was occurring just as the development of CCRCs began to slow. Assisted living facilities became the new focus of the older consumer, the financial world, and many state regulators. The late 1990s saw an explosive period of growth in freestanding assisted living communities as part of a Wall Street–backed burst in new construction. Hundreds of new assisted living facilities sprang up across the country. While state governments kept a wary eye on the many new facilities, there was widespread public support for them because of the large numbers of older adults who could be cared for at the assisted-living level with no expenditure of increasingly limited Medicaid dollars. For many state policy makers, the emergence of assisted living facilities was a dream come true. Not only did these brand new facilities have modern, state-of-the-art facilities and services, but also in almost every state it was the older consumers and/or their families who were responsible for paying for care and services, not the government.

This frenzy of expansion has inevitably given way to a slowdown, or in some cases even rollbacks, as the realities of the marketplace and the challenges of providing quality care and services have hit home for many new providers, yet the sheer numbers of older adults in need of a supervised living environment have helped to keep many of these new assisted living facilities operating with high occupancy.

Although assisted living facilities will continue to play an important role in the provision of care to older adults who need some degree of supervision and assistance with activities of daily living, it is unlikely that another 1990s-style boom in assisted living development will occur. With the exception of Sunrise Senior Living Corporation and a few other smaller, national assisted living developers, the field has settled into a period of limited growth or even retrenchment, depending on the local market and the number of assisted living units that were constructed.

The slowdown in assisted living development may also have been impacted by the growing realization among older adults and their families that, while freestanding assisted living is often an attractive alternative for people who need assistance with activities of daily living, the absence of a full continuum of care also means that a resident might be asked to move out of the facility should his or her care needs change and begin to exceed the level of care and services allowable in the assisted living setting. The potential for an additional move for the resident, often to a nursing home where additional long-term care services might be available, serves to reinforce the advantages of CCRCs and other continuum-of-care models.

## RETIREMENT COMMUNITIES TODAY (2007)

For the seniors of today and, most likely, those of tomorrow, the continued growth and evolution of retirement communities will depend to a large degree on the leadership of not-for-profit organizations. The church-affiliated, not-for-profit organizations that primarily founded the senior-living field are still the predominant providers. They have been joined by other not-for-profit organizations, many of which are affiliated with hospitals and health systems (e.g., colleges and universities), as well as other community-based organizations that have begun to sponsor and develop new communities. Indeed, with the exception of a few national for-profit companies primarily affiliated with the hospitality industry, including Hyatt and for a short while Marriott, it is not-for-profit organizations that sponsor the over-whelming majority of retirement communities. Depending on which retirement living organizations are counted, estimates place the numbers at approximately 96% not-for-profit and 4% proprietary. Included as part of this discussion are senior-living organizations providing a continuum of care that includes independent living (apartments and/or cottages) and a range of long-term care services, which might include assisted living residences, skilled nursing care, and other services and amenities.

As noted earlier, after a relatively healthy period of growth during the 1970s, '80s, and '90s, the pace of new CCRC development has slowed. This slowdown may be a natural part of the industry's maturation, but also it has been driven by the emergence of a decidedly antidevelopment position on the part of many community leaders and localities across the country. Although not specifically directed at developers of retirement communities, the policy changes have affected them as well. These have included increasingly restrictive zoning regulations and environmental approvals, as well as lawsuits and other legal mechanisms designed to challenge any new residential projects with delays or prohibitions. The familiar "not-in-my-backyard" stance that has become a hallmark of modern life in many parts of the United States has had a chilling effect on the development of new CCRCs (and other large-scale residential development projects). It is currently estimated that, despite the profound impact of changing demo-

**Figure 5.1.** Residential development of all types is becoming more difficult as localities across the United States use regulatory impediments and open space initiatives to limit growth.

graphics and the market demand for new senior-living options, only about 40 new CCRCs have opened in each of the past 5 years (2002–2007). Moreover, it is taking longer and longer for sponsors and developers to navigate the regulatory minefields found at the local level. Where once it was not uncommon for a CCRC project to take about 5 years from inception to opening, it is now more likely to be 7 or 8 years.

There are more and more signs popping up in the state of New Jersey (and elsewhere in the Northeast) that proclaim: "Another 50 acres Saved from Development" or "Your Municipal Government Has Protected this Farmland from Development." This is all a part of a growing preservation movement that seems committed to slowing or stopping development of all types. Amazingly, widespread support for antisprawl measures is common, despite the fact that over 95% of the United States remains completely undeveloped (Gertner, 2006). In and around large cities across the country, however, the perception among citizens is that undeveloped land is dwindling and must be protected at all costs. It is difficult to argue with efforts to protect the environment and to preserve green space in and around cities and suburbs, yet the need for retirement housing options for the aging U.S. population will only grow in the coming years. These conflicting forces will, in all likelihood, clash as the need for more senior-living options continues to rise.

Fortunately, CCRCs and other senior housing projects remain among the most reasonable land-use options, at least from the perspective of the general public and, therefore, of many municipal leaders. The reasons for this support are fairly straightforward: $50 million to $90 million in construction (for a medium-sized CCRC); 120 to 140 new jobs when the CCRC opens; no additional children in area schools (unlike most multifamily, residential-development projects); sizable payments-in-lieu-of-taxes (because the vast majority of new CCRCs are not-for-profit) that go toward municipal services; and campuses that usually are attractive places and make good neighbors.

Historically, the preponderance of not-for-profit organizations in residential long-term care has reflected the tendency of older adults and their families to trust the local church or other religiously affiliated organization with what often amounts to their life savings, rather than an individual, a company, or a publicly traded corporation. Deciding to live the last years of one's life in a retirement community is not a decision that generations of elderly individuals have taken lightly, neither from a lifestyle nor from a financial perspective. Not only have the financial aspects of the decision been key, but also the decisions about what type of organization one could trust for services and health care over a period of many years. The long-standing local roots of not-for-profit organizations have afforded families a degree of security and comfort. Fortunately, with very few exceptions, this trust has been well placed.

With the exception of a very small number of CCRCs that in the early years of the industry ran into financial difficulties for reasons associated more with incompetence than malfeasance, the track record of the industry has been sterling. In the few cases, mostly in the late 1970s, when not-for-profit CCRCs ran into financial difficulties, it was often the religiously affiliated parent organization that stepped in to address the problems.

The success of retirement communities has been tied in large part to an increasing level of sophistication in the planning and financing of CCRCs during the past 35 years. A dedicated group of financial analysts, bankers, underwriters, consultants, and developers with a specific focus on senior-living projects has led the way in improving both the planning of communities and the marketing and development process to minimize the risks not only for older adults who live in the communities, but also for the not-for-profit organizations that sponsor them. The strengthening on the financial side of CCRC development has been accompanied by refinements in market research and marketing techniques. Combined, these improvements in due diligence undertaken by CCRC sponsors before deciding to pursue the development of a new retirement community have reduced risks for all stakeholders.

As retirement communities have evolved, so also has their regulatory environment. From the early days, when state governments were mainly concerned about whether the creation of new nursing home beds was supported by certificates of need, a wide range of state statutes have been designed to regulate the development and operation of CCRCs. State governments have been much more involved in the regulatory front than the federal government, whose oversight has focused primarily on the not-for-profit status of sponsors and on the method for calculating interest on resident entrance-fee deposits.

The most prescriptive and restrictive state statutes are ostensibly about consumer protection. The laws and regulations tend to focus on the protection of assets for older adults who are either considering living in a new community that is under development (and will be making a financial deposit to reserve space) or who are living in operating communities. The most active state governments in this regulatory sphere typically impose a range of reserve requirements on the sponsors to cover operations and future health care costs. These reserve accounts are usually in addition to a range of financial reserves that operators must maintain for reasons found in their bond financing or loan documents. Alone or in some combination, the state agencies involved in overseeing CCRCs tend to be the state insurance department, health department, attorney general's office, and the department of aging.

The growth of state regulations has certainly helped to increase protections for older consumers, but an argument can also be made that the maturation of the industry, including its financial consultants, developers, marketers, and underwriters, has played just as important a role in ensuring that communities are well planned, well financed, and well run. It is probably safe to conclude that the combination of all of these factors has contributed to the development of a robust industry that inspires confidence among the elders who live in these retirement communities.

## PROGRAMS AND INNOVATIONS

As the senior-living industry has matured, the sponsors, managers, and developers have shown a greater willingness to listen to the desires voiced by consumers for new services, programs, and amenities. Numerous changes and innovations in the buildings and physical plants of retirement communities have occurred. The programs and services found within these evolving communities have also kept pace with changing ideas.

### IMPROVED INTERNAL PROGRAMS AND SERVICES FOR RESIDENTS

The trend in the design of the physical plants and building components of CCRCs has been toward more independent-living units (i.e., apartments or cottages) to meet the desires of the residents. Most CCRCs offer a range of different apartment types, from one-bedroom units and one-bedroom units with dens to large two-bedroom cottages with full dining rooms and dens. The square footage can vary widely depending on the unit type, ranging from 750 to over 2,400 square feet. Among the most common features are walk-in closets, separate laundry rooms, and eat-in kitchens. Most developers and architects work closely throughout the development process to adjust the numbers and mix of different units to meet demand. Also, flexibility is built into the process so that residents can make adjustments to unit layouts and features.

The community center of the modern CCRC, the place where most programs, services, and amenities are offered, has perhaps changed the

**Figure 5.2.** Cottages or patio homes are a feature of many suburban CCRCs.

most. Much like the town hall or village green of the past, these centers are places where the residents of a community gather for meals, social and intellectual stimulation, exercise, and other activities. An average CCRC—that is, one with about 225 independent-living units, a health center, and a mix of skilled nursing and assisted living units—may have a community center with 50,000 square feet of space or more. Modern additions to the community center feature computer rooms, Internet cafes, salons, spas, and state-of-the-art fitness centers, including Olympic-size swimming pools. Whatever features reflect the interests of today's older adults can be found.

The dining experience at CCRCs has also evolved to reflect a combination of both choice and quality. Not only is its daily social focus acknowledged, but also the impact that proper nutrition has on the health and well-being of residents. The staid, formal dining rooms of early CCRCs have evolved into a wide range of dining options, including restaurant-style dining, the café or bistro, the Internet café, and the "grab-and-go" take-out menu in the style of modern upscale supermarkets such as Whole Foods or Trader Joe's. In many CCRCs, residents may stop at the retirement community's pub or cocktail lounge to meet friends before dinner. On other days, delicious, high-quality gourmet food—previously pre-

**Figure 5.3.** Jefferson's Ferry, the first CCRC on Long Island, New York, features a large, attractive community center with the latest amenities.

pared and flash frozen—may be picked up and taken back to the resident's apartment or cottage for reheating. On holidays or other special occasions, residents can reserve the large private dining room to host groups of family members or friends.

The focus on flexibility in dining services has carried over into the scheduling of meals and the requirements of meal programs. With the advent of computerized meal-tracking systems that use ATM-style cards to track meals or dollars spent, CCRCs can now offer residents the opportunity to choose when and whether to have a meal in one of the dining areas or to cook in their own apartments. Gone are the days when every resident had a meal plan requiring at least one meal per day at the main dining center. And the old-fashioned approach of scheduling one or two seatings in the formal dining room has also faded away. In general, residents are now able to eat when they please and in one of many different venues.

With the roots of CCRCs in religious organizations, it is not surprising that many communities have strong spiritual programming. This includes not only weekly worship services for a number of different denominations, but also bible study, discussion groups, and other opportunities for residents to embrace their own particular religious faith.

The arts are another area that lend themselves to wonderful programming and services in CCRCs. Most communities embrace a wide variety of

**Figure 5.4.** The social life at a CCRC may include cocktails before dinner at the project's pub.

the performing arts, including theater, dance, and music. From plays and musicals performed by CCRC residents themselves to recitals by local musicians to shows featuring "off Broadway" talent, the schedule of performances slated for the CCRC's theater or auditorium is usually full.

Often residents will find a special room set aside for woodworking and an art studio for painting, sculpture, and other artistic outlets, providing a wide range of opportunities for creative activity. Other examples of creative outlets for residents include, photography, gardening, embroidery, dried flower arranging, and quilting. It is not uncommon for residents who move into CCRCs to realize that they have the time and the support to pursue artistic interests that may have been delayed or deferred due to work and family responsibilities. The results can be spectacular. Paintings and sculptures of museum quality can be found in many CCRCs. Resident-created photography exhibits and art shows are also hosted, while the woodworking talents of other residents can be seen in various pieces of furniture used in lounges and other community center spaces. Some resident associations use the sale of handmade furniture, quilts, and crafts created by residents as a means of fundraising or to support social activities at the community.

With today's increased focus on health prevention and healthy living, it is not surprising to find a large variety of programs related to physical fitness and wellness. Some communities have state-of-the-art fitness programs, including workout rooms outfitted with equipment designed spe-

**Figure 5.5.** The dining room at CCRCs is a place for daily social interactions as well as nutritious meals.

cifically for older adults. Personal trainers are available to provide advice and encouragement and to ensure the proper use of fitness machines. Communities that have the space for swimming pools commonly have aquatic exercise and fitness programs. Several well-known CCRCs have expanded their aquatic programming to allow nonresident seniors to access their facilities and programs. The cost of pool upkeep and the salaries of professional trainers have been funded in part by charging membership fees to these nonresident participants. This practice has not only helped underwrite the design and development costs, but also raised the standards of the programs. A side benefit is often seen in the marketing arena, as many local seniors gain a better understanding of the CCRC's caliber of facilities, staff, and programs, and subsequently consider the CCRC as a living option when they might not otherwise have done so.

The development of fitness and wellness centers has matured for CCRCs, particularly as a specialty of architectural design and programming. Indeed, quite a number of firms now specialize in assisting CCRCs, developers, and sponsors of new communities in the appropriate use of existing space or in the design of new areas for these programs. The results

**Figure 5.6.** Indoor swimming pools are a focal point for aquatic fitness programs, water aerobics, and lap swimming.

are often impressive. They include bright, spacious rooms with high-tech equipment and professional staff. Additional features may include adjacent spa areas and salons offering massages, manicures, and pedicures. No longer are fitness or wellness areas an afterthought of the development process. Rather, they are becoming a focal point in the design of new communities. With the baby boomer generation waiting in the wings for its long-anticipated move into the retirement arena, progressive sponsors are trying to accommodate not only the desires of today's older adults, but also the anticipated wants of the boomers of tomorrow.

## ENGAGING WITH THE LARGER COMMUNITY

Opening up their health and fitness programs to the outside community is just one way that CCRCs reach out to their larger communities for the benefit of those communities as well as the enrichment of their residents.

Among residents of retirement communities can certainly be found a desire to live with one's peer group, but also to remain active with all generations. Numerous intergenerational programs have therefore been created to afford residents the opportunity to interact with children of all ages. Mentoring programs with area high school students, for example, are built around the professional backgrounds and life experiences of residents, and can be enriching for both age groups. Foster grandparenting programs are also common, matching residents with younger children who have no living grandparents or older role models. In some CCRCs, the residents have embraced programs to fight illiteracy through reading programs for preschool children. Other CCRCs offer on-site childcare for their staff, which allows opportunities to create fulfilling interactions between the generations.

Lifelong learning has been recognized as a goal by many older adults, and modern CCRCs are becoming renowned for their programming for educational and intellectual stimulation. There are myriad examples of CCRCs that have developed formal and informal links to local colleges and universities. The symbiotic relationships that have developed have led to adjunct professorships for residents, mentoring programs for students, and the ability for seniors to earn degrees and audit classes for personal growth and development. Lectures on a wide range of topics are presented regularly at the CCRC's auditorium or theater.

Internships and career-development programs created for college students at CCRCs are almost too numerous to mention. Nursing, social work, business management, exercise physiology, gerontology, geriatric medicine, art, computer science and information technology, and communications are just a few of the disciplines that have created programs at CCRCs that give students real-world experience in the working world and with older adults. It is not just the students who benefit, of course, but also the CCRCs and their residents, who gain tremendously from their interactions with this younger generation as it moves into new careers and vocations.

The natural symbiosis between retirement communities and institutions of higher learning has been so great that currently more than 40 CCRCs have either been sponsored by or formally affiliated with colleges and universities, their alumni associations, and/or their foundations. According to Ziegler Capital Markets Groups, the number of college- and university-affiliated retirement communities continues to grow (Brod, 2003). Perhaps the most common model is when an affiliated organization (e.g., alumni, retired faculty, or a foundation) sponsors the new CCRC project and works collaboratively with the administration of the institution of higher learning to create a cooperative relationship. Once successful retirement communities are developed, the college or university will often see an increase in donations, legacies, and other financial support from the CCRC's residents and their estates. Additionally, the residents who have had past links to the college or university can enjoy a reconnection with their alma mater through wide-ranging educational options and attendance at cultural and/or sporting events.

In another common model, a not-for-profit organization creates a retirement community in close proximity to an institution of higher learning but initially has no formal affiliation. Over time, through a focused program of outreach and cooperative interaction, the relationship between the two entities begins to develop naturally. Membership on the CCRC board may be offered to the president, dean, or other senior-level staff at the school as a way of facilitating connections. Also, retired faculty and staff may be among the resident population and can play an important role in building relationships and creating programming.

Older adults want to stay connected to the outside world in ways other than education. Numerous social accountability activities are initiated by the CCRC sponsors and residents, such as environmental activities, political actions, and fundraising for various charities that play important roles in supporting the broader locality. Residents of CCRCs bring their passions for charitable entities and causes to their new home and their new neighbors. The results can be impressive: fundraising campaigns, new community resources and ideas, and expanded public support for diverse issues and causes.

Supporting environmental issues is an example of the social activism of CCRC residents, wherein they work cooperatively among generations to ensure accountability in the protection of natural resources. At the urging of residents, some CCRCs have developed strong recycling programs. Other CCRCs, also following the lead of their residents, have become leaders in their local communities to support local environmental causes. Residents of CCRCs have sponsored, for example, the protection of wetlands, improvements to parks and hiking paths, habitat protection for endangered species, and environmental education programming.

Politics are also alive at CCRCs. Politicians have recognized the potential opportunities for campaigning at retirement communities. Debates, candidates' nights, and other political forums are often scheduled at CCRCs. This is a function of three important factors: the CCRC has the space for these events (i.e., large auditoriums and theaters), the population of potential voters living there is large, and the voting rate of older adults tends to be higher than other age groups in our society. Given these factors, it is not surprising to find many CCRCs serving as polling places during local, statewide, and national elections.

CCRCs can also serve as the focal point for local meetings of other not-for-profit organizations and community groups. The community library, rotary club, community chest, local business council, and other area organizations find CCRCs to be an ideal location for meetings. This is an easy way for a CCRC to strengthen its relationship with local community leaders and their organizations. An outgrowth of providing free meeting space can be new programming or services that are developed to serve the residents of the CCRC or the broader community.

Building and strengthening such community ties can be particularly instrumental in instances when a battle erupts, as can occur in any community, between the CCRC and the community at large over taxes, traffic, or other operational issues. Having allies among community leaders and other not-for-profit organizations can be helpful in lessening the impact.

## PUBLIC POLICY BENEFITS OF CCRCS

In discussing the modern CCRC, it can be demonstrated that not only do residents enjoy a wide range of benefits, but also society as a whole. Most notably, when CCRC residents pre-fund their own future long-term care needs through the payment of an entrance fee, they are reducing or, in the case of Type A contracts, eliminating the possibility that the state and/or federal government will be paying for any future nursing home care with Medicaid funds. Given that an estimated 80% of the more than $150 billion spent on nursing home care is currently funded through the Medicaid program, CCRCs can have a tremendously positive financial impact. That impact is even more profound when one considers that in addition to the care provided in nursing homes, more than 7 million Americans, mostly family members, provide 120 million hours of unpaid care to frail elders living in their own homes or elsewhere in the community, according to the 1994 National Long-Term Care Survey. If these informal caregivers were paid, the additional cost of long-term care would range from $45 billion to $94 billion a year (Stone, 2000).

With the advent of Medicaid estate planning and other legal means of transferring personal assets so as to access Medicaid-funded long-term care, older adults have faced the dilemma of finding a way to protect their savings while also being able to receive and pay for care when they need it. With the cost of skilled nursing care in some parts of the country rising to over $350 per day, a 6- to 12-month stay in a nursing home has the potential to wipe out a lifetime of savings and to impoverish spouses and other family members. The understandable desire to legally shelter assets has driven many families to attorneys who specialize in this practice. In doing so, however, these older adults have limited their residential living options because the number of Medicaid "beds" is limited in many long-term care settings and the care associated with them can be substandard.

From a societal point of view, the Medicaid funding that is intended to pay for the health and long-term care needs of the poor is being diverted to pay for the care of middle- and upper-income Americans who can find legal ways to shelter or transfer their assets. If more CCRCs were available, and if older adults and their families were better educated regarding the quality of living, the lifestyle, and the financial benefits of CCRCs, there would be stronger incentives for them to consider this option as a way to invest and protect their assets while funding their own retirement and possible long-term care.

## THE FUTURE OF RETIREMENT COMMUNITIES IN THE UNITED STATES

The demographic challenge facing the United States is vast. As of 2006, more than 36 million people were over the age of 65. This represents 12.3% of the population. Meanwhile, like a giant tsunami poised to overwhelm everything in its path, 78 million baby boomers will reach age 65 in a 20-year period between 2010 and 2030 (U.S. Bureau of the Census, 2005). Aside from questions about their financial ability to afford to retire and, indeed, the ability of the federal government and the Social Security System to remain solvent during those years and beyond, two of the great unanswered questions are: Where will all of these retirees live and who will provide any needed long-term care and services?

Society often hedges its bets about the future by presuming that advances in technology will lead to increased efficiencies that can overcome unmet problems. While there will undoubtedly continue to be advances in a wide range of technologies that impact the provision of care and services to older adults, including many that will increase efficiencies and effectiveness, the simple fact remains that millions of people will, at some time, be living in retirement settings that will require some oversight and assistance. With the sheer numbers involved, the challenges for senior-living providers will be creating enough residential living options and finding staff to provide the needed care and assistance.

For the 2,400 existing CCRCs and the 40 new ones that will be built each year for the next few years, there will certainly be sufficient numbers of older adults in the marketplace. Getting those elders to move from their own homes, however, remains the biggest obstacle. In fact, with so many baby boomers likely to be considering retirement-living options in the near future, programs such as continuing care at home or the longstanding Friends Life Care at Home model may warrant further examination and possible replication.

The original Friends Life Care at Home program was founded in 1985 by two Quaker-sponsored organizations in the Philadelphia suburbs. Funded by a grant from the Robert Wood Johnson Foundation and the Pew Trust, Foulkeways and Jeanes Hospital partnered to create a program of "continuing care without walls." Three key findings that encouraged the founding organizations to implement the program were that (1) older adults were highly interested in guaranteed lifetime health care; (2) social activities available in residential settings outside their own homes were not of particular interest; and (3) people of modest incomes who were living in a CCRC were interested in a plan that would allow them to live in their own homes (Barbour, 1998). The program serves older adults through a network of contracted providers of adult day health care, home care, homemaker assistance, emergency response, and meal delivery as well as referral settings in assisted living and skilled nursing facilities. There is a one-time enrollment fee that is based on the age of the enrollee and his or her selection of a particular level of benefits. Admission criteria screen potential participants by measuring their ability to live independently.

The success of this program, and others like it, offers hope that new models of care may be found that can provide services to people in the place they most often desire to live—their own home. With the limitations on development of new retirement communities and the rising cost of land and building materials, it will be incumbent upon society to find inventive ways to address what is likely to be a shortage of retirement-living options.

## CONCLUSION

The existing CCRCs, particularly those built during the growth years of the late 1970s and '80s, will need to remain flexible and creative in finding methods of overcoming the problems that are beginning to arise from aging physical plants and buildings. Across the country, a number of CCRCs are undertaking significant redevelopment and repositioning projects designed to renovate or replace older structures. This type of activity will be important with the passing years if the current CCRCs are to remain viable and attractive to today's seniors and the baby boomers in the future.

With many redevelopment projects underway, sponsors and their development consultants are working diligently to design new building and community spaces that can offer the types of living spaces, programs, and services desired by the senior marketplace. Without a crystal ball that can clearly delineate the types of programs and services that will be in vogue in the future, however, the most practicable approach will be to redevelop the older CCRCs with a high degree of flexibility built into their community spaces. While apartments and cottages can usually be retrofitted with more modern appliances and technological devices, the large community center spaces present a challenge. Once constructed, it is more difficult to make significant changes to these physical spaces without incurring large costs. Therefore, the design of program spaces is being done with an eye toward the future.

In 2006 and 2007, New Life Management & Development, Inc., conducted more than two dozen focus group sessions with over 400 older adults for a variety of different not-for-profit clients around the United States. Some interesting insights have been gleaned that may help to guide planning for the future. When older adults were asked about the programs, services, and amenities that would be important to them in a new retirement community, the answer was: Everything! High percentages of focus group attendees indicated that they wanted quality health care, an indoor swimming pool, a state-of-the-art fitness center with personal trainers, hiking and walking trails, elegant dining options, a computer room, a library, group travel options, a pub, and housekeeping. In short, they wanted everything possible that could be designed into the new CCRC. These participants considered themselves healthier and more active than other older adults in the community. They felt financially secure for a variety of reasons, not the least of which was that the value of their homes had appreciated significantly in recent years.

While this unscientific sample can provide some interesting insights about today's elders, the troubling aspect of this brief analysis is that it does not provide any information about what the baby boomers will want in the future. Given the common public knowledge of this generation, it is not too much of a prediction that if today's seniors are demanding, then the baby boomers will be much more so. Boomers will want options and they will want choices in every aspect of their senior-living experience. They will want all that is being offered to today's seniors and more. Besides the impact of their sheer numbers, a particular generational nuance that has distinguished baby boomers has been a propensity to upend societal foundations as the generation has moved through its life cycle. From shortages of hospital nurseries when they were born to shortages of classrooms as they entered schools to insufficient jobs as they entered the workforce, boomers have forced society to make often substantial adjustments as they have moved through every stage of life. It is therefore probably inevitable that it will again be the case as they move into retirement.

For the senior-living field, the aging of the baby boomers will present the last great societal challenge before that generation becomes an interesting footnote to history. Retirement communities will try to prepare for the onslaught. The best advice it seems may be to remain flexible and open to change as the needs of baby boomers become known. And while there should certainly be an increased focus on the creation of new CCRCs around the country, the realities of a slower development process for new projects should temper any expectations that the senior-living industry will be able to build its way out of any shortages of living units. Creativity in new programming and redevelopment of older campuses may indeed become the best way for society to address these looming challenges.

## REFERENCES

American Association of Homes and Services for the Aging & American Association of Retired Persons. (1988). *National continuing care directory*. Glenview, IL: Scott, Foresman & Co.

American Association of Homes and Services for the Aging & Ziegler Capital Markets Group. (2004, March). *AAHSA Ziegler 100—The nation's 100 largest not-for-profit multi-site senior living organizations*. Report issued at the AAHSA Future of Aging Services Conference, Washington, DC. Available at http://www .zieglerassetmanagement.com/display/router.aspx?docid=666.

Barbour, C. (1998). Futurescape: Long term care without walls. *Nursing Homes Magazine, 3*.

Brod, K. L. (2003, September). University related senior living or senior living related universities? Paper presented at the annual meeting of the American Association of Homes and Services for the Aging, Chicago, IL.

Gertner, J. (2006, March). Home economics. *New York Times Magazine*.

Gordon, P. A. (1993). *Developing retirement communities: Business strategies, regulation, and taxation*. New York: Wiley.

Mills, R. E. (Ed.). (1996). *Long term care investment strategies: A guide to start-ups, conversions and strategic alliances*. Chicago, IL: Irwin Professional Publishing.

Stone, R. I. (2000). *Long-term care for the elderly with disabilities: Current policy, emerging trends, and implications for the twenty-first century.* New York: Millbank Memorial Fund.

U.S. Bureau of the Census. (2005). National population projections. Washington, DC: U.S. Bureau of the Census.

6

# NATURALLY OCCURRING RETIREMENT COMMUNITIES
## Thriving through Creative Retrofitting

*P. Annie Kirk*

THE NUMBER OF INDIVIDUALS turning 65 years of age in the next two to four decades has profound implications for housing developments, the retrofitting of homes, in-home service delivery systems, neighborhoods, community planning, and policy making for many parts of the United States. Approximately 1 in 7 Americans were 65 or older in 2000, and this ratio is projected to increase to 1 in 5 by the year 2030, according to current projections (U.S. Bureau of the Census, 1999). The many dimensions and impacts of this shift will call for ongoing discourse and collaboration between public health experts, land use planners, and designers of the built environment. Social service organizations acknowledge what looms on the horizon and are working in concert with state and federal governments to initiate demonstration projects to learn more about what is needed and what works in prevention and support services. Planners, designers, and policy makers are being tapped for innovations in infrastructure that are responsive and sensitive to a varied constituency, not just to older adults. The marketplace, having taken notice of a whirl of activity, has ignited and is attempting to define and address the baby boomer consumers who are coming of age for retirement.

According to a 1999 National Nursing Home Survey by the Centers for Disease Control and Prevention, only 18% of the oldest older adults (those over the age of 85) in the United States were living in skilled nursing facilities, while the remaining 82% percent were residing in the community, living out the common desire to grow old, or "age in place," in one's own home and surrounding community (Centers for Disease Control and Prevention, 1999). These citizens, living among other older adults, are aging in their own homes by virtue of several factors: their own preference, the advancements of modern medicine to help manage chronic pain and illness, and the availability of various forms of conventional support services. However, given the dawn of retirement for the baby boomers, the dramatic increase in the number of older adults living "in-community" over the course of the next 50 years will not only stretch service delivery systems, but also the housing market. Challenges mixed with opportunities will present themselves, and every community across the United States will likely experience some associated change caused by interventions designed to meet the societal demands of an aging population. Civic operations, on the whole, will be pushed in directions not previously seen and policies will have to be modified, if not created. How the physical environment is planned, altered, and designed will come under even greater scrutiny than under current practices. Individuals will personally experience the effects of an aging population as demographics force designers, public health professionals, land-use planners, and builders to find new directions, solutions, and collaborations. The overall challenge will be one of balancing traditional environmental needs with the immense social demands that have become characteristic of baby boomers for resource-laden, people-oriented, creative, health-promoting, and sustainable outcomes. The aging baby boomers and their adult children will play significant roles in the innovation, testing, and implementation of new practices and policies. Housing and support services will see a new dawn as baby boomers crest retirement.

Creativity will be essential to meet the challenges of the aging population. Some of these challenges include the number of older adults among the current population; the wave of older adults on the horizon who will be reaching retirement age; the current and forecasted experience of the adult children of these older adults (coined the "sandwich" generation [a generation of people who are caring for their aging parents while also supporting their own children]); and the nation's current federal, state, private, and not-for-profit health care systems. A critical question, posed by Karen Alexander, Director of Eldercare Service at United Jewish Communities of

Metrowest in New Jersey, is "How can we transform communities that were initially designed for young families and healthy adults into places that embrace, engage, and support older residents?" (Alexander, 2006, p. 191). The challenge is ". . . to create livable communities, with appropriate and affordable housing, adequate options for mobility, and the community features and services that can facilitate personal independence and continued engagement in civic and social life," according to Elinor Ginzler, Director of Livable Communities in the Office of Social Impact at the American Association of Retired Persons, in her statement before the Senate Committee on Health, Education, Labor, and Pensions Subcommittee on Retirement Security and Aging (Ginzler, 2006). This is *the* challenge and a call to action—the need for cross-disciplinary collaboration so that sound, applicable, and practical planning and design of the built environment can be achieved. Designers, researchers, public and community health experts, planners, and policy makers must work toward progressive, ingenious, and holistically informed solutions that transcend and traverse disciplines.

## NATURALLY OCCURRING RETIREMENT COMMUNITIES—A PRIMER

An entire array of older adult living arrangements exists in the United States. As a group, these living arrangements form a field of study that has been explored by many disciplines and they have become a significant and growing commodity in the economy. Public health and welfare personnel, policy makers, geriatricians, home health care workers, advocacy groups, social services organizations, transportation designers, land planners, and religious leaders in faith communities all have a stake in the living accommodations provided for and the health and quality of life experienced by older adults. Along the continuum of housing and care alternatives for older adults is one that will be explored here in greater depth: naturally occurring retirement communities or NORCs.

The term *NORC* was first introduced in 1985 by Michael Hunt and Gail Gunter-Hunt, and was used to broadly describe a sociological phenomenon of aging and of place wherein apartment buildings, neighborhoods, and developments not originally designed nor programmed with aging adults in mind have nevertheless evolved over time to house concentrations of 50% or more residents who are older than 50 years of age (Hunt & Gunter-Hunt, 1985). While identified more than 20 years ago, the

NORC has received little attention as an actual "retirement community." Yet with significant growth in the emergence of these communities across the United States, new inquiries and innovations are being made to determine what actually occurs "on the street" in the form of accommodation, reward, and support. How do NORCs currently function? What is their social and physical infrastructure? What services do residents require to thrive in these communities? What sets one NORC apart from another in terms of "thrive-ability" (an older adult's ability to thrive in-community)?

The increased growth of NORCs has not been premeditated nor achieved by outside migrations into these communities. These are not planned retirement and assisted-living communities designed as "destinations." Instead, they arise out of the aging of their existing residents within a concentrated area or building complex. The overall aging in the U.S. population is reflected in the continuing growth of NORCs.

NORCs are in various stages of emergence and recognition across the United States and are a living example of the universal desire to age in place in one's home and community. A study conducted in 2005 by the American Association of Retired Persons (AARP) confirmed that "89% of those polled reported that they want to stay in their current residence for as long as possible and 85% want to stay in their community for as long as possible" (American Association of Retired Persons, 2005, p. 3). NORC residents have stayed in place, raised families, developed long-time friendships, built businesses, and worked in the community or city while their homes and neighborhoods have aged along with them. These residents are an established component of the matrix of the larger community, district, town, and/or city. They possess "institutional knowledge," having borne witness to the political, civic, and commercial changes that have affected the neighborhood over time.

NORCs occur just about anywhere across the United States. Almost any individual has or will come into contact with them, either by being situated near a NORC or by knowing an elder who resides in one. These communities are unlike the retirement destinations in states such as Florida and Arizona that are planned and designed to attract a migration of older adults who have reached or passed "retirement age." Unlike retirement destinations, NORCs are understood as a place of "home," chosen, moved into, and settled into years prior to retirement age. The residents have no desire to relocate to any other place. Some experts question the need to support residents who choose to remain in-community, while others explore how to sustain the desire of older adults to age in their locale of choice. To address these questions, it is first necessary to understand the evolution of the NORC and the demographics of its residents. Then, one can examine the benefits afforded a city by the residents of a NORC, the financial windfall to the city or community provided by its existence, and the positive by-products that can emerge for the whole community from "retrofitting" the social and physical landscape.

## EVOLUTION

The residences in NORCs, whether in rural, suburban, or urban areas, were generally built in the 1940s and '50s and were designed to serve a mix of age groups. Over time, and likely due to differences in preferences among generations, fewer and fewer younger families moved in or stayed in-residence within these particular communities. Over the past century, neighborhoods in the United States have often been settled over relatively brief eras (e.g., World War II), and a particular generation has become dominant in one community or another. No two NORCs are alike in structure or geographic makeup. These communities have also evolved within a full continuum of housing options: Some are apartment buildings, garden cottage complexes, single-family homes, streets, neighborhoods, districts, developments, suburbs, zip codes, and rural/farming communities. According to the AARP, about 27% of older adults in the United States in 2004 were living in a NORC environment (AARP, 2004). These residences were not constructed with an eye to the physical and psychological effects of aging (e.g., blindness, mobility limitations, social isolation, depression, memory loss), nor to the potential for modifications or retrofitting that may be required for the aging physical structures and for the demands of ongoing home ownership on a fixed income (e.g., property taxes, upkeep, utility costs). Additionally, accessibility within and in and out of the setting (e.g., transportation, mobility, universal design) may not have been considered when the municipal infrastructure in the surrounding community was developed.

Efforts to resolve these unforeseen needs have given rise to a second classification for NORCs, which is distinct from the 1980s sociological definition: In the local legislatures of cities such as New York and Chicago, *NORCs* are locations "to which government in collaboration with private housing entities provide socially supportive services to defined geographic concentrations of seniors," whereby funding to support transportation, social and recreational programs, and home visits is made available (Kennedy, 2006, p. 33). Out of this distinctly legislative designation arose two differentiations that are important in testing and delivering services:

One is an *open NORC*, which has multiple owners or management entities, such as a neighborhood of one- or two-bedroom family dwellings, and the other is a *closed NORC*, which is a one-owner/management entity, such as a condominium, apartment building, or mobile home park.

Older adults living in NORCs are surrounded by a context they have known for many years and in which they have become quite comfortable. The surrounding neighborhood serves as an extension of "home" and is often referred to as such. NORCs are rich in potential resources for health promotion, socialization, and supporting independence. However, differences in geography and site-specific context are important when examining the ability of a community to support older adults in their quest to remain independent and in their neighborhoods, now and through the next 40 years when the baby boom population peaks. In the urban context, the sense of "home" may be the physical home structure; the local grocery store, drugstore, bank, and post office, as well as the accessibility of public transportation to support errands and social activities. In 2002, the Robert Wood Johnson Foundation identified 5,000 NORC apartment buildings across the United States. The largest of these NORC complexes, Co-op City in Bronx County, New York, housed nearly 8,000 residents (Feuer, 2002). In contrast to urban-based NORCs, suburban older adults rely on the automobile to maintain their errand and social circuit, traveling some amount of distance even for one errand. According to the 2000 U.S. Census, suburban Cook County, Illinois, with 13.4% of its population age 65 and older, ranked the highest in older adults, higher than the national average for suburbs and, surprisingly, for urban areas (U.S. Bureau of Census, 2000).

Larger NORCs, which took form during the 1950s movement toward developments, towns, or townships, were originally built adjacent to large cities. These inner-ring communities developed mainly in the Midwest (Ohio, Michigan, Illinois). They are considered to be the "first suburbs," and comprise a fifth of the U.S. population (Adler, 2006). The cities, towns, and suburbs of larger NORCs face a number of policy issues, according to a study by the Brookings Institute in Washington, DC (Puentes & Warren, 2006). Services, programs, and zoning changes are being sought in these first suburbs to assist and support older adult residents in remaining in their homes, in dealing with rising property taxes, and in paying for the increasing costs of energy and other utilities. These first suburbs are feeling the pressure to remake themselves and, because of their large size, government agencies and coalitions will need to step in to shape policy for them.

## DEMOGRAPHICS

Having little in common as far as locale, the unifying element of NORCs is the disproportionate number of adults over the age of 60 residing in-community for an extended length of time. According to a profile gathered in 2004, "one third (7.4 million) of the nation's 22.6 million householders age 65 and older have lived in the same residence for at least 31 years" (Bryan & Morrison, 2004, p. 3). Of these households, 94% are homeowners, with 72% of the residences located in metropolitan areas and 17% located in central cities. Fifty-eight percent are members of family households and 42% are members of nonfamily households (Bryan & Morrison, 2004). The demographics of the NORC residents vary in relation to income, educational history, marital status, ability and mobility, race, and cultural background.

## NORC BENEFACTORS AND BENEFITS—MANY SIDES OF THE COIN

Unlike other older adult housing counterparts that are planned communities or buildings, NORCs are part of the matrix of the city of residence and consist of neighborhoods, individual postal addresses, and private residences with no particular confines or separation between citizens of a NORC and fellow citizens living adjacent to a NORC. Because of this integration in the everyday city fabric, both a NORC's citizens and its very assembly afford many benefits to the larger community. For example, according to census data, older adults move less frequently than younger people, with only about 5% of adults over the age of 55 moving in a given year (U.S. Bureau of the Census, 2005). This provides a city with neighborhood stability and avoids the sometimes problematic escalation in property values and housing costs that are associated with migrant retirement communities. These benefits are also attractive incentives for younger families interested in moving into a community but seeking affordable housing. About one half of those over the age of 55 who do move, do so within the same county (Ginzler, 2006).

A reticence to relocate on the part of NORC residents supplies a solid tax base that benefits the community in many ways. On the whole, NORC residents are considered to have stable incomes (Social Security income and pensions) and to be "positive taxpayers" who use fewer services than they pay for through taxes (e.g., school districts, criminal systems, recreational and natural areas) (Crompton, 2001). In particular, local school systems are supported by these NORC dollars from residents who do not draw on or demand services (i.e., have no children of school age enrolled in the school systems). These stable, positive taxpayers are likely providing a deposit base into local investments and banking institutions that in turn fund new development of community amenities (e.g., recreational opportunities, support services, accessibility, beautification, safety). Socially, these long-standing residents contribute to and are active in churches as well as local philanthropic and service organizations. Within the commercial realm, maintaining this constituency within its locale of choice creates possibilities for new businesses and services in the area that in turn create positive financial growth for the community at large. And finally, retirees place little pressure on the local job market as new jobs and businesses develop.

NORCs can and should be regarded as a vital and necessary part of the community as a whole. Municipalities will find that, by accommodating the needs of and supporting the residents of one demographic to remain in their homes, a ripple benefit effect will be experienced by other city constituents (e.g., consistent funding for schools, universal accessibility, volunteerism). As this happens, municipalities will likely be able to efficiently meet the various demographic demands simultaneously.

## RETROFITTING THE PHYSICAL AND SOCIAL LANDSCAPE: SMALL- AND LARGE-SCALE NORC INTERVENTIONS

The Older Americans Act of 1965 and the creation of Medicare spawned an era of community-based services designed to meet the health-maintenance and social needs of aging adults. Some of these services include social work case management, referral services, home meal delivery, and recreational/ social programming headquartered in senior centers. These programs, paired with advances in medical technologies, have extended life expectancies so that a segment of the U.S. population lives comparatively well into their 80s. With the numbers of older adults expected to rise sharply to 85 million people over the age of 55 by 2014, there is a significant burden looming for service providers and health systems (Emrath, 2007). According to a 2003 survey by the AARP, community-based services will be expected and demanded by 82% of adults over the age of 45 who not only want to remain in their current home, but also expect to receive services necessary to do so (AARP, 2003).

## CREATIVITY ON THE NEIGHBORHOOD
## RESOURCES SCALE: LOCALIZED STRATEGIES AND EXAMPLES

Over the course of the last three decades, organizations have aligned to support the concept of aging in place. Organizations such as the AARP and United Jewish Communities (UJC) have rallied and created demonstration projects based primarily on a social model as opposed to a medical model. They have examined services in terms of "what is needed and what works."

Federal funding has been provided through the Older Americans Act for NORC demonstration projects. As of 2003, the federal government had provided approximately $10 million to fund such efforts (Jaffe, 2003). Many of these projects have been initiated and coordinated by the UJC, the umbrella organization for the Jewish Federation of North America and one of the oldest health and social services networks that strives for innovation in the conception and implementation of community-based preventive and support services for older adults. The UJC continues to initiate and lead the movement as the strain of a growing aging population continues. As of 2004, the Jewish population of older adults was close to 20%, compared to a national average of 11%–12% for people over age 60, making it imperative to plan for future needs (Alliance for Children & Families, 2004).

In collaboration since 2002 with the U.S. Administration on Aging and local services providers, the UJC continues its commitment with its national Aging in Place Initiative, which taps the lessons learned from its mid-1980s urban service model and applies them in suburban areas, reaching 29 communities as of 2004. These NORC demonstration projects seek to respond to differences in geography and scale as well as to the uniqueness of specific communities, moving beyond modifications to the home (grab bars, access ramps) to determine which service model would best serve the community at large. A cookie-cutter approach is never viable, nor is seeking and creating entirely new services. Instead, older adults are empowered to play major roles in identifying needs, after which existing services are coordinated to gain efficiencies through a wide range of community representatives (e.g., hospitals, governments, places of worship, businesses, transportation providers).

Based on geographical differences, two distinct service-delivery programs have emerged that strive to support older adults who wish to remain independent and to age naturally in their own homes rather than in institutional settings. The NORC Supportive Service Program (NSSP) is a community-level demonstration project that grew out of the NORC

Aging in Place Initiative. It started as a volunteer group seeking not-for-profit service providers, charitable support, and government investment from New York City and state. In 2007, approximately 80 NSSPs had taken shape across the United States. Typically found in more urban environments, an NSSP forms partnerships by drawing from the surrounding community network of long-established relationships to transform a community that was not originally intended as a "good place to grow old." NSSPs strive to operate on a proactive (prior to crisis) basis and to foster alliances through shared history, experience, and interests to obtain support services for a NORC. A primary strategy of an NSSP is to partner with older adult residents to promote self-governance and "coalition" lobbying efforts. This method is effective in cities and other high-density settings.

In the more suburban locales, a "basket-of-services" delivery system has been used on a one-to-one basis for residents who are geographically grouped in outlying areas. The Association for the Planning and Development of Services for the Aged in Israel, for example, created the Supportive Community Program (SCP), in which households are registered and pay a membership fee (which may be subsidized) for an array of core services, including house calls, an emergency switchboard, household repairs, and social activities. Additional fees, or "for-fee services" (e.g., transportation services), may be added to the package, offering customers flexibility.

A collaborative approach in programming for a NORC is often what is required to reach the goal of eliminating service duplications. Within the last 5 years, NORC service-development and delivery models have called for a rethinking of the way services are delivered. A proactive approach allows communities to build and develop ideas and services specific to each unique NORC setting and demographic. Seniors are eager to contribute meaningfully to their communities (Alliance for Children & Families, 2004). This involvement serves as a quality-control check and also prevents the all-too-common isolation and associated depression that can occur with older adults. Over time, NORC programs may help to stabilize neighborhoods, improve property values, reduce older residents' isolation, and postpone institutionalization (Lanspery, 1995). Notable are the increasing indicators that NORC support services offer the opportunity to positively affect health promotion and disease prevention (Kennedy, 2006).

The focus of stewards of the built environment and of policy makers who are developing innovations for aging baby boomers must be two-fold: (1) they must work with NORCs to modify zoning laws to promote supportive and temporary housing, respite apartments, and group residences; and (2) they must make sure all future planning and retrofitting promotes healthy social and physical activity within the community (e.g., curb cuts, longer-timed walk signals) (Lanspery, 1995). Incorporating empowerment by including resident participation and quality-control checks into the process of designing products to be used in the physical landscape (e.g., paving, signage) will prove to be viable and necessary. Services provided to older adults in NORCs are site- and population-specific. Providing services to a single or a high-rise complex will be different from services provided to older adults in an entire zip code area.

Services, interventions, and products must be considered for the overwhelmingly large aging segment of the U.S. population, with the understanding that home and community are the preferred "retirement" locale. What can be learned from existing communities that have an abundance of older adults and that are attempting to match services with needs? What must be affirmed or reworked in the realm of community and land-use planning so that civic infrastructures operate in tandem with support-service delivery? Across the board, creative and sustainable alterations are being sought to accommodate the changes in physical, mental, and social needs as well as the familial concerns of NORC residents. It is the implementation of localized delivery of social services, network building, referral, and health promotion and management, offered in a context that also provides assistance with transportation, housing upkeep, and shopping, that have been most successful. Yet, what of the physical landscape interventions on the micro and macro scale?

## CROSSING THE HOME FRONT THRESHOLD IN RETROFITTING

All NORCs will need to make the adaptations necessary inside the home environment to help conserve human energy and physical exertion, which will make life easier and less stressful for older adults to get out of the house and go into the community. A NORC demonstration project in St. Louis, Missouri, which was facilitated by the Jewish Federation and Washington University's Center for Aging, and was led by John C. Morris, professor of neurology, found that by removing small barriers and providing modest retrofitting measures (ramps, minimum pressure facets) within the home interior, older adults were able to continue to comfortably age in their own homes. Not enough research has been done, however, to demonstrate the profound positive impacts that can be achieved from simple retrofitting within the home environment. Consequently, current federal, state, and local policies fail to support these modifications. There is also a lack of acknowledgment of the tangible benefits of retrofitting at the macro level of a community. Susan Stark, an occupational therapist, noted that simple home modifications help older adults continue to perform daily activities on their own. She found that the true disability one experiences with aging is not the stroke or failing eyesight or weakening limb, but the mismatch between the person and his or her environment. Stark cited an example of a large-scale mismatch, specifically in federal policy, in which Medicare reimburses for an aid to assist a person getting in and out of the bath, yet does not reimburse for a bath bench that would allow the person to continue to function independently (Stark, 2003).

In 2002, anticipating the housing needs of the aging baby boomer generation, a coalition of organizations, including the National Association of Home Builders Research Center, the 50+ Council, the Remodelers Council, and the AARP, launched the Certified Aging-in-Place Specialist (CAPS) program. The only one of its kind nationally, the CAPS program trains individuals in specific aging-in-place physical modifications as well as design and technical solutions to common barriers within the home environment that can inhibit safe, independent, and comfortable lifestyles for older adults. Suggested modifications can take many forms, including

- Widening doorways for walkers and wheelchairs
- Modifying door, sink, and bathing utility handles
- Modifying door swings
- Providing grab bars and seating in bathing areas
- Providing ramps inside and outside the home.

All CAPS interventions take into account the needs of the older adult population, international building codes and accessibility standards, and the principles of universal design (i.e., design that is user-friendly and easy for all to navigate). Sensitivity training and innovation are applied so that most modifications suggested by CAPS "blend seamlessly into a home so visitors will never know the real purpose of the renovation" (Butler, 2006, p. 1). Interior designers, landscape architects and designers, architects, and home builders continue to answer the urgent call to improve home safety and apply universal design principles that make performing activities of daily living in their own homes easier for older adults. Resources such as the book *Residential Interior Design for Aging in Place* offer retrofitting suggestions, case studies, and explanations of site-specific modifications for designers and builders (Lawlor & Thomas, pending 2008). The Universal Design for Better Living program was developed by Mary Yearns, Associate Professor and Extension Housing Specialist at Iowa State University, because few homes were built to handle the changing mobility and accessibility needs of aging homeowners. This educational program demonstrates how the concepts of universal design are being incorporated into new products and features within the home to support independence and to reduce the likelihood of aging adults becoming "prisoners in their own homes . . . unable to fully participate in community life" (Yearns, 2002, p. 1).

As proponents come forward to address the topic of retrofitting specific home environments, attention must also be given to retrofitting beyond the home to help older adults as they cross their own threshold and step out into the community. Land planners and designers, municipalities, policy makers, and social-service providers must work in concert with design experts of microenvironments (i.e., the home) to carry independence-enhancing adaptations forward from the threshold to the sidewalk and thence into the macroenvironment of the community.

## LARGER-SCALE CREATIVITY: WHAT PUBLIC HEALTH OFFICIALS, POLICY MAKERS, DESIGNERS, AND PLANNERS CAN DO

Cities across the nation are seeking measures to provide livable communities for all residents. First, understanding the natural aging process, and then grasping the enormity of the aging population and the needs it will raise and how to address these is critical for policy makers. It is, however, merely the first step on a long road to providing a livable, "thrive-able" community fabric. One must come to understand the communal and likely vicarious benefits of supporting NORCs by way of providing services, service delivery options, and a supportive physical infrastructure. Kennedy (2006) noted that

> Without urban policy that promotes the ongoing social integration of seniors, including accessible transportation, zoning, senior-friendly signage, safe traffic patterns, safe environments for exercise, and opportunities for seniors to assert greater involvement in community decision making, the hoped for benefits of NORC residents will not be realized. (p. 35)

In *A Report to the Nation on Livable Communities: Creating Environments for Successful Aging*, the AARP defined *livable communities* as consisting of "affordable and appropriate housing, supportive community features and services, and adequate mobility options, which together facilitate personal independence and the engagement of residents in civic and social life" (AARP, 2005, p. 18). Improving transportation access and infrastructure, sidewalks, and connections; providing bike-friendly streets, more walking paths, and comprehensible signage and wayfinding; and slowing traffic for NORC residents within the large community context are paramount to meeting the demands of the largest "retirement-in-place" group the United States has ever seen (Wilkinson et al., 2002). Land stewards and policy makers must be sensitive to the natural conditions of aging, such as sensory disabilities (blindness, deafness, severe vision or hearing impairments) and physical disabilities (those that limit walking, climbing stairs, and carrying objects), among others.

So what can public health officials, designers, and municipalities do? They need not look too far. The 2005 White House Conference on Aging selected its top 50 resolutions as core goals for federal lawmakers and other government officials to follow as they craft future policies affecting the nation's older adults. Among the resolutions were ones that

- Expand opportunities for developing innovative housing designs for seniors' needs (Res. 14)
- Encourage redesign of senior centers for broad appeal and community participation (Res. 15)
- Encourage community design to promote livable communities that enable aging in place (Res. 18)
- Support older drivers to retain mobility and independence through strategies to continue safe driving (Res. 21)
- Ensure that older Americans have transportation options to retain their mobility and independence (Res. 22)
- Support older adult caregivers raising their relatives' children (Res. 26)
- Promote economic development policies that respond to the unique needs of rural seniors (Res. 29)
- Attain adequate numbers of healthcare personnel in all professions who are skilled, culturally competent, and specialized in geriatrics (Res. 40)
- Promote innovative models for noninstitutional long-term care (Res. 42)
- Improve access to care for older adults living in rural areas (Res. 53)
- Develop a national strategy for promoting new and meaningful volunteer activities and civic engagements for current and future seniors (Res. 56)

- Develop incentives to encourage the expansion of appropriate use of health information technology (Res. 62)
- Develop a national strategy for supporting informal caregivers of seniors to enable adequate quality and supply of services (Res. 67)
- Improve state- and local-based integrated delivery systems to meet 21st century needs of seniors (Res. 71).

These are clear directives. Now, practical application fused with evidence that has been derived from NORC demonstration projects and input from older adults must be explored.

*Transportation, Signage, and Wayfinding.* As witnessed by NORC service demonstration projects, transportation options must be well thought out in order to meet the needs of older adults, as independence and mobility go hand in hand. Ninety-eight percent of older adults identify independence as "extremely important" (Millar, 2005). According to needs assessments and focus groups conducted by the Jewish Family Service of Los Angeles, "many older adults can't access public transportation or are frightened to ride the bus. Even taxis and medical vans pose a problem for people whose mobility impairments prohibit them from meeting the driver at the curb" (Alliance for Children & Families, 2004, p. 9). A 2004 Baltimore NORC study of services found that overwhelmingly mobility options proved to be the greatest need of residents in the area. Specific travel needs ran the continuum, as many older adults were dispersed across the area. Alternatives and supplemental transportation services were considered necessary to continue delivery of valuable services (Baltimore Metropolitan Council, 2004).

Most adults are aging in the suburbs without the efficient service-delivery infrastructure found in more densely populated urban settings. Can the urban delivery models transfer to the older adults living at the end of cul-de-sacs and snowy driveways (Alexander, 2006)? The UJA-Federation and United Jewish Communities are actively exploring how to articulate and distribute services that cross a variety of geographies, whether the walk-up apartment complex, the suburb, or the single-family home. Currently underway, the "NORC without Walls" initiative extends the practices of the NSSP program to a target base of 1,800 single-family homes totaling more than 900 older adults.

For the looming wave of baby boomers, transportation services must be multimodal. Normal changes in the mobility, gate, and agility of older adults should factor into planning a well-timed crosswalk light and narrowing the designs of streets and intersections. Offering alternative means of transportation, such as bikeways, will be critical to relinquishing dependence on the automobile for the short, one-errand trip. The St. Louis NORC demonstration project identified trouble spots within its community (e.g., intersections with confusing signage) as well as valued destinations, such as smaller supermarkets, that do not require older adults to walk too far.

In general, baby boomers are active and are expected to want to remain so. The 2003 AdvantAge Initiative National Survey of Adults Aged 65 and Older found that an overwhelmingly large majority of older adults surveyed (96%) had participated in at least one civic activity in the past three years, 36% were engaged in volunteer work, and many provided caregiving to a family member or friend (Simantov & Oberlink, 2004). Connectivity must therefore be designed into the fabric of communities, as social services will continue to be the backbone of health promotion and maintenance. Removing barriers so that NORC residents may be social as well as participate in leisure and volunteer activities will foster the tremendously valuable civic contributions of this generation.

***Repurposement and Redevelopment.*** Development of new housing comes with a high price point and during a time when availability of open land is ever-diminishing in rural, suburban, and urban areas. These factors affect older adults as well as young or first-time homebuyers. It will be increasingly important to be innovative in "repurposing" existing structures to accommodate not only the demands of an aging population, but also to perpetuate an intergenerational living environment for the enhancement of the entire community. The need to house older adults of modest or low incomes also cannot be ignored. Surveys conducted by the Jewish Family Service of Los Angeles on two NORCs revealed that many residents spend 75% of their income for housing, which leaves little to cover all other expenses (Jaffe, 2003).

It will continue to be a high priority to work toward more compact, higher-density, mixed-use, and activity-friendly communities, as demonstrated by the NSSPs. The size and compactness of NORCs facilitate economical service delivery and outreach, and also encourage social interaction and mutual support among residents (Landsberg et al., 2002). By supporting zoning and development of affordable housing for older adults near services, amenities, and shopping areas, cities can send a clear message of support and encouragement to their older adult citizens. Redevelopment of property, combined with a centralized service delivery through the adaptation of mixed land use, provides outstanding opportunities for all sides of the table: property owners and developers with the inclination for refurbishment; neighborhoods and districts seeking infrastructure investment; and lower-income older adults requiring safe, affordable, and accessible housing, which can all be set in a walkable, nonautomobile-dependent context.

**Health, Leisure, and Recreation Promotion.** Health benefits are higher within NORCs where physical and social environments facilitate greater activity and promote feelings of well-being (Masotii et al., 2006). This is good news for communities, municipalities, health providers, and insurers alike, not to mention for stewards of landscapes that promote health. By turning "amenities," as they are currently understood, into "necessities," planners and landscape architects can positively affect the outcome of the aging explosion. Attractiveness (tree-lined streets, public gardens, green spaces), accessibility (universal design), safety, controlled traffic (traffic calming), sidewalks, and crosswalks, among others variables have been identified as important factors in whether or not older adults will get out of their homes and walk (Michael & Landfair, 2004). A 2004 study reported in the *American Journal of Health Promotion* found that urban neighborhoods that offered a variety of services with ample pedestrian access were associated with increased walking among older residents (Patterson & Chapman, 2004). A study in 2001 confirmed what many landscape architects and park advocates already knew: Residents who lived adjacent to a greenway or park were more likely to meet the Surgeon General's recommendations for physical activity than those who did not (Brownson et al., 2001).

*Active living* is a concept rising out of the public health domain that integrates physical activity into everyday routine. This concept is gaining increased recognition as a means to avoid certain types of preventable diseases and improve overall quality of life. As recently as 2001, older adults (age 65 and older) reportedly had the highest inactivity rates (U.S. Department of Health and Human Services, 2001). Policy makers and land stewards must work with health providers to create environments that invite and stimulate NORC residents to continue to be or to become physically active, as called for in the 2001 *National Blueprint: Increasing Physical Activity Among Adults Age 50 and Older* (sponsored by the AARP, American College of Sports Medicine, American Geriatrics Society, The Centers for Disease Control and Prevention, The National Institute on Aging, and The Robert Wood Johnson Foundation) (Robert Wood Johnson Foundation, 2001). The physical environment of a community plays a significant role in the choice to "go outside" and be active. In the past, however, the community environment has been overlooked for its potential role in supporting active lifestyles. Growing research suggests that the built environment does influence people's physical activity levels (Bors et al., 2004). Evidence of this can be seen in destination senior-retirement communities that offer gyms, walking trails, and spa-like facilities with support staff. Some destination communities are replicating what New Urbanism and research have called for: a condensed layout of the community with services and destinations that make for a more walkable community. As research indicates, when green spaces and pedestrian-friendly access are in close proximity to residences, people living nearby tend to be active and live longer (Takano et al., 2002).

Green space and related amenities in the urban environment can serve many functions. For example, in the United States the hobby of gardening has consistently ranked high. Therefore, putting community gardens in city green spaces that are located near NORCs affords great opportunities for physical and social activities for the residents. These gardens may offer therapeutic services, such as those provided by an occupational therapist, nutritionist, or horticultural therapist, and may work to facilitate group activities and to monitor the healthy aging of the surrounding community. These gardens provide a platform for social interaction at whatever level a participant selects. The efforts already being undertaken by park bureaus to collaborate with community and therapeutic garden proponents, as well as with health providers, to bring these services to the public realm show signs of promise. Research indicates that involvement in nature reduces stress, lowers blood pressure, balances circadian rhythms, allows for the absorption of vitamins through sunlight, and improves health (Ulrich, 1999). The creation of environments that promote an interaction with nature is essential to a community's overall health and well-being, for the old and the young. Green spaces within NORCs that offer year-round exposure to nature, gardening, and horticultural activities would promote strength and endurance, coordination, mobility, cognition, social skills, leisure time, adaptive strategies, and community integration for residents, and moreover would provide a restorative experience for the community at large. A 2007 study found that social and emotional isolation (being single, having few friends, and participating in few activities) increased the risk of older adults developing dementia by approximately 51% (Wilson et al., 2007). This number is staggering to comprehend. Promoting opportunities for older adults to remain socially, emotionally, and physically active in a community therefore is a matter of public health and will improve the overall quality of life for older adults.

Creative solutions lie in the hands of local governments, policy makers, philanthropists, voters, landscape architects, and planners. By advocating comprehensive planning and design that encourage recreation and social interaction and that are sensitive to the context of each city, agencies providing support services to older adults can become investors in the community's economic health and well-being. Research has shown that there is a strong social element in recreation:

> Indeed, a primary purpose of participating in recreation activities for many people is to facilitate socialization. Thus, encouraging retirees to stay in their home environment where there are extensive existing social networks should be easier for communities than recruiting to the area new retirees who face the formidable challenge of creating new social networks. If excellent recreation opportunities are available in the home environment, one of the primary reasons that retirees leave an area will disappear. (Crompton, 2001, p. 67)

Going by per-capita disposable income, the 55 to 59, 60 to 64, and 65 to 69 age cohorts are wealthier than any other five-year age-range cohorts in the United States. Providing for and supporting the aging in place of baby boomers is, suffice it to say, a good thing for their communities. As many of the nation's first suburbs struggle to meet the demands of an aging population, they must at the same time strike a balance in competing for and attracting younger residents. Meeting the needs of a vital, new, young population must be integrated with the demands of the older residents. From employing the tenets of universal design to retrofitting a city infrastructure, any modifications must meet the needs of all people in the community. In the end, older adults as well as young families should be able to enjoy activities within the community.

*Location, Location, Location.* Public health and social service providers can lend wisdom to landscape architects and planners by identifying barriers to health in built environments that decrease activity and quality of life. Working in concert as they serve their older adult constituents, these disciplines may assess the suitability of a built environment infrastructure and, in turn, the sustainability of the community at large. Developing strategies of health promotion through savvy, holistic planning and retrofitting of NORCs will have positive effects on the growing numbers of older adults. The NORC that has no gardens or green spaces, sidewalks, curbs, public seating, leveled paving, signage, nor appropriate lighting poses a hazard to older adult residents and creates social and physical barriers to accessing physical activity, social stimulation, health services, and continued community involvement, which evidence shows are essential elements for older adults to thrive and age in place. Such denuded community environments will not be tolerated by the baby boom generation, which is expected to be healthier and more active than the generations that came before it.

Oregon Health and Science University professor Yvonne Michael and fellow researchers Mandy Green and Stephanie Farquhar found that local shopping and services, traffic and pedestrian infrastructure, neighborhood attractiveness, and dependable public transportation influenced levels of activity among older adults (Michael et al., 2006). By developing land-use policy and planning that assist NORC residents to age in place by means of good neighborhood design that includes plenty of accessible amenities, younger generations also stand to benefit from the overall "attractive" character of a neighborhood that is simply a good place to live and raise a family.

Successful aging may be defined in many ways and, at best, is subjective to depict. A healthy NORC, however, has been determined to be an environment that facilitates greater physical and social activity through design, planning, and programs, and that promotes feelings of well-being. In 2006, Masotti et al. reviewed low-cost measures that aid in promoting healthy aging in NORCs. They recommended that local municipalities enact policies that not only stimulate, but also continually support the development and retrofitting of healthy NORCs, and that by doing so the improvements and modifications are a boon for all (Masotti et al., 2006).

*Of Money and Support.* Former Massachusetts governor Mitt Romney signed a law that would provide counseling for Medicaid beneficiaries on options for private or at-home care. This innovative law sought to discern the better option for older adults who are considering nursing home care. Providers anticipated a reimbursement windfall for services that would support the older adults in their homes instead of in nursing homes, whenever appropriate. This legislation is an example of earnest attempts by lawmakers, providers, and insurers to look for funding and service alternatives for the baby boom explosion, especially because nursing home facilities will not accommodate all of them. At the national scale, ongoing research and scientific evidence of the value of all forms of creative retrofitting (home interiors, social services, physical landscapes and networks) will be required in order to influence policy makers and legislators to provide the tax credits, means of affordability, and backing from the insurance industry that will be necessary to support it. The Bush administration unfortunately questioned the efficacy of monies spent on NORC demonstration projects, but funding must nevertheless move forward and be secured for the preventive services that NORC model programs deliver and for retrofitting of the physical landscape not only to provide successful delivery of services, but also to tap resources that are abundant in the landscape and built environments. NORC programs and services married with sensitive enhancements in the physical environment will work in unison to delay the need for more expensive long-term care options for the large baby boom cohort. Federal and state governments, along with insurance companies, are likely to follow Massachusetts' example to buffer the burden of long-term care expenses. (In October 2006, Congress included NORC programs in the reauthorization of the Older Americans Act, yet at the time of this publication, funds had yet to be appropriated by Congress.)

## NORC BUSINESS IS BIG BUSINESS

The marketplace has turned its eye toward NORCs as a source of profits in the provision of targeted services to support older adults in their desire to age in place. Creativity will guide strategies and implementation. It is widely believed that, with practical ingenuity, services aimed at supporting independence will alleviate the burden on institutional settings as well as on family members. Cost savings to individuals, families, communities, and state and federal governments will be seen immediately as decreases in the number of unnecessary admissions to institutional care are tallied. Enclaves of older adults in a geographic area may prove to be very lucrative in the business realm. NORCs offer a natural point of entry into the older-adult market that can be reached through personal recommendations or word-of-mouth marketing techniques that are a part of the close-knit character of these communities. Advancements in adaptive strategies and retrofitting, centralized services promotion, and delivery of products and services might fill a growing gap between the number of aging baby boomers and the services and facilities needed for these boomers, as well as provide the deeply treasured sense of control, freedom, and privacy sought by the aging baby boom generation. Technologies such as remote telemonitoring, for example, can provide peace of mind to on-call caregivers or adult children who live far away and who need reassurance that an older adult is living safely in a NORC.

In conjunction with advances in technologies, a savvy market must explore whether older adults will pay for "no-walls CCRC" (continuing care retirement community) services in order to remain in their homes.

Perhaps a new twist on "to-go menu" as it relates to care services is on the horizon. After all, many who have moved to a CCRC environment have transitioned from a local community. Perhaps neighbors, who are living safely, independently, and comfortably within their own homes, might explore the idea of a "no-walls CCRC" by visiting a friend or former neighbor in their new "digs" or have coffee and lunch and pick up laundry, all as part of the local CCRC support services extension or "services to go" from neighbors who return to their own homes. Sunrise Senior Living, one of the largest for-profit older adult care providers, began including light housekeeping and personal grooming for a fee as part of in-home care medication management. Others businesses that are offering nonmedical home care, and who are likely on the trail of something soon to be in great demand, are Home Instead (http://www.homeinstead.com) and Comfort Keepers (http://www.comfortkeepers.com).

## CONCLUSIONS

The Census Bureau predicts that by 2030, 20% of the U.S. population (71.5 million people) will be older than 65, compared to less than 13% in 2007 (U.S. Bureau of the Census, 2005). This phenomenon has profound implications for housing development and retrofitting, in-home service delivery systems, neighborhoods, and community planners in many parts of the United States. The result of this explosion will mean that many older adults who desire to age in place in their own homes will not just have the option, but will be required to do just that. As stated by Todd Ephraim, Executive Director of Jewish Family and Children Services in Kansas,

> Delivering services to the elderly in the next 5, 10, 15, or 20 years is going to be critical. . . . We're really going to focus on how we do that, because there's not enough housing out there to house all of the people who are going to be demanding it. So we're going to have to deliver services where seniors live—in their homes and in their apartments." (Jaffe, 2003)

NORCs, which are neither intended nor planned communities for older adults, are going to become the de facto retirement communities for the United States. The desire, preference, and ability to stay in one's own home for as long as possible depend on the safety and functionality of the home, the local support services designed to accommodate older adults, and the ability of the civic infrastructure to be "activity friendly." It is one thing for planners and designers to solve for access, safety, and independence within one's home through support services and physical interventions; it is another thing to examine the community in which the home exists and what the community has in place to engage and support older adults. Grab bars and ramps have an important place on the continuum of considerations for those who wish to age in place. The emancipation and independence of older adults aging in place, however, must be served on a much larger, more complex, and comprehensive scale. A steady review of solutions at the micro and macro level must be continually pursued. Ongoing multi- and interdisciplinary discourse on the benefits of well-designed green spaces, gardens, streets, and modal systems must occur. Comprehensive solutions for older adult thrive-ability must be met with a focus on practicality, aesthetics, and sensitive, forward-thinking public policy. Interventions, support programs, and retrofitting solutions must be fluid and dynamic and allow for adaptation for both the country's oldest older adults and the baby boomers who are just on the horizon. Finally, the demands of a vital, new, young population must also be integrated with the demands of older residents to serve the needs of all.

Given the nearly universal desire to remain in one's home, it is likely that "paradise" has already been found in the homes and neighborhoods of many older adults and the baby boomers on the cusp of retirement. This paradise consists of established, long-term, local social support systems of like-minded neighbors with similar interests. Ever since their entry into the U.S. population, baby boomers have stimulated revolution in thought, services, and environments. Collectively, this generation revolutionized the arts, culture, and music industries. This generation made famous various lifestyle choices and spirited radical changes in the U.S. economy. So it is reasonable to expect the boomer personality to take hold of housing options as this generation grays.

As active as boomers have been in shaping their communities through grassroots activism, and as a generation that holds more disposable income than previous generations, why wouldn't the boomers demand that the social and physical environments of their NORCs respond to their needs? Governments, policy makers, designers, and health care and social services providers will be forced to align, collaborate, and conceive of the means and measures necessary to accommodate baby boomers who are choosing to age in their homes and their communities. Boomers will expect a smooth transition through the aging process, adapting to limitations imposed by the natural aging process, yet seeking to enjoy life to the fullest, living independently within their own communities. Those 85 million baby boomers by 2014 will demand barrier-free environments in their communities, both in service delivery and in the physical landscape. Policy makers and municipalities will be forced to be proactive in examining current and future land and urban planning to promote age-friendly and activity-friendly environments. In a presentation to the National Association of Home Builders in 2002, AARP's Executive Director, William Novelli, summed up the desire of baby boomers: "They want to live well and they want to live comfortably and they want to live in familiar surroundings" (Novelli, 2002). Director Novelli went on to remind all that "People 50 [and older] are more than a third of the population, but they own 80 percent of financial assets and they dispose of 50 percent of discretionary income, and the 50 [and older] population is going to double in the next 35 years" (Novelli, 2002).

A new paradigm is afoot for NORCs. The baby boom generation will strive to empower communities to solve and prevent problems by engaging the leadership and becoming involved at the local level. The demands they place on their communities will force social services agencies and the purveyors of the physical landscape to work together in unexpected new ways. According to Fredda Vladeck, founder of the first NORC program and director of an aging-in-place initiative for the New York research and grant-making foundation the United Hospital Fund, "we need to go back to transforming our communities into good places to grow old" (Vladeck, 2007).

Private residences, the most dominant and overlooked forms of senior housing, have become the core of many natural, unplanned communities of collective aging and are increasingly regarded as viable and potentially more practical venues of housing and care for older adults than traditional institutionalized settings. If those who desire to age in their own home can be supported to do so, fewer burdens will be felt by the institutional care industry, and it is quite likely that these older adults will thrive. "Home" and its provision of autonomy, identity, memory, control, choice, independence, and security, coupled with a long-established surrounding landscape rich in social resources, are under examination by the aging experts in the United States. Identifying, developing, and maintaining the resources, supports, and services necessary to foster "home" as a retirement ingress rather than egress is the challenge ahead as millions of baby boomers approach retirement age over the next few decades. Widespread and collective ingenuity must be solicited from the surrounding community and from associated disciplines to master this imminent challenge. In the name of societal well-being and public health, it will be vital to understand, predict, and explore how social and medical needs can be met within the larger intact neighborhood context and built environment. In striving to accommodate the staggering numbers of aging adults, the United States as a whole must explore the effects, composition, and implications of NORCs in the larger context of older adult environments; there is much that NORCs can offer to other venues of older-adult housing and care. These communities sit positioned to be a resource and a model of efficiency without losing individual character or uniqueness. As these communities gain more attention and support, fostering the most natural of the age-in-place scenarios, the creative innovations that emerge for the social and physical landscapes likely will be "borrowed" for continuing care retirement and assisted-living communities as well as for nursing homes. Ongoing research on aging is required to continue to understand the cross-discipline implications. How will the "young old" age differently from the "old old," for example? How will the redeveloped urban areas be reused once this tidal wave of aging passes? How should independence be defined, determined, and examined in the early part of this century and, consequently, how might independence be expressed in the later half of this century?

Clearly it is time to become creative and to collaborate on multiscaled retrofitting necessities in the social and physical landscape so that NORC residents can thrive in place. Designers and land planners working with policy makers have a responsibility to determine what is right and meaningful for each unique NORC. They must "make way" by removing barriers in the physical landscape of the community at large for those working hard to deliver professional and neighborly social services that have the tremendous potential to make life-changing impacts on the quality of life for older adults aging in place.

## REFERENCES

Adler, J. (2006). Seniors find "first suburbs" are a natural place to retire. Retrieved April 2006, from http//www.chicagotribune.com/classified/realestate/realestate/chi-0604090151apr09,0,3588450.story?coll=chi-classifiedrealestat-hed.

Alexander, K. (2006). Naturally occurring retirement communities—An introduction. *Journal of Jewish Communal Service, 81*(3/4), 191–193.

Alliance for Children & Families. (2004). Creative thinking leads to enhanced living—Keeping older adults in the neighborhood. *Alliance for Children & Families Magazine*, Summer Special Section, pp. 6–9.

American Association of Retired Persons. (2003, May). *These four walls—Americans 45+ talk about home and community.* Report prepared by Mathew Greenwald & Associates, Inc., for AARP. Washington, DC: American Association of Retired Persons.

American Association of Retired Persons. (2004, January). *State of 50+ America survey.* Report prepared by AARP Policy and Strategy Group. Washington, DC: American Association of Retired Persons.

American Association of Retired Persons. (2005, May). *A Report to the nation on livable communities: Creating environments for successful aging.* Report prepared by AARP Public Policy Institute. Washington, DC: American Association of Retired Persons.

Baltimore Metropolitan Council. (2004). *Naturally occurring retirement communities in the Baltimore region.* Task Report 04-10. Baltimore: Transportation Planning Division.

Bors, P., Altpeter, M., Luken, K., & Marshall, V. (2004). 10 Strategies to promote active living. *American Journal on Active Aging,* Jan.–Feb., 34–35.

Brownson, R. C., Baker, E. A., Housemann, R. A., Brennan, L. K., & Bacak, S. J. (2001). Environmental and policy determinants of physical activity in the United States. *American Journal of Public Health, 91,* 1995–2003.

Bryan, T. M., & Morrison, P. A. (2004, April). New approaches to spotting enclaves of the elderly who have aged in place. Paper presented at 2004 Population Association of America Meeting, Princeton, NJ.

Butler, V. (2006). 1,000 NAHB members trained for specialized aging-in-place remodeling. Retrieved August 2006, from http://www.nahb.org/news.

Centers for Disease Control and Prevention. (1999). *The national nursing home survey: 1999 summary,* series 13, no. 152. Washington, DC: U.S. Government Printing Office.

Crompton, J. L. (2001). *Parks and economic development.* Planning Advisory Service Report No. 502. Chicago: The American Planning Association.

Emrath, P. (2007, February). *Profile of the 50+ housing market.* Washington, DC: National Association of Home Builders.

Feuer, A. (2002). Haven for workers in Bronx evolves for their retirement. Retrieved August 2006, from http://query.nytimes.com/gst/fullpage.html?res=9D07E7D9133BF936A3575BC0A9649C8B63.

Ginzler, E. (2006, May 16). Aging in place and naturally occurring retirement communities. Statement before the Senate Committee on Health,

Education, Labor, and Pensions Subcommittee on Retirement Security and Aging.

Hunt, M. E., & Gunter-Hunt, G. (1985). Naturally occurring retirement communities. *Journal of Housing for the Elderly, 3*(3/4), 3–21.

Jaffe, A. (2003). Aging in place: Jewish groups seek federal funds to serve growing senior population. Retrieved April 2006, from http://www .zwire.com/site/news.cfm?newsid=10014156&BRD=1425&PAG=461 &dept_id=154733&rfi=6

Kennedy, G. J. (2006). Naturally occurring retirement communities: An expanding opportunity for health promotion and disease prevention. *Primary Psychiatry, 13*(8), 33–35.

Landsberg, G., MacLearen, C., & Schwartz, H. (2002, September). *The accomplishments, issues, and prospects of supportive service programs in naturally occurring retirement communities.* Report prepared for the Fan Fox and Leslie R. Samuels Foundation. New York: Ehrenkranz School of Social Work, New York University.

Lanspery, S. (1995). The supportive housing connection. Retrieved April 2006, from http://www.homemods.org/library/pages/aaa.htm.

Lawlor, D., & Thomas, M. (September 2008, pending). *Residential interior design for aging in place.* New York: Wiley.

Masotti, P. J., Fick, R. Johnson-Masotti, A., & MacLeod, S. (2006). Healthy naturally occurring retirement communities: A low-cost approach to facilitating healthy aging. *American Journal of Public Health, 96*(7), 1164–1170.

Michael, Y., & Landfair, F. (2004). Building community partnerships to create walkable neighborhoods for seniors. In *Improving the Health of Our Communities through Collaborative Research*, p. 29. Northwest Health Foundation conference proceedings. Portland, OR: Northwest Health Foundation.

Michael, Y. L., Green, M. K., & Farquhar, S. A. (2006). Neighborhood design and active aging. *Health Place, 12*(4), 734–740.

Millar, W. (2005). Mobility options that will enable freedom, opportunity, and independence for older adults: A vision of our transportation future. Retrieved August 2006, from http://www.apta.com/research/ info/online/mobility_options.cfm.

Novelli, W. D. (2002, May). Baby boomers: Helping aging boomers to age in place. Paper presented at the Seniors Housing Symposium, sponsored by the National Association of Home Builders, Orlando, FL.

Patterson, P. K., & Chapman, N. J. (2004). Urban form and older residents' service use, walking, driving, quality of life, and neighborhood satisfaction. *American Journal of Health Promotion, 19*(1), 45–52.

Puentes, R., & Warren, D. (2006, February). *One-fifth of the nation: A comprehensive guide to america's first suburbs.* Paper presented at the Brookings Institution Metropolitan Policy Program, Washington, DC.

Robert Wood Johnson Foundation. (2001). National blueprint: Increasing physical activity among adults age 50 and older. Retrieved January 2006, from http://www.rwjf.org/files/publications/other/Age50 BlueprintSinglepages.pdf.

Simantov, E., & Oberlink, M. (2004). When older adults are involved in the community, the benefits are mutual. Retrieved January 2006, from http://www.vnsny.org/advantage/fact/AI_FS_Involvement.pdf.

Stark, S. (2003). NORCS. Retrieved April 2006, from http://medicine .wustl.edu/~wumpa/outlook/summer2003/occupationaltherapy.html.

Takano, T., Nakamura, K., & Watanabe, M. (2002). Urban residential environments and senior citizens' longevity in megacity areas: The importance of walkable green spaces. *Journal of Epidemiology and Community Health, 56,* 913–918.

Ulrich, R. S. (1999). Effects of gardens on health outcomes: Theory and research. In C. Marcus and M. Barnes (Eds.), *Healing gardens: Therapeutic benefits and design recommendations* (pp. 27–86). New York: Wiley.

U.S. Bureau of the Census. (1993). Population projections of the United States, by age, sex, race, and Hispanic origin: 1993 to 2050. *Current Population Reports*, pp. 25–1104. Washington, DC: U.S. Government Printing Office.

U.S. Bureau of the Census. (2000). *National Population Projections.* Washington, DC: U.S. Government Printing Office.

U.S. Bureau of the Census. (2005). *National Population Projections.* Washington, DC: U.S. Government Printing Office.

U.S. Department of Health and Human Services. (2001). Healthy People 2010. Retrieved April 2006, from http://www.healthypeople.gov/document/html/objectives/22-10.htm.

Vladeck, F. (2007). Programs offer seniors option to age at home. Retrieved February 2007, from http://www.usatoday.com/news/nation/2007-01-16-norc_x.htm?csp=34.

White House Conference on Aging. (2005). *2005 White House council on aging final report.* Retrieved April 2006, from http://www.whcoa.gov/ about/about.asp#report.

Wilkinson, W.C., Eddy, N., MacFadden, G., & Burgess, B. (2002). *Increas-*

*ing physical activity through community design: A guide for public health practitioners.* Washington, DC: National Center for Bicycling & Walking.

Wilson, R. S., Krueger, K., Arnold, S., Schneider, J., Kelly, J., Barnes, L., Tang, Y., & Bennett, D. ( 2007). Loneliness and risk of Alzheimer disease. *Archives of General Psychiatry,* 64(2), 234–240.

Yearns, M. (2002). The universal design for better living program. Retrieved April 2006, from http://www.ncoa.org.

7
_____

# COHOUSING AND SHARED HOUSING

*Laura Bauer Granberry*

ACCORDING TO A 2006 REPORT released by the U.S. Census Bureau, in 2011 the baby boom generation will begin to turn 65, and by 2030 it is projected that 1 in 5 people will be age 65 or older. Combined with the fact that families have become smaller in recent generations and that adult children may be scattered across the globe, the question becomes, where will this burgeoning population live and who will provide care for them as they age? Gone is the assumption that a person will live out his or her life with extended family. New social and physical support models are being designed that embrace all ages in codependent networks of care.

Akin to the communes of the 1960s, today's cohousing options often feature older adults and help promote connection, independence, and dignity. Day-to-day responsibilities are shared by all residents, who co-own their community. As an alternative to cohousing, shared housing allows seniors to share their home or choose to live in the home of another adult or family. The roommate(s) may or may not be of the same generation.

This chapter explores these options in detail to identify what needs to happen to ensure that cohousing and shared-living arrangements become workable, long-term alternatives to nursing homes or other institutional settings.

## COHOUSING

The concept of cohousing was introduced in the United States in 1988 through the book *Cohousing: A Contemporary Approach to Housing Ourselves,* by husband and wife architects Charles Durrett and Kathryn McCamant (Durrett & McCamant, 1988). They spent a year studying and photographing over 50 cohousing communities in Denmark. The concept has spread quickly. The first cohousing neighborhood in the United States, completed in 1991, was Muir Commons in Davis, California. Worldwide, there are now hundreds of cohousing communities. According to Durrett, "The reason cohousing works at all is that everybody looks out for their own interests, but people also learn to look out for other people's interests as part of that equation."

In the article "Building a Cohousing Community," McCamant and Durrett described cohousing as such:

> In many respects, cohousing is not new. In the past most people lived in villages or tightly knit neighborhoods. Even today people in less industrialized regions typically live in small communities linked by multiple interdependencies. Members of such communities know each other over many years; they are familiar with each other's families and histories, talents, and weaknesses. This kind of relationship demands accountability, but in return provides security and a sense of belonging. Cohousing offers a contemporary model for re-creating this sense of place and neighborhood, while responding to today's needs for a less constraining environment. . . . Most cohousing communities have attached dwellings clustered around pedestrian streets or courtyards. Generally they are new construction because it is difficult to create the desired relationships between spaces in existing buildings. Nevertheless, two communities have adapted old factory buildings and another an old school building. While all the newly constructed Danish developments are low-rise in scale, in both Denmark and Sweden high-rises as well as sections of huge housing projects have been converted to cohousing to overcome impersonal environments that encouraged vandalism and high turnover. (McCamant & Durrett, 1989, pp. 42–47)

Cohousing is a form of intentional neighborhood in which residents actively participate in the design and operation of their own community. Cohousing communities usually consist of private, fully equipped dwellings but differ from typical suburban neighborhoods by also including extensive common amenities, such as a common house and recreation areas. These unique features create ample opportunities for spontaneous interactions between residents. In cohousing, residents know their neighbors well and enjoy a strong sense of community that is typically absent in contemporary cities and suburbs. Most communities also forge a strong partnership with a professional development team. Together they create a custom-built, resident-managed, close-knit neighborhood that offers a healthy balance of privacy and community.

In *Senior Cohousing: A Community Approach to Independent Living*, Durrett identified six qualities that all cohousing communities have in common (Durrett, 2005):

1. *Participatory process.* Residents organize and participate in the housing development planning and design process and are responsible as a group for final decisions.

2. *Deliberate neighborhood design.* The physical design encourages a strong sense of community.

3. *Extensive common facilities.* An integral part of the community, common areas are designed for daily use as well as to supplement private living areas.

4. *Complete resident management.* Residents manage the development, making decisions of common concern at community meetings.

5. *Nonhierarchical structure.* There are no real leadership roles. The responsibility for decision making is shared by the community's adults.

6. *Separate income sources.* If the community provides residents with their primary income, it is a significant change to the dynamic between neighbors and defines another level of community beyond the scope of cohousing.

Cohousing communities are usually designed as attached or single-family homes along one or more pedestrian streets or clustered around a courtyard. They range in size from 7 to 67 residences, the majority of them housing 20 to 40 households. Regardless of the size of the community, there are many opportunities for casual meetings between neighbors as well as for deliberate gatherings, such as celebrations, clubs, and business meetings.

The common house is the social center of a community, with a large dining room and kitchen, lounge, recreational facilities, children's spaces, workshop, laundry room, and frequently a guest room for visitors. Communities usually serve optional group meals in the common house at least two or three times a week. Cohousing residents are free to choose which activities they want to do. The need for community members to take care

**Figure 7.1.** Toddlers greet an adopted "grandpa" at the Macklin Intergenerational Institute in Findlay, Ohio.

of common property builds trust, support, and a sense of working together. Because neighbors hold a commitment to a relationship with one another, almost all cohousing communities use consensus as the basis for group decision making.

## THE PHYSICAL ENVIRONMENT
## AND CAREGIVING RELATIONSHIPS

At the Building Community Capacity for Caregiving expert panel meeting sponsored by the Johnson & Johnson/Rosalynn Carter Institute Caregivers Program in August 2002, renowned architect Elizabeth Plater-Zyberk gave a presentation emanating from the belief that a significant parallel exists between the organization of the physical environment and social relationships. She stated that this parallel is being expressed through a contemporary movement called the New Urbanism, which brings to the practice of city and town design empirical knowledge and generally accepted observation and experience about human interaction in place-based communities. The principles of New Urbanism maintain that social relationships such as connectivity and interdependence are influenced by neighborhood characteristics such as physical proximity and diversity of use. Plater-Zyberk further proposed that place-based community is the ideal context for many aspects of caregiving.

In a paper written about her presentation, Plater-Zyberk described caregiving as a social relationship that can be facilitated or hindered by the physical environment:

> It is easy to imagine ease or difficulty of caregiving in a home, for instance, or in a nursing facility. But beyond the activity that takes place inside a building, what about the larger context for caregiving? What about access to, or delivery of, care in the context of community? The image springs to mind of being driven to the medical facility, or the caregiver driving to the home. But what about the lower threshold of need for which the effort of dislocation may seem excessive, such as the drop-in visit or the casual monitoring by neighbors of one's needs? In recent years, social scientists have succeeded in making the case that the well-being of the individual is related to the integrity of the family, and that families in turn benefit from the support of an interactive community. The aphorism "It takes a village to raise a child" has become a universal refrain. In turn, the sustenance of community requires the commitment of the individual to the common good of [his or her] neighbors. After years of promoting autonomy as a benchmark of mental health, we are beginning to hear from psychologists that interdependence may be a more fruitful approach to human relations. One individual's behavior can have a salutary effect on group comportment—or conversely, a demoralizing one. In the United States, we have been dealing with the experience of broken families, living in broken neighborhoods, in declining core cities. The detrimental impact of these situations on the individual is well documented. What may be less well understood is that this is a threat to the well-being of the city and to society at large. Fortunately, recent experience shows that the reverse process is true, too: Deteriorated neighborhoods are renewed one building and one street at a time. It might be further suggested that social connectivity can be similarly strengthened, one person, one family at a time.

In a cohousing community, residents know who lives six houses down because they eat common meals with them and accept the offer of a ride from them if their car is in the shop (or they do not own one). Residents begin to trust one another enough to leave their children with each other. Residents listen to what each other has to say, even if they do not agree with each other; yet they sense that they each experience the feeling of being heard.

## COHOUSING MODELS

Cohousing residents generally aspire to "improve the world, one neighborhood at a time." This desire to make a difference often becomes a stated mission, as the Web sites of many communities demonstrate. For example, at Sunward Cohousing near Ann Arbor, Michigan, the goal is to create a place "where lives are simplified, the earth is respected, diversity is welcomed, children play together in safety, and living in community with neighbors comes naturally." At Winslow Cohousing near Seattle, the aim is to have "a minimal impact on the earth and create a place in which all residents are equally valued as part of the community." At EcoVillage in Ithaca, New York, the site of two adjoining cohousing neighborhoods, the goal is "to explore and model innovative approaches to ecological and social sustainability." Many other communities have visions that focus specifically on the value of building community. Sonora Cohousing in Tucson, Arizona, seeks "a diversity of backgrounds, ages, and opinions, with our one shared value being the commitment to working out our problems and finding consensus solutions that satisfy all members." Tierra Nueva Cohousing in Oceano, California, exists "because each of us desires a greater sense of community, as well as strong interaction with and support from our neighbors."

Koinonia Farms is a unique cohousing community in rural southwest Georgia. *Koinonia*, a word taken from the ancient Greek, is translated as *fellowship* or *community*. Founded in 1942, Koinonia's principal work in the early days was to provide resources and education for impoverished sharecroppers in the area, and the farm workers who were hired were paid equally and ate and worshipped together regardless of race—a decidedly dangerous ideation in the Deep South at the time. Due to this belief in brotherhood, as well as in its pacifism and economic sharing, the community endured boycotts, threats, sabotage, and bullets. Koinonia survived to become not only the birthplace of Habitat for Humanity, but also several other social justice projects.

Koinonia resides on 573 acres of land and is home to fields of crops, pecan orchards, an organic garden, two villages of partnership housing, community housing, a main farm, a museum, store, woodshop, ceramic shop, bakery, dining hall, office, and wooded areas, including a Peace Trail.

Residents live as a community, praying, studying, working, and serving others on a daily basis.

During a visit to the farm, I interviewed two senior residents, Dave and Ellie Castle. Ellie told me that Koinonia is an

Open, intentional Christian community . . . it is intergenerational, inter-religious, and interracial. There is a wide variety of people with differing economic situations and educational experiences working and living together out of spiritual intention and compassionate care for one another. Living is very simple at Koinonia, and the different ages and large variety of cultures is much different from what one would find in a standard retirement home. Many of us at this age find this type of situation to be a relief; I feel looked after and cared for. Making accommodations for the many varying religious holidays, cultural food preferences, etcetera, represented by members of the community makes life at Koinonia a rich learning experience. Here you need to think more intentionally to find ways to express neighborliness—you don't just come and enjoy it without giving back.

Ellie's husband Dave agreed,

Koinonia is a place you can get hooked on very easily. There's a spirit here that's inviting. People may not have much materially, but what everyone

**Figure 7.2.** Koinonia Farms in rural southwest Georgia.

**Figure 7.3.** Residents studying daily work assignments.

does have is the ability to respond to the needs of others. You come here wanting to help somebody, and the first thing you know, you have received more than you could ever have imagined.

Although all community members share in the daily work assignments necessary to keep the farm and all of its operations running smoothly, "work is more an excuse to be together and share your hearts," said Dave. Foy Valentine, a volunteer at Koinonia in the 1940s, shared the lessons that he learned there:

> Faith is victorious, even if it is dynamited.
>
> Courage is contagious, even if cowardice is characteristic.
>
> Compassion is communicable, even if it gets turned out of the church or crucified.
>
> Friendship is forever, even after the grass grows over the red clay mound.
>
> Giving is better than getting, even if my need is great.

A new variation of cohousing is senior cohousing, or cohousing designed specifically for active adults age 55 and older. Senior cohousing residents can choose to grow older meaningfully, consciously, and independently in a self-managed, close-knit community. Senior cohousing neighborhoods are built with the future in mind. Using universal design principles (user-friendly, barrier-free, accessible, easy for all to navigate), each living space can transition from a home for an active lifestyle to one that supports growing needs for accessibility. Common areas, indoors and out, are designed to provide easy access and recreation for all levels of physical ability. Studio residences can be included in a community's common house to provide living quarters to home health aides whose services may be shared by several residents, allowing members to remain at home for all but major medical emergencies.

This new kind of "commune" exclusively for the elderly began as a movement by seniors to avoid institutionalization. There are now about a dozen of these cooperative housing developments for older adults in development in the United States, from Sante Fe, New Mexico, to St. Petersburg, Florida. Janice Blanchard, a gerontologist and housing consultant in Denver, predicted that "Baby boomers are going to want to re-create the peak experience of their lives. Whether a commune or a college dorm, the common denominator was community." Universal themes emerge when senior cohousing residents are asked about their experiences: opportunities for emotional growth, loss of isolation and fear of loneliness, and renewal of spirit.

Charles Durrett focused on this new sub-specialty of cohousing designed specifically for an older population in his book *Senior Cohousing: A Community Approach to Independent Living*. Durrett found that when interviewing people about senior cohousing, some broke down in tears. He felt that there were two obvious reasons for the response:

> First, these folks in senior cohousing were not in denial. They are grappling with growing older. You can't avoid the issue of mortality. It was very emotional for them. Second, they were considering their alternatives to cohousing: regular assisted living, living in some kind of institution, becoming increasingly isolated by staying in a single-family home, moving in with one of their children, or maybe shared housing. In any case, they would have lost their independence, and would have been much more subjected to the whims of others. (Cohen, 2005, p. 33)

Durrett made the following distinction between regular cohousing and senior cohousing:

> Regular cohousing is extremely conducive to families raising a young child, when the parents' world revolves around them, and for young adults, with their careers. Seniors have done all that; they're off the career

treadmill, and now they want a world that revolves around them. You can't blame them.

Based on decades of Danish experience in designing senior cohousing communities, Durrett divided the creation of a senior cohousing community into four distinct but interlocking parts: Feasibility, Study Group I (group formation), Study Group II (participatory design process), and Study Group III (policy). Feasibility is simply taking the time to consider the big-picture details. A complete and exhaustive overview of a potential project in a given area is the first job. Some points to consider are the following:

- Where are the multifamily zoned sites?
- What uses can be rezoned to multifamily?
- What are the constraints?
- Are there wetlands, artifacts, archeological remnants, natural amenities, bird habitat, and so forth that need to be protected?

Study Group I (group formation) is where prospective residents will grow into cohousing and discover for themselves how suitable cohousing is for them. They do this by sitting down and working through the issues of their project with their prospective neighbors. Participants establish the key social foundations and agreements in their community (co-care limits, decision-making procedures, legal agreements) before the process of planning for and building their homes actually begins.

Study Group II (participatory design process) begins after the senior cohousing group members complete Study Group I and identify a site. Now the group and their architect create design criteria. This program is broken down into the site program, the common house program, and the private house program. After these three steps are completed, there is a design closure workshop, and the plans are submitted to the city for approval.

In Study Group III (policy), the group needs to address key issues that affect both the economic and social health of the community. Everything from co-care policies (What are the extents and limits to care that residents should be expected to provide to other residents?) to dinner policies need to be decided in advance and identified as rules of the cohousing community.

In addition to the planning stages taken as a group, the individuals who will reside in the community must take responsibility for their own personal health as well as financial and legal planning. They should talk about these matters and have a plan in place for their continued care. It is important to make their wishes known, and have any necessary paperwork in place. They should become familiar with local laws, as these can be very different from one state or municipality to another. Issues such as informed consent, living wills, and power of attorney can be difficult to understand, so finding someone trustworthy to explain the options is vital. Planning ahead relieves others of trying to guess what a person wants under certain circumstances and guards against assuming that others are aware of one's wishes.

Those seniors who are actively involved in the creation of meaningful and supportive communities list as their priorities the ability to actively participate in designing how they will live the rest of their lives—owning their own homes, retaining their assets, managing their own neighborhoods, and arranging for the kind of care they want. Overarching ideals differ from community to community. ElderSpirit, a senior cohousing community first conceived by former nuns and located in Abingdon, Virginia, has a focus on "ecumenical and diverse spiritual practices, community service, and fun." Most of the residents of Glacier Circle in Davis, California, belong to a Unitarian Universalist Church and say that they are seeking a "loving, supportive, and tolerant lifestyle that supports aging in place and conscious aging." Community members at Silver Sage Village in Boulder, Colorado, share academic backgrounds as well as political and civic pursuits and are also interested in Rabbi Zalman's "Spiritual Eldering" teachings.

## RURAL SENIOR-HOUSING COOPERATIVES

The need for new senior-housing options in rural areas will continue to grow as the population ages. Statistics show that 70% of all seniors in the United States live in rural communities. Because the upper Midwest is home to the greatest number of cooperatively owned housing units anywhere in the country, the U.S. Department of Agriculture funded the Cooperative Development Services (CDS) to conduct a feasibility study that looked at the need for affordable senior-housing cooperatives in rural Wisconsin. It has worked with specific communities there that are considering developing senior-housing cooperatives. According to the CDS Web site (http://www.cdsus.coop), current initiatives include development of an ongoing system of board and member education as well as training for senior-housing cooperatives to enable them to more effectively share information about best practices in cooperative governance and management and in the development of a network of public and not-for-profit service providers to work with communities in the creation of new senior-housing cooperatives. With the University of Wisconsin Center for Cooperatives as its partner, the CDS expects to be an active player in the development of cooperative growth. In 2001, CDS published *Developing and Sustaining Rural Senior Cooperative Housing*, a how-to manual designed for use by rural communities that wish to explore the possibility of developing a cooperative senior-housing project (Cooperative Development Foundation, 2001). The manual is also designed to be useful for cooperative development practitioners and housing developers. Developers are taking note that while intergenerational cohousing is a relatively small market, cooperative housing for seniors has far more market potential based on the simple fact that people are and will continue to live longer and longer lives.

The manual *How to Start a Senior Housing Cooperative* outlines several types of housing cooperatives and includes research findings that indicate that senior-housing cooperatives offer a supportive, close community that helps prevent isolation; provides an affordable housing alternative that enables seniors to retain their equity by reinvesting it; allows seniors to maintain a measure of control over their lives; and takes advantage of economies of scale to keep service costs down. The use of a building manager, either full- or part-time, was recommended to help coordinate social activities, hire housekeeping staff, assist residents with transportation needs and maintenance, and arrange for personal and home care with outside contractors as needed. The manual states that senior-housing cooperatives provide their community with a mechanism to turn seniors' single-family homes over to younger families. The long-term economic impacts come from enabling young families to stay in town, where they will buy their groceries and other necessities as well as pay real estate taxes. The most impressive finding is that keeping seniors in the communities in which they have lived and worked has significant community benefits: they continue to contribute to the tax base through real estate taxes at the cooperative, they continue to leave their money in place at their rural banking institutions, and they continue to make important contributions to their local churches and other community institutions. If the seniors leave for greener pastures elsewhere, everyone suffers. According to gerontologist Gerald Glaser,

> [T]he essential benefit of the cooperative is that it provides an economic structure and social framework that fosters self-reliance, self-control and

determination, [and] interdependence and cooperation among the resident members, even among those with severe chronic conditions. As gerontologists, we know that these factors contribute directly to continued independent living, successful aging, and the enhancement of longer life." (Glaser, 1981, p. 3)

## SHARED HOUSING

Another housing option for seniors is shared housing. Although many people have lived in shared-housing arrangements over the years, this option for seniors has received far less publicity than cohousing. With shared housing, seniors can share their own home or share the home of another. In either setting, the others living in the home may or may not also be seniors. Professional organizations have begun to spring up that specialize in matching individuals together based on a senior's needs and the potential roommate's abilities to adequately help in providing for those needs. Some of these organizations conduct extensive screening beforehand and also provide services afterward to help the arrangement work out in everyone's best interests.

Shared housing is an affordable and attractive alternative for a senior struggling with financial concerns who may also fear losing independence. Shared housing offers security, companionship, mutual support, and affordable housing. This arrangement can help enhance the health and well-being of not only the senior, but also of all others living in the home.

While it may be an intentional decision to advertise for a roommate or decide to live as a roommate in another's home, some shared-housing arrangements develop naturally between acquaintances. Anthony Akins and his wife Edna decided to share their home with an elderly woman who Anthony saw regularly on his rounds as an insurance salesman in rural southwest Georgia. Anthony noticed that the sweet-natured Miss Hattie Mae Rhodes had several insurance policies from different companies. A thorough review led him to conclude that Miss Hattie, a widow living alone with no family members to assist her, was being financially exploited. Anthony began keeping regular tabs on Miss Hattie, and she told him of other situations in which other individuals were clearly taking advantage of her trusting nature. In one instance, she agreed to sign as a reference for a neighbor's automobile loan application only to find later that she had signed paperwork actually purchasing the vehicle for the person.

Anthony regularly took his wife Edna with him when he visited Miss Hattie. They would often go to the store to get her groceries or assist in other ways. During one visit, they noticed that Miss Hattie had not been eating and had lost weight that she could ill afford to lose. When they questioned her, the Akins learned that nightly gang activity was occurring right outside Miss Hattie's home and she felt "scared all the time." This had severely affected her eating habits. The Akins began visiting Miss Hattie more frequently, and she became a loving grandmother to their recently adopted twin daughters. As they also had no family living in the area, the Akins decided to approach Miss Hattie with the idea of moving in with their family on a full-time basis. Miss Hattie took a few weeks to decide, and then took them up on their offer. The Akins enclosed their garage and brought Miss Hattie's most prized possessions to give her comfort and make her feel at home. That was 6 years ago, and Miss Hattie is now an integral part of the Akins' family. Now 96, Miss Hattie continues to help with daily household chores and enjoys cooking, gardening, and looking after the twins.

Surprisingly, although Miss Hattie is African-American and the Akins family is white, family and friends are supportive of the arrange-

**Figure 7.4.**    Edna Akins and Miss Hattie.

ment. Miss Hattie does admit that some of her black friends from the local senior center are jealous that she has such a loving, caring family to call her own. Miss Hattie lost her husband, Marion Rhodes, 23 years ago and her only child, Marion Jr., died in 1932 at age 6. Having a family again has "meant the world to me," states Miss Hattie. "I'm there to see the girls off the school bus, and I just love spending time with them." Edna Akins agrees that it has been a "win-win" situation for all of them. "Miss Hattie has seen so much and been through so much . . . she is the last of a vanishing legacy—a strong, southern, black woman who worked hard, faced intolerable cruelties not only from whites, but from members of her own race, and survived on a deep well of faith and a bucket of sheer, gut-drawn determination," said Edna. "Our family has learned so many valuable lessons from her; she is a wonderful role model for our little girls."

A senior deciding to live with another person or family, based on mutual needs, lifestyle, and concern, is one way to experience shared housing. Another is for the senior to be the one who decides to take in a roommate or roommates. According to http://www.seniorresource.com, questions that a senior should ask him- or herself to determine if sharing his or her home is a viable option are:

1. Do you live alone?
2. Could you use additional income?
3. Would you like to reduce housing costs?
4. Do you need help with chores?
5. Are you willing to share your home?
6. Are you willing to help out to lower your rent?

According to A Blueprint for Action: Developing a Livable Community for All Ages, the vast majority of Americans want to remain in their communities as they age (MetLife Foundation, 2007). Contrary to popular belief, only a small minority actually moves to warmer climates upon retirement. Fewer than 5% of those 65 years of age and older reside in nursing homes. Instead, most Americans choose to age in place within the same communities where they have long lived. Every community, from fast-growing suburbs to more stable rural areas, will have to adapt to a maturing population. Shared housing is an excellent way for seniors to successfully age in place.

Another excellent resource on shared housing is the National Shared Housing Resource Center (NSHRC), a not-for-profit organization fueled by volunteers. The NSHRC serves as a national clearinghouse for consumer inquiries regarding shared-housing programs; provides technical assistance for program start-up, problem solving, and marketing strategies through literature, site visits, and a national conference; informs other allied organizations about shared housing; maintains a national directory of shared-housing programs; and produces a shared-housing newsletter as well as other publications and resources. According to NSHRC, shared-housing programs include not only the previously-mentioned matching programs, but also shared-living residences, where a number of unrelated people live cooperatively in a large home. Several publications are available from NSHRC that can assist in making the transition to shared housing.

Innovative local and state agencies have also begun developing programs to assist seniors in the shared-housing process. One program that helps match seniors with unrelated adults in mutually beneficial home-sharing arrangements is the Housing Options for Seniors Today (HOST) Homesharing Program of the Office for Aging in Tompkins County, New York. Governor George Pataki also created a Web site (http://www .seniorhousing.state.ny.us) devoted to senior housing to aid seniors in finding affordable housing across New York State. The site is a comprehensive, Internet-based listing of nearly 1,100 senior-housing developments that includes active-adult communities, senior housing, supportive senior housing, enriched housing, adult homes, assisted-living programs, continuing care retirement communities, dementia facilities, shared-living residences, naturally occurring retirement communities, intergenerational housing, and single-room occupancy sites. As the need for senior-living options in the United States increases, other states are sure to follow New York's lead in helping seniors locate affordable housing in their communities.

## CONCLUSION

Although there are many benefits to cohousing and shared-living for seniors, many challenges will continue to exist for seniors who decide to try them. Older adults who initially are in good health when undertaking a new housing option may eventually become ill or incapacitated, needing more care than other residents or their roommates can help to provide. Senior cohousing communities should ensure that these issues are addressed during the initial planning stage for their community's development to avoid conflict and misunderstanding later. Seniors who share their home with others or who become roommates in another's home must make their wishes known as well.

Harkening back to the conclusions of Elizabeth Plater-Zyberk, the physical environment can be restructured according to principles of benefit that have been proven across history, namely locating daily needs within walking distance of residence. She states,

> This is a place where a child can walk or be walked to school; adolescents can engage friends in the socializing process under the watchful eye of neighbors on porches or business owners who know their parents; the young single can find a small apartment above the shop or next door to it; the young couple can purchase a small house; the parent caretaker and the home worker are within a short walk of informal company at a neighborhood park, on the main street, or at a place of worship; the empty nester can move to a smaller residence without leaving the community; the elder person can find support from caring neighbors who are nearby.

Although strides have certainly been made in the past two decades, the United States is still ill-prepared for the graying of America that has already begun. By the year 2030, 39 states will have as many retirees as Florida had in 2007. It makes sense to invest time, money, and energy in the re-creation of the neighborhood of yesteryear, where people looked out for and assisted one another. Surging energy prices are taking a huge toll on U.S. senior citizens. Many pay up to 35% of their incomes just to cover utility bills. Gas prices are affecting seniors' ability to perform daily activities, such as shopping for groceries and going to doctor's appointments. Even those who no longer drive are being negatively affected: home health care workers and volunteers delivering needed services such as Meals on Wheels are quitting their jobs and dropping out from volunteering when they can no longer afford rising gas costs. The seniors who depend on these services have no one to fill the gaps left behind.

The bonds created through cohousing or shared-housing options can help facilitate the work of all caregivers and provide a renewed understanding of what former First Lady Rosalynn Carter has stated many times: "There are four kinds of people in the world: those who have been caregivers, those who are currently caregivers, those who will be caregivers, and those who will need caregivers." We cannot afford to wait to take responsibility for the needs of ourselves and of our communities.

## REFERENCES

Cohen, R. (2005). The next phase: Senior cohousing. *Communities Magazine* (Summer), pp. 33–39.

Cooperative Development Foundation. (2001). *Developing and Sustaining Rural Senior Cooperative Housing.* Washington, DC: Cooperative Development Foundation. Available at http://www.cdf.coop/usda_report.html.

Durrett, C. (2005). *Senior Cohousing: A Community Approach to Independent Living.* Berkeley, CA: Ten Speed Press.

Durrett, C., & McCamant, K. (1988). *Cohousing: A Contemporary Approach to Housing Ourselves.* Berkeley, CA: Ten Speed Press.

Glaser, G. (1981). Housing Cooperatives for the Elderly. Presentation to the President's Commission on Housing, Washington, DC, December 3. Available at http://www.seniorcoops.org/glaser.html.

McCamant, K., & Durrett, C. (1989). Building a Cohousing Community. *In Context* #21 (Spring), pp. 42–47. Available at http://www.context.org/ICLIB/IC21/McCamant.htm.

MetLife Foundation. (2007). *Blueprint for Action: Developing a Livable Community for All Ages.* Washington, DC: National Association of Area Agencies on Aging and Partners for Livable Communities. Available at http://www.aginginplaceinitiative.org/index.php?option=com_content&task=view&id=18&Itemid=47.

# 8

# Outdoor Environments Supportive of Independence and Aging Well

*Jack Carman and Edward Fox*

A LARGE PROPORTION OF AGING AMERICANS who currently live independently do not live in communities that will support their independence or promote healthy lifestyles as they continue to age. Other chapters in this book have previously highlighted the need for public policy makers, planners, designers, and community leaders to look ahead and anticipate the demands that will be placed on communities by today's aging baby boomers and to prepare for how best to use or adapt public and private resources to support the overall well-being of older adults to maximize their continuing contributions to their communities. Not only the housing options, but also the outdoor environments in which these are located will play an important role in how successfully today's older adults will age.

## SENIORS' BASIC PHYSICAL, EMOTIONAL, AND OUTDOOR NEEDS

The design and development of housing and outdoor environments must be sensitive to and respond to the aging process. Older adults become more and more familiar with the body's reduced sensory capacity, such as farsightedness, reduced depth perception, night blindness, and hearing loss.

Imagine how a senior experiences these sensory difficulties when walking on a street in the general community. As one ages, the brain and nervous system tend to slow down, reducing recognition and reaction times, orientation, and short- and long-term memory. One of the more significant effects of sensory and nervous system reductions to seniors is the increasing difficulty to operate a car safely. In the fast-paced, suburban environments that are designed and programmed for the automobile instead of for pedestrians, the car holds baby boomers and the rest of the United States hostage.

In addition to the physical and mobility changes associated with aging, baby boomers will face personal and social challenges that can be aggravated or ameliorated by the design of the built and natural environments. Changes in one's independent and self-sufficient lifestyle affect one's ego, self-esteem, feelings of control over the environment and over one's life, feelings of worth and belonging, and even one's ability to touch and communicate with others. What will happen to aging "independent" baby boomers when they can no longer drive? Will they drop out of society to be shuttled from place to place like invalids, or will they choose to adapt their lifestyles to include walking and mass transit? The latter choice, which maintains a healthy, independent, and affordable lifestyle, is more likely and is often the more desirable option.

Unfortunately, the modern development community has not planned or built this type of human-scaled and pedestrian environment for much of the United States. Probably the majority of this book's readers cannot step outside their buildings or homes and walk just 5 or 10 minutes to get a loaf of bread, meet a friend for an activity, or enjoy a neighborhood park. If it takes more than 5 or 10 minutes to walk from home to any public destination, imagine what it would be like to live without a car or to be dependent on someone else to provide transportation. Even for an independent senior baby boomer, imagine making a trip with impaired senses or memory, diminished cardiopulmonary capacity, or stiff joints. Almost 60% of those age 65 years or older report one or more physical limitations in mobility (National Center for Health Statistics, 2002).

People do not live exclusively indoors. Most people venture outside at least once a day—to fetch the newspaper, to go to the store, to visit family and friends, to enjoy a beautiful day, and, more often than not, to go to work. These outdoor destinations involve parks, gardens, city streets, playgrounds, and sidewalks. Whatever the reason for stepping out of the front door and off the porch, some person is venturing into his or her community at any given moment. There is a great need for older adults to maintain a connection with nature and the world around them. It is vitally important that individuals become more aware of and make better use of outdoor environments.

One of the important reasons people go outside, besides the need to collect goods and to travel from one point to another, is the need to maintain a connection with nature. Edward O. Wilson describes our connection with nature as the *biophilia hypothesis* (see Chapter 4). One's mood changes if it is cloudy or rainy, one dresses depending on what the weather will be like that day, and one may even alter certain plans depending on the weather. People plan their vacations based on climatic conditions and decide how much time to spend in an outdoor environment depending on the season. People don't always appreciate, however, all the benefits they can experience from 'visits' with Mother Nature. Parents tell their children to go outside and play because they know inherently that fresh air and sunshine are good for healthy bodies (and they are not just trying to get some peace and quiet), but for some reason the same concept is not applied to adults, and especially to older adults.

Researchers have long documented the physical benefits of walking as a form of exercise. Exercise can "improve and maintain health, prevent disability and hospitalization, improve blood lipid profiles, and reduce body fat" (Schneider, 2004, p. 46). A research study found that "People who live in walkable neighborhoods . . . are more likely to know their neighbors, participate politically, trust others, and be socially engaged" (Southworth, 2005, p. 248). Walking is relatively inexpensive, does not require special equipment (except for good shoes), and the scenery is always changing. Walking can help maintain and possibly improve the physical and mental abilities of an individual. Combined with a greater interest in their health and well-being, the coming wave of baby boomers who will be reaching retirement age will want to maintain or increase their levels of exercise.

The importance of exercise cannot be overstated. Physical activity can help reduce the risks of type 2 diabetes and cardiovascular disease (Jenum et al., 2006). In older women, regular long-term physical exercise, including walking, is associated with significantly better cognitive function and less cognitive decline (Weuve et al., 2004). Mobility loss in older adults can be reduced by walking at least 1.5 to 2 hours per week (Visser et al., 2002). It is very important that older adults understand the benefits of exercise so that they can continue to live active lives. Exercise does not always have to involve joining a health club. The most effective form of exercise is simply stepping out of one's front door and walking. Plus, exposure to the outdoor environment allows for the natural absorption of Vita-

**Figure 8.1.** Wide sidewalks set away from streets and car traffic encourage physical activity. (Courtesy of Jack Carman)

min D, balances circadian rhythms, reduces stress, and lowers blood pressure, among many other health benefits. The creation of appropriate outdoor environments is vitally important in encouraging and maintaining a healthy, active lifestyle. Encouraging physical activity in older adults requires a broad-based approach, including safe community design, community-level resources, workplace promotion efforts, and other interventions (Van der Bij et al., 2002).

Most people would prefer to live in a walkable neighborhood. Opportunities for social interaction and neighborhood connectivity increase as people spend more time walking around their neighborhood. Older adults are no exception and they may have more time to walk and get involved in different aspects of their community. Walking to specific events and destinations will foster greater involvement. The stereotype of the retired person will dissolve as older adults participate in such activities as walking clubs, evening strolls, or taking their grandchildren for a walk (Evanson et al., 2002).

Society must adopt the mindset that sidewalks are an integral part of a community, that walkable neighborhoods encourage and maintain phys-

**Figure 8.2.** Enjoying a walk in the park with grandchildren along a safe sidewalk and street crossing. (Courtesy of Jack Carman)

ical activity that is vital to all, and that people have the right to walk anywhere they may want or need to go. The car should not take prominence over the pedestrian. Communities, with the help of developers and land-use planners, must take a close look at and consider alterations to the built environment to remove some of the barriers preventing residents, young and old, from getting closer to nature.

## BEST PLACES TO RETIRE?

What will older adults face as they grow older and face the possibility of supportive services? Most people do not wake up one day and declare that it is time to move to a senior community. The decision to move to a more supportive environment is a gradual process and is influenced by one's peers, one's health, changes in family structure, economics, and many other factors. People who are over the age of 65 want to continue to be a part of and remain actively engaged in their community. Most people enjoy the life they have created and want to continue to live and remain socially involved in their community. Baby boomers will continue to be major consumers for themselves, their children, and their grandchildren. In addition, they have the disposable income to spend on these three generations. The underlying question is how to create senior-friendly environments that enable seniors to participate in and enjoy their neighborhoods, and where seniors can drive, bike, and/or walk to wherever they want to go. Aging baby boomers will not passively accept the role that society has previously defined for their parents.

Current research on senior-friendly communities examines the attributes of a community based on retirement perspectives. However, the notion of "retirement" is changing every day. The Social Security Act of 1935 established the concept of most Americans retiring with an old-age pension. This became a reality for most following World War II, boosted by labor union and veterans benefits programs. The thinking was that a person who reached 50 years of age was entering the twilight years of life. Such is not the case today. Baby boomers look at age 50 as the start of the second half of their lives. Based on lifestyle changes, longevity, goals, finances, and many other factors, people will not face retirement the way previous generations have. They may work longer, work part time, start new careers, return to school, do volunteer work, or choose some combination of any of these alternatives. When baby boomers start to retire, their sheer numbers will be difficult to replace with new workers. Employers will need the boomers to continue to work in some capacity because their sudden retirement will leave a void of experienced personnel that cannot be filled fast enough. Research conducted by the American Association of Retired Persons (AARP) indicated that 8 in 10 baby boomers plan to work at least part-time past traditional retirement age (Novelli, 2002). To paraphrase the Oldsmobile car slogan, "This is not your father's retirement." Or, more in keeping with how the later stages of life are now viewed by many older adults, "This is not your father's fulfillment."

With that retirement perspective in mind, one could review several of the many popular "place-rated" articles and books. In 2005, for example, *Money Magazine* ranked 1,300 cities on how they respond to "senior issue" criteria, such as housing, health care, cost of living, community age and education profiles, weather, personal health and safety (e.g., air pollution and crime risk), and leisure and cultural amenities (*Money Magazine*, 2005). The last criterion reviewed the number of local theatres, restaurants, golf courses, libraries, and museums within a 15-mile radius. The magazine has an interactive Web site that allows one to enter a town name to see how it ranks. Similarly, Armstrong (2004) ranked places by climate, cost of living, taxes, housing costs, crime rate, and health care statistics. Bland (2005) judged community-retirement desirability based on 12 criteria: landscape, climate, quality of life, cost of living, transportation, retail services, health care, community services, cultural activities, recreational activities, work/volunteer activities, and crime. Savageau (2004) rated retirement areas by 6 main categories: ambiance, cost of living, climate, personal safety, public services, and the local economy.

Climate and weather are geographic-related issues. Public services and costs of living are regional economic issues. There is little that individuals or communities can do to alter these conditions at the local level. Other senior choice issues, such as housing and transportation, cultural and recreational amenities, and "ambience," deal with the built and outdoor environment, which can be changed at the local level. Diana Wheeler, a planner in Alpharetta, Georgia, created a R.E.C.I.P.E. for developing and maintaining desirable senior communities: "Customer-driven" communities concentrate on *R*ecreation, *E*ducation, *C*ulture, *I*mage, *P*ersonal health, and the *E*nvironment as critical elements in successful senior-sensitive areas (Wheeler, 2005). Her approach incorporates the ideals of smart growth design and planning, which are now used to improve communities across the United States (see the discussion of smart growth principles under "Senior-Friendly Design Principles").

Wheeler's approach to customer-driven community and recreation planning is being encouraged by senior-oriented and non–senior-oriented smart growth groups. For example, the Florida Department of Elder Affairs' Community for a Lifetime program supports a Web-based network of best practices. AARP's 2005 *Livable Communities: An Evaluation Guide* includes handy survey evaluation checklists for a number of senior-related issues: transportation, walkability, safety and security, shopping, housing, health services, recreation and cultural amenities, and community services (American Association of Retired Persons, 2005). The checklists identify areas in which the public and private sector can improve local conditions and services to make them more senior-friendly. The guide also provides references for more information on and resource contacts for these issues.

Although many programs and resource guides such as those described above use similar criteria, a senior's lifestyle choice is not a simple matter of statistical analysis. It is a personal and subjective decision as well as one based on individual needs, preferences, and realistic options. In many cases, seniors will choose to remain in their current communities for a number of personal reasons, or will have no choice but to stay where they are now. Seniors who flock to place-rated communities may find them to be no better than where they currently reside. Unless they are well-planned and well-designed smart growth communities, new housing and neighborhoods in these "destination" senior areas may become sprawling, traffic-snarled, and overpriced versions of a senior's charming, original residence.

## AGE-APPROPRIATE COMMUNITIES

Previous generations of seniors had accepted the limited number of living options available to them. Today's housing market challenges people with a growing number of senior-oriented communities from which to choose. Baby boomers will redefine the choices of how to age and the settings in which to age. They have already redefined the various stages of their lives and reshaped their world accordingly. How this segment of the marketplace will embrace retirement and the "golden years" will undoubtedly be different from what current retirees face today.

As this book was being written in 2007, most local suburban land-use and zoning controls perpetuate mass-market, post–World War II-era, single-family detached housing "products." Although many seniors may own their homes outright (i.e., do not have a mortgage), they may be unable to afford the maintenance and property tax costs they were able to afford before they went into retirement. Case law has affirmed that seniors are a special class of residents for whom local governments may create or modify zoning standards to meet their special needs or living arrangements (low- and moderate-income households are another special class). It is important to understand the various housing options that are available to seniors today and what the coming baby boom retirement wave will experience.

Baby boomers no longer accept the "old folks' home" as their only senior-housing option. A large variety of housing forms are available today for seniors, depending on their personal needs, incomes, and lifestyle choices. Many choose to live in the same home from their 40s through their 80s, until the time they may become dependent on specialized care. Some choose to downsize their living arrangements, moving into smaller homes or those with fewer stairs, often in the same neighborhood or community. Some seniors elect to relocate to age-restricted, independent-living communities. The most common of these are residential communities that are deed-restricted to prohibit nonsenior owners and occupants (usually under the age of 55).

Many active senior housing developers today design homes that meet the special needs and preferences of seniors, such as single-story or split-level arrangements to reduce stair climbing, first-floor master bedrooms, wider doorways, and other barrier-free features. Community rooms and activities are included as part of an association fee, along with outdoor main-tenance, security services, and so forth. These age-restricted communities could be in single-family districts or multi-family structures of stick-built or manufactured construction. Other than those subsidized by religious and charitable organizations or local governments, this type of independent housing is a very expensive alternative, and often out of reach for many seniors. These insular and isolated seniors-only communities cloister their residents from children and people of other age groups and lifestyles who cannot or choose not to live there. An alternative independent-living option, among many others, is the naturally occurring retirement community (NORC). NORCs are different from other seniors-only housing developments and retirement communities because developers have not designed them as elder communities; they have evolved over time to be that way (see Chapter 6 for a detailed discussion of NORCs).

The private market also has responded to meet the needs of seniors who are no longer able to live independently. Common market-based con-gregate senior-housing forms include assisted living, intermediate care, and continuing care retirement communities. Skilled nursing and demen-tia residences, often managed by a hospital or religious organization, are expanding senior special needs living care, as are adult foster care and adult group home facilities. These choices also are expensive propositions for sen-iors, their families, and caregivers. Often, the transition from independent-living to a dependent-living situation is dramatic, brought on by a catastrophic condition, accident, or circumstance. Adjusting a senior's independent-living arrangement often prevents these circumstances from happening (see the discussion of long-term care settings in Chapter 1).

By looking at how residential dwellings are organized, residents and local governments can begin to formulate ways to create a more cohesive support network that provides seniors with choices for appropriate, afford-able, and adjustable independent lifestyles. Most U.S. housing outside of older urban centers is in zoning districts where local governments permit only single-family dwellings. This house form and restrictive zoning policy was created for nascent baby boomers at the dawn of the "nuclear family" era and had been perpetuated as baby boomers had their own children. Today, the typical nuclear family house and neighborhood finds itself in an America where only 24% of households are "nuclear" (i.e., two married parents with children). For seniors, the census reports are even more alarming: 25% of all people age 60 or older live alone (He et al., 2005). How can seniors endure cleaning, maintaining, repairing, heating and cooling, and paying taxes on a single-family house that becomes more of a physical, mental, and economic challenge as they age? Statistics show that seniors are moving away from the neighborhood and intergenerational community life. The 2005 American Housing Survey estimated that out of the roughly 22.2 million American households with a person 55 years of age or older, 2.4 million (10.6%) reported living in an age-restricted community. This is a 25% increase from 2001, when 8% of comparable households lived in age-restricted communities (U.S. Department of Housing and Urban Development, 2005).

The United States must rethink the ways in which housing and neighborhoods are built and rehabilitated for senior baby boomers, just as it did 60 years ago for infant boomers. This means returning to communities where networks of "traditional" and "modern" families look out for their neighbors in this global village in which we all live and interact. These new, neighborhood-based choices, which offer diversity in suburban single-family zoning districts, can meet senior and nonsenior needs. They offer independent-living choices while maintaining household and family-style social networks that are important to people of all ages and lifestyles. They also allow seniors to share responsibilities for cleaning, maintaining, repairing, heating and cooling, and paying taxes on their home, as well as for preparing meals, shopping, caring, nursing, fellowship, companionship, and so forth. Senior baby boomers currently do not have very many ways to redefine the meaning of house and family. They must and will ultimately demand greater independent-living choices.

Some of these options have been around for decades. In a cohousing situation, for example, two or more related or unrelated people can share a house as well as their respective living expenses and housekeeping duties, as many baby boomers did when they were in their 20s. The NBC sitcom *Golden Girls* depicted the social dynamics of independent living, companionship, and senior issues in a shared-housing or cohousing arrangement. Shared housing connotes that each resident is a cohouseholder with defined responsibilities, according to his or her ability. This is different from other independent-living housing options, such as senior boarding houses, single-room occupancy houses, dormitories, or hostels. In these units, the residents are tenants and are generally not responsible for housekeeping functions. They may share bathrooms, kitchens, dining rooms, and common areas, but they do not expect to share in "ownership" responsibilities.

Many local governments are averse to both types of tenant-style housing forms, particularly in established single-family neighborhoods, and prohibit them due to potential or perceived nuisance complaints from neighbors who fear stereotypically bawdy "nonfamily" behaviors. There is no evidence, however, to support the belief that seniors in shared-housing dormitory structures will wreak havoc in established single-family neighborhoods. The development of subsidized and market-based senior apartment housing continues to occur in downtown and high-density districts. Local governments, however, are sometimes reluctant to permit senior-oriented alternative-housing forms in single-family "bedroom" zoning districts. Courts in California, New York, New Jersey, and Michigan are redefining local zoning codes by changing the definition of traditional "family" as it pertains to single-family residential districts (Howe et al., 1994). Other jurisdictions consider seniors a special class of people who should be able to live in alternative-housing forms and living arrangements in single-family districts. These trends in progressive zoning for people with special needs, such as seniors and people with disabilities, may provide future seniors with more choices and the housing development and care-taking communities with more opportunities to build and operate their alternative-living arrangements.

Two other types of senior-friendly, independent-living "conversions" in single-family housing districts are the accessory apartment and elder cottage housing opportunity (ECHO). Accessory apartments can be as simple as converting a garage into a senior suite or making an addition to a primary dwelling. These senior units can be fully separated living units, thus creating two dwelling units or a duplex in one structure. Alternatively, residents can share some facilities with the primary dwelling, such as the kitchen. The latter case essentially would be like building a spare bedroom and renting it out to a senior family member or other trusted senior. ECHO housing is a self-contained living unit, placed on the side or rear of an existing single-family dwelling and removed when no longer needed. These satellite units provide affordable short- and medium-term senior-housing opportunities for families who want to stay together. Again, many local governments prohibit these types of conversions or "intrusions" into the fabric of single-family residential districts because they are afraid of potential nuisance complaints from nonseniors as well as of issues related to architectural design, overcrowding, waste management, traffic, off-street parking, and regular health code inspections.

Some local governments are beginning to address senior-housing issues through the application of specialized zoning measures, much as they have for other special purposes, such as environmental protection and affordable housing. By proactively planning for and regulating senior-housing development applications, local governments can reduce the number of zoning variance requests for these otherwise prohibited units. The most common of these tools are conditional use or special-use permits, which would allow an ECHO unit, for example, on an existing occupied lot as long as it meets a series of predefined criteria. These types of permits could apply in all zones, or only in special overlay or "floating" zones, where the local government wants to encourage such development. Exclusionary zoning standards can mandate senior housing set-asides or contributions to a senior-housing construction or rehabilitation fund. Incentive zoning tools may provide density or height bonuses, clustering or special subsidies, or financing for senior housing. Communities also are using "smart-code" and "illustrated" zoning documents, such as those developed by the Congress for New Urbanism, to educate and require developers to build these types of living environments (see http://www.smartcodecentral.com/index.html). These documents include many of the design principles discussed below.

## SENIOR-FRIENDLY DESIGN PRINCIPLES

There are four fundamental design philosophies for planning, building, and maintaining senior-friendly outdoor environments. The first are the principles of *smart growth*, which are used to advance policies governing transportation and land use planning for urban areas that benefit communities and preserve the natural environment. Smart growth advocates land use patterns that are compact, transit-oriented, walkable, and bicycle-friendly, and that include mixed-use development with a range of housing choices. This philosophy keeps density concentrated in the center of a town or city, combating suburban sprawl (Nozzi, 2006). The second philosophy, *defensible space*, examines how designers can enhance outdoor environments to be safer and more secure, which is a critical issue for seniors. This is important because changing outdoor environments in response to the diminishing physical and cognitive abilities of seniors helps them to feel more independent, engaged, and self-confident while also lessening their risk of becoming potential targets or victims of crime. The seven core principles of the third design philosophy, *universal design*, expands the basic horizons of the 1990 Americans with Disabilities Act (ADA). Whereas the ADA's accessibility guidelines focus on "separate but equal" handicapped accessibility, universal design principles stress a bottom-up approach of redesigning public, semi-public, and private environments and material objects so that they work for all people. The premise of the fourth design philosophy, *sustainable and green design*, while not senior-specific, is that current resource-wasteful methods of designing and building environments and structures must be replaced with renewable methods that society can afford over the long term. This issue is critical for seniors who want to minimize resource use and costs for themselves as well as for future generations.

## SMART GROWTH DESIGN

Design professionals, social advocates, environmentalists, builders, and community groups have been working together for the past decade to reverse patterns of unsustainable, sprawling, auto-oriented development in the United States. The concept of smart growth harkens back to the sustainable, walkable, and livable design patterns of America's historic communities and those of great cities of the Old World in Europe, Africa, and Asia. Sir Winston Churchill characterized the importance of design when he said, "We shape our buildings, and afterwards our buildings shape us." While hard to define, many have adopted the following 10 planning principles as the core of smart growth:

1. Direct development toward existing communities
2. Preservation of open space and farmland
3. Mixed land uses
4. Distinctive and attractive places
5. Compact building design
6. Range of housing choices
7. Variety of transportation choices
8. Walkable neighborhoods
9. Community and stakeholder collaboration in development decisions
10. Predictable and cost-effective development decisions.

Several of these principles are significant issues for aging baby boomers. One of the most important, ensuring a wide range of housing choices, is a major focus of this chapter and others in this book. Mixing land use, another key smart growth principle for retiring baby boomers, means building different structures (e.g., housing, commercial, and civic) in close proximity to one another (i.e., usually within the same building). Mixing land uses creates great streets, public spaces, and pedestrian-oriented places where people can meet and experience the community. The travel destination cities of the Old World and the charming historic towns of early America were mixed-use districts. These are places where people walk, bicycle, or take mass transit as alternatives to driving. They are diverse, exciting, lively, and safe places where people look out for one another, young and old alike.

Distinctive and attractive communities are ones where the builders respect local and regional architectural traditions and natural features—elements that define a community, reinforce its identity, and make people feel as though they belong. They are places that have "memory" and that are memorable, much like the historical communities people visit on holiday. Distinctive and attractive communities convey a special ambiance that many retirees seek in their golden years. Architectural beauty and quality landscape design are no accidents. They require well-defined community standards, attention to detail, and continued maintenance. These efforts show a community commitment to place; that is, public awareness of and participation in creating and maintaining a place mean that people care about the community and about one another, which can contribute to a renewed sense of self. Such communities are important for seniors, who need to feel a sense of control over their environment and of belonging. At a time when they recognize the temporal nature of their own lives, being a part of and committed to a place that has an air of permanence is comforting.

*Compact building design* means minimizing a structure's footprint and impact on the environment by building vertically, close together, and within short, walkable neighborhood blocks. By designing buildings compactly, they become more resource efficient, affordable, and "human-scaled." The human-scale factor of design cannot be overemphasized. Human-scaled buildings and environments are pleasing, relaxing, and comforting places, in contrast to the anonymity and impersonal nature of modern commercial sprawl or colossal architecture. Again, they are like the places of the Old World and of early America that people enjoy traveling to and visiting. People want to live in and belong to a neighborhood, which is usually a compact collection of homes, supporting uses, and public amenities—a place where one can walk 5 or 10 minutes and be somewhere. They also support population densities that sustain mass transit systems.

The U.S. Environmental Protection Agency's (U.S. EPA) smart growth policies glossary defines a "walkable" neighborhood as one that is located within an easy and safe walking distance to goods (e.g., housing, offices, retail) and services (e.g., transportation, schools, libraries) that a community resident or employee needs on a regular basis. Walkable neighborhoods are characterized by mixed land uses, compact buildings, inviting pedestrian corridors, and a streetscape that serves a range of users (e.g., pedestrians, bicyclists, transit riders, automobile drivers). When one recalls the charming hometown neighborhoods and downtowns of old Hollywood pictures, he or she remembers how everyone walked from one place to the other. Although a comfortable 5-minute walk for an average adult is about one-quarter mile, these figures may be less for seniors, depending on their ability. The Partnership for a Walkable America, in association with the Pedestrian and Bicycle Information Center, the U.S. Department of Transportation, and the U.S. EPA, publishes the *Walkability Checklist: How Walkable Is Your Community?* and resource guide for pedestrians (see http://www.walkableamerica.org). AARP publishes a similar checklist,

**Figure 8.3.** Walkable neighborhoods encourage interaction. (Courtesy of Jack Carman)

*Livable Communities: An Evaluation Guide*, that is geared toward seniors. The *Portland Pedestrian Design Guide* (1998) is one of the best pedestrian design guides (see http://www.portlandonline.com/shared/cfm/image.cfm?id=84048).

Two organizations have codified more detailed, design-based smart growth criteria and implementation guidelines. The Sacramento-based Local Government Commission's Center for Livable Communities developed the Ahwahnee Principles at a smart growth conference at the Ahwahnee Hotel in Yosemite, California. The center has a very interactive Web site that provides detailed guidance and reference materials on many sustainable-development practices, such as their "health and physical activity" programs, which are very applicable to aging baby boomers (see http://www.lgc.org/ahwahnee/ahwahnee_principles.pdf). The Chicago-based Congress for New Urbanism has a similar program that teaches people how to implement the practices of smart growth and New Urbanism (see http://www.newurbanism.org/newurbanism/smartgrowth.html).

The International City Management Association (ICMA) and the Smart Growth Network provide additional information on smart growth practices in *Getting to Smart Growth I: 100 Policies for Implementation* and *Getting to Smart Growth II: 100 More Policies for Implementation* (see http://www.smartgrowth.org/search/default.asp). The New Jersey Smart Growth Gateway's Web-based information clearinghouse includes a checklist for proposed developments, municipal planning, community design, and so forth (see http://www.smartgrowthgateway.org).

Although these planning design and development guidelines are not senior-oriented, per se, they do specify that smart growth communities must be ones with housing and transportation choices geared toward a variety of households and consumers, especially seniors. Requirements for mixed land uses and walkable neighborhoods provide the opportunity for active living and healthy communities that are desired by and needed for all seniors. Smart growth principles geared toward open-space preservation, mixed land uses, and distinctive and attractive places, as well as toward the other planning principles noted above, are essential elements in the creation of community ambience, image, and amenities that are used as criteria by most place-rated references.

## Defensible Space

The concept of defensible space is critical for senior citizens and others who need to feel safe and secure outside their homes. Criminologist C. Ray

Jeffrey developed a multidisciplinary practice of crime prevention through environmental design (CPTED), which seeks to deter criminal behavior by limiting opportunities to stalk and strike potential victims by changing natural landscapes and built environments. The three basic principles of CPTED are natural surveillance, natural access control, and natural territorial reinforcement (Jeffrey, 1971).

Natural surveillance limits criminal opportunities by increasing one's ability to observe the normal and abnormal activities of a site, neighborhood, or district. Increasing a place's "visibility" means more people can look out and look after each other. Communities can encourage safe and protected social interaction in public and private spaces and discourage potential criminal activity by incorporating natural surveillance into the design of a place's physical features. Mechanical and technological measures, such as closed-circuit cameras, can augment natural surveillance techniques, as can additional personnel, such as police and neighborhood watch patrols. Natural surveillance design practices include the following:

- Placing windows overlooking sidewalks and parking lots and leaving window shades open
- Encouraging vehicular and pedestrian traffic to pass by building entrances and exit points
- Using transparent shelters and vestibules at house and building entrances and transit stops
- Installing lighting that eliminates blind spots, glare, and deep shadows and that enhances visibility along pathways, stairs, building entrances and exit points, parking areas, transit stops, and other public and semi-public areas
- Planting fully mature trees, shrubs, flowers, and groundcovers for all seasons that will not obscure public and semi-public surveillance areas.

Natural access controls delineate public and private spaces and define who does and does not belong in a space. Increased anti-terrorism controls at airports and public buildings are an extreme example of this form of design in its most unnatural setting. The challenge for designing intergenerational and senior-friendly outdoor environments is how to incorporate site access and flow that feels normal and "natural" when constructing building entrances, fencing, lighting, and landscaping. Some natural access control practices include:

**Figure 8.4.** Thoughtful design elements (wide sidewalks, benches, and adequate lighting) along store-fronts create safe, walkable communities. (Courtesy of Jack Carman)

- Constructing single or clearly identifiable points of entry
- Installing waist-level open fencing or plantings and locking gates between public and private areas to allow surveillance and social interaction among neighbors (e.g., high-cyclone fencing, opaque fencing, and razor wire connote a lack of regular surveillance and social interaction)
- Planting low, thorny shrubs around basement and first-floor windows and trimming tree branches to limit access to upper floors and roofs
- Incorporating structures or landscaping that lead people to reception, anteroom, or security checkpoint areas.

Natural territorial reinforcement occurs when people become attached to their environment and demonstrate that they will protect it from intruders. This principle is achieved through regular physical site maintenance that shows personal or group investment in or "ownership" of a property, as well as through the repeated use and enjoyment of a place. When a site becomes physically deteriorated, vandalized, or abandoned, it shows that no one cares or "belongs" to the place anymore. People do not tolerate criminal and undesirable activities in outdoor environments that are designed to reinforce a positive social territory and in which people feel a personal stake. Natural territorial reinforcement clearly delineates public and private spaces to create a sense of ownership. More important, it requires designing and building outdoor environments that people would enjoy and choose to care about, such as those environments created in accordance with the principles of smart growth and universal design (see the discussion on universal design below). Some other natural surveillance design practices include:

- Planting trees and/or community gardens that attract and maintain people's interest and respond to the seasons
- Installing amenities, such as a sculpture, seating, or refreshments, in public areas
- Scheduling and controlling social activities, programs, and events in public areas.

In his groundbreaking book, *Defensible Space: Crime Prevention through Urban Design* and his successive work, the late architect and city planner Oscar Newman challenged design professionals to create communities where people felt secure and actually were secure (Newman, 1972). The results of

**Figure 8.5.** Amenities such as fountains, benches, and neighborhood parks are essential elements of all communities. (Courtesy of Jack Carman)

his implementation and expansion of the basic CPTED principles are nationally renowned. The Institute for Community Design Analysis continues his work by assisting communities and groups in redesigning their outdoor environments for public safety and security, while enhancing the attractiveness and livability of those places. Newman's *Creating Defensible Space* provides case studies and an expert review of defensible space issues, principles, and techniques (Newman, 1996). In his 1975 book, *Design Guidelines for Creating Defensible Space*, Newman outlines four basic defensible space principles:

- *Territoriality:* The idea that one's home is sacred
- *Natural surveillance:* The link between an area's physical characteristics and the residents' ability to see what is happening
- *Image:* The capacity of the physical design to impart a sense of security
- *Milieu:* Other features that may affect security, such as proximity to a police substation or busy commercial area.

## Universal Design

The design of various environments should incorporate the principles of universal design, whether they are for able-bodied individuals, people with disabilities, or seniors. Universal design respects, values, and strives to accommodate the broadest possible spectrum of human ability in the design of all products and environments (Young & Pace, 2001). The declaration of the Rights and Responsibilities for older persons by the International Federation on Aging in 1990 states that "fundamental human rights do not diminish with age and . . . older persons are at risk of losing their rights and being rejected by society unless these rights are clearly identified and respected" (International Federation on Aging, 1990). To protect the rights of older persons, the built environment should:

- Maximize *independence*
- Enable full *participation* in society
- Enhance the provision and process of *care*
- Provide a platform for *self-fulfillment*
- Enhance individual *dignity*. (Sandhu, 2001)

Ron Mace, founder of North Carolina State University's Center for Universal Design, College of Design, defines universal design on the center's Web site as "the design of products and environments to be usable by all people, to the greatest extent possible, without the need for adaptation or specialized design." The center's goal is "to simplify life for everyone by making products, communications, and the built environment more usable by as many people as possible at little or no extra cost." The center promotes the following seven basic principles of universal design and publishes a guide for implementing them:

1. *Equitable use*: The design is useful and marketable to people with diverse abilities.

2. *Flexibility in use:* The design accommodates a wide range of individual preferences and abilities.

3. *Simple and intuitive:* Use of the design is easy to understand, regardless of the user's experience, knowledge, language skills, or current concentration level.

4. *Perceptible information:* The design communicates necessary information effectively to the user, regardless of ambient conditions or the user's sensory abilities.

5. *Tolerance for error:* The design minimizes hazards and the adverse consequences of accidental or unintended actions.

6. *Low physical effort:* The design can be used efficiently and comfortably and with a minimum of fatigue.

7. *Size and space for approach and use:* Appropriate size and space is provided for approach, reach, manipulation, and use, regardless of the user's body size, posture, or mobility.

Universal design principles should not be confused with the technical construction guidelines required under the ADA, which is a civil rights law that prohibits discrimination against "a physical or mental impairment that substantially limits a major life activity." No person with a disability may be discriminated against the "full and equal enjoyment" of the goods, services, facilities, or accommodations of any place of "public accommodation." Public accommodations include government facilities and most educational, recreational, lodging, dining, and commercial facilities, but do not include private homes, private clubs, religious properties, and other exclusions. The ADA contains specific technical guidelines for everything from parking stalls to stairs to bathroom sinks (U.S. Department of Justice, 1994).

A coalition of housing developers, senior advocates, and the state of Georgia developed the EasyLiving Home Certificate of Approval to encourage the incorporation of universal design principles into basic home design. Although not fully ADA-accessible, EasyLiving homes must be "visitable"—a senior or person with a disability must be able to visit someone living there. Certified EasyLiving homes must have:

- *Easy entrance:* A zero-step outside entrance for safe and easy access
- *Easy passage:* Ample-width doorways (minimum 32 inches) throughout the main floor, including the entrance, and ample-width interior doors (minimum 32 inches) on the first floor, including the bathrooms
- *Easy use:* At least one bedroom and a full bathroom on the main floor.

Homebuilders find these homes "easy to build, easy to visit, and easy to sell." After all, access into or out of a residence or building can be one of the most limiting factors for an older individual. The National Association of Home Builders has created the Certified Aging in Place Specialist (CAPS) program, which encourages designers to "make homes more user-friendly for ALL ages and populations . . . and to set standards and provide more opportunities for everyone in the community." The CAPS program promotes independent living for seniors and aging in place for everyone (see http://www.nahb.org/generic.aspx?genericContentID=9334).

## SUSTAINABLE AND GREEN DESIGN

A fourth consideration in the design and construction of outdoor elder-friendly environments is sustainable or "green" building practices. Sustainable design and development practices are like those for smart growth: They are not elder-specific, but will benefit seniors and other generations alike. The U.S. Department of the Interior's National Park Service promotes sustainable design practices to "reduce negative impacts on the environment and the health and comfort of building occupants, thereby improving building performance" (see http://www.nps.gov/dsc/d_publications/d_1_gpsd.htm). These are important considerations for environmentally-conscience, as well as health-conscience and fiscally-conscience, baby boomers. According to the U.S. General Services Administration, the basic objectives of sustainability are "to reduce consumption of nonrenewable resources, minimize waste, and create healthy, productive environments" (U.S. General Services Administration, 2007).

According to the U.S. Green Building Council, a national sustainable development advocacy and design accreditation organization, a sustainable approach to design should create buildings and interiors that

1. Are healthier for people and enhance productivity
2. Can be built at market rate and cost much less to operate
3. Use less fossil fuels, thus conserving energy, generating less global pollution, and saving on operational costs by requiring less maintenance
4. Use less water
5. Manage waste at the highest productive level
6. Reduce impacts on both developed and undeveloped land
7. Minimize the use of materials and use materials with the lowest environmental impacts.

According to the council, American buildings account for 36% of total energy use and 65% of electricity consumption, 30% of greenhouse gas emissions, 30% of raw materials use, 30% of waste output, and 12% of potable water consumption. Sustainable development is important to baby boomers because much of their future housing and many of their destinations (e.g., retail, entertainment, health care facilities) will be new construction. Green buildings and outdoor environments make good sense in a national economy with limited resources and for senior households with limited budgets. Many states and utility companies have programs that reward green developers and consumers, ranging from reduced rates on electric bills to discounts on compact fluorescent light bulbs. The U.S. Department of Energy's Office of Energy and Renewable Energy is the national clearinghouse for such programs. The U.S. Green Building Council's Leadership in Energy and Environmental Design (LEED) Green Building Rating System® program recommends standards for new commercial construction and major renovations, existing buildings, commercial interiors, core and shell buildings, neighborhood developments, homes, and other specialized building types and uses (see http://www .usgbc.org/). Standards are being developed for outdoor environments, such as streetscapes and landscapes.

## SENIOR-FRIENDLY OUTDOOR ENVIRONMENT DESIGN AGENDA

This section identifies senior-related design concerns related to four major outdoor issues: placemaking and wayfinding, landscapes, the pedestrian realm, and personal and mass transit. It references organizations that are addressing these issues and begins a design agenda for rethinking the way we design, build, maintain, and operate these environments.

## PLACEMAKING AND WAYFINDING

A place is a location (presumably a neighborhood, downtown, or local park) where a person feels welcome. It is an inviting area that encourages one to interact and socialize with others. It draws one out of the home and entices one to enter into outdoor environments, where the general mainstream of life's activities occurs. Those activities occur in public spaces, typically in built environments, where people shop, dine, and generally maintain a connection with the world around them. One of the ways that this connection is accomplished is through networks of safe, paved pedestrian or bicycle pathways that link people to their chosen destinations. The process of designing the "quality of life" of those destinations is *placemaking*. The ability of people to navigate those destinations in a secure and comfortable manner is *wayfinding*. In senior-friendly outdoor environments, one should experience both of these from a "human-scale" or pedestrian point-of-view.

The scale and placement of buildings within a community can influence the location and design of the public pedestrian rights-of-way that are used to move through the built environment (e.g., paved walkways and sidewalks). Within all districts of a community, residential, commercial, and retail, there needs to be space available to incorporate sidewalks. Local zoning ordinances should require buildings to be located adjacent to each other to encourage walking and pedestrian activity, such as an average residential density greater than eight dwelling units per acre and a commercial floor area ratio that exceeds 1.0. Within residential areas, houses should be situated so that they have a view of the streets and pedestrian spaces. Sidewalks should connect all areas so that people can walk throughout the community. Existing residential subdivisions, downtowns, civic areas, and park districts should be retrofitted wherever possible to include pedestrian paths and sidewalks. Studies show that residents in a high-walkability neighborhood engaged in about 70 more minutes per week of moderate and vigorous physical activity than residents in a low-walkability neighborhood (McCann, 2005). People are inclined to walk more frequently, up to twice as often, when the communities have connected sidewalks and pathways (Active Living Research, 2005).

Among all of the things that can be done to change the physical characteristics of a neighborhood, conveying that the sidewalks and pathways are safe and accessible for older adults is very important. If people do not believe that the path they take to the store is accessible and safe for basic pedestrian travel, they will not use it. Interference in or competition for access routes by cars can discourage pedestrian travel. The level of dominance of cars must be reduced to a point that people feel that they "own" their communities and that the "livability" of the community increases (Ewing, 1999). Communities should conduct surveys throughout their various neighborhoods to determine the walkability of a particular community. One such survey, How Walkable Is Your Community?, which was mentioned earlier, reviews the connection of paths from start to finish, such as whether the paths are blocked by signs, poles, plantings, tree branches, frequent driveway crossings, problems with dogs, lighting, lack of places to sit, and many other site features that may impede use by older adults. People are motivated to walk when they have something pleasant to look at and possibly a friend to walk with them during their travels. "Perceived environmental aesthetics and convenience and walking companions," such as a spouse, a friend, or a pet, will result in an increase in walking and a more positive experience (Ball, 2001, p. 440).

Walking around neighborhoods can be a treat to the senses. There are sights, sounds, and smells that are almost indigenous to a particular area or city. The sound of a person's footsteps as he or she travels along a walk has a distinctive noise. The sounds of a church bell ringing out on the hour or signifying a morning service define the neighborhood and alert people to a community event. The pleasant smells of a restaurant or bakery can stir up the senses. There are smells that can transport a person instantly back to his or her childhood or evoke memories from other times. After all, it is the sense of smell that is the most powerful of all the five senses. The song of a bird echoing down the street or drifting into residents' windows is a pleasant sound throughout the year. A sidewalk restaurant, a cluster of park benches, or the front steps of a building are places to catch up on what is happening in the neighborhood. These cultural amenities and vernacular architecture stimulate the senses and create a feeling of belonging when a person walks through a neighborhood.

An important yet under-appreciated element of the outdoor environment is semi-public space, such as the front porch or building foyer in the built environment or the front yard in the natural environment. Semi-public spaces encourage people to interact with the other people in the neighborhood. Senior-friendly houses should be set relatively close to the sidewalk in order to allow a resident to see others walking by and, in turn, to provide security and safety for those walking or riding bikes. Residents

**Figure 8.6.** Enjoying the paper under a shelter in a downtown setting. (Courtesy of Jack Carman)

can decorate a porch for the seasons, thereby adding visual interest as well as a potential conversation-starter for someone walking by. A swing, wicker furniture, a table with ice tea, holiday banners, awnings, a ceiling fan, and wind chimes are but a few of the embellishments that enliven the semi-outdoor living space. Modern zoning practices and an automobile-oriented culture have repositioned the home farther away from roads and sidewalks, and air conditioning and televisions have drawn people off of their front porches. There needs to be a rethinking of social spaces and the design of homes that fosters greater interaction among the members of a community.

Public entrances to civic buildings as well as to commercial and employment centers must be designed to be easily visible, welcoming, and accessible from the street and sidewalk. Entrances should be on grade or provide a minimally sloped ramp that would easily accommodate a person in a wheelchair or walker, with no steps and no slopes greater than 3%. Raised doorsills, if necessary, should be flat and easily mountable. The doors should have a minimum 5-foot-long landing graded away from the building at a maximum of .05%. The width of the walk leading up to the building should have a minimum 4-foot width to allow a person to navigate easily, especially if he or she is using an assisted-mobility device. A path should be free of protrusions and overhanging branches (*Portland Pedestrian Design Guide*, 1998). Seniors and others appreciate sufficient entry lighting as well as places, such as a bench, table, or ledge, on which to sit or rest packages while they search for their keys.

Designers improve wayfinding mostly through appropriate signage. The design of signage varies depending on purpose: to identify a retail establishment, offer directions, alert people to specific conditions, or provide wayfinding information. Corporate branding policies often dictate specific styles; however, many will work with local governments and communities that have particular design preferences. Whatever the rationale for creating signage, it has to be visible for an older adult, otherwise sales, safety, or comfort, or a combination of all three, will dissuade a person from visiting or returning to a particular area. The lettering must be large enough to enable seniors to see the sign clearly, and the sign must be appropriately sized to help make it more visible. Lettering styles, symbols, numbers, and graphics should be in a bold, simple typeface (e.g., Helvetica). The color contrast between the lettering and the background must be distinct. Any glare created by the surface or finished materials of the sign must be reduced or eliminated so that the sign is legible. Raised lettering and braille typefacing will help those individuals with diminished eyesight. Voice-activated signs and information kiosks can facilitate wayfinding and provide information. The height of the signs should be appropriate to the person walking along the sidewalk or riding in a passenger vehicle. According to the American Automobile Association, increasing the size of traffic signals for cars and adding signalized left-turn lanes has resulted in a reduction in the number of collisions (Saranow, 2005).

## LANDSCAPES

Landscapes are outdoor human environments, and the most critical element of the outdoors involves pedestrian-friendly design. One truly cannot appreciate the beauty of Mother Nature in a car, nor can a person who is adjacent to or surrounded by large, fast-paced, air- and noise-polluting internal-combustion engines. Landscapes are designed for the enjoyment of people, not cars. The landscape provides opportunities for people to reconnect with nature and to experience its sights, sounds, smells, textures, movement, and life force; to think about their own spirit and those of others; to recollect past events and to aspire to future dreams; to remember family and friends; to forget, relax, and refresh; to feel comfort and relief—to be human.

Senior-friendly environments incorporate senior-design considerations of pedestrian and vehicular circulation, as well as the urban design elements of placemaking and wayfinding. Successful senior-friendly outdoor landscapes involve the best practices of barrier-free access, sensory design, and therapeutic gardening. These practices must be incorporated into all senior-living environments, as well as into those living environments designed for other generations. The design of a senior-friendly landscape is dependent on the basic conditions of types of soil, shade, climate, and topography as well as on location and outdoor function. A well-designed landscape has the power to re-create self and society by affecting human conditions and moods through sensory stimuli.

The Province of Ontario's Ministry of Municipal Affairs and Housing provides barrier-free design guidance for public outdoor and recreational facilities and stresses the role of municipal leadership in public accomodation (Ministry of Municipal Affairs and Housing, 2005). The ministry maintains that other amenities of the public environment, such as "picnic tables, benches, drinking fountains, and play areas, should be universally designed and in good repair" (http://www.mah.gor.on.ca/Page1290.aspx). It cautions that the proper placement of street furniture, such as benches, lampposts, public signage, transit stops, telephone booths, planters, drinking fountains, café seating, paper boxes, and street lamps, are critical to barrier-free use and enjoyment along sidewalks, walkways, and outdoor paths. The ministry also recommends fencing and landscaping to orient and direct seniors and people with disabilities, placing signage at comfortable reading heights and with universal iconography, and using tactile lettering and fonts in easy-to-read sizes, typefaces, and colors.

The U.S. federal government's DisabilityInfo.gov Web site provides links to housing, transportation, and community life resource information that offer guidance and standards for improving accessibility for seniors and people with disabilities in all 50 states. The recreation section within the "community life" link indicates how outdoor facilities can become compliant with the U.S. Architectural Barriers Act of 1968 and the ADA. The National Center on Accessibility in Bloomington, Indiana, a joint project of Indiana University and the National Park Service, promotes research, training, and technical assistance focused on enhancing parks, tourism, and recreation accessibility across the United States. The Robert Wood Johnson Foundation's Active Living by Design provides programs, reference materials, and community toolkits "to increase physical activity through community design" through their Web site (see http://www.activelivingbydesign.org). Because the primary focus of many of the foundation's programs is encouraging seniors and other generations to get outside, it provides guidance for making better landscape design and pedestrian-amenity choices.

Most people think only of the visual beauty of landscapes. While no one would deny nature is beautiful to look at, there are many other ways to experience the outdoor environment. For example, trees are the thread woven throughout a neighborhood, making them a tapestry of life and of visual interest. By purifying the air, trees are the lungs of a community. They also provide shade for homes and for residents, thereby helping people maintain a connection with the natural world. Street trees and shade trees also offer an important social component to a community by fostering greater social contact and interaction among residents. Residential buildings that have a higher level of vegetation had 52% fewer total crimes, 48% fewer property crimes, and 56% fewer violent crimes than buildings with low levels of vegetation (Kuo et al., 2002). This is particularly important for many seniors who are afraid of crime or who have impaired eyesight and other conditions that may limit their mobility. Green spaces foster greater contact among residents and use of these areas as well as contribute to the social cohesion and validity of a neighborhood (Sullivan, 2004).

Thrive, a not-for-profit social and therapeutic gardening organization in Reading, England, has the slogan "Using Gardening to Change Lives." It provides guidance in making gardening and landscape appreciation easier for blind and visually impaired people by stressing orientation, which is, of course, a key element in wayfinding and placemaking and is also critical for seniors with memory and dementia problems. Thrive recommends that gardens, and by extension outdoor landscapes, be visually beautiful, barrier-free, simple, and devoid of curves and intricate patterns. They should use gentle ramps and slopes as well as handrails for steps, if unavoidable. Thrive suggests the use of raised edgings, borders, and planters along paths to guide and orient people, as well as changes in pathway materials, such as gravel or bark, that provide additional color, texture, and sound stimuli. When using materials and natural elements for reference landmarks and orientation, Thrive recommends using selective vivid colors and bold materials for plants, furniture, and ornaments; distinctive yet sparing scented, sound, and tactile features to avoid confusion; and plants that are thornless, are easy to maintain, require little pruning, and do not overhang in the pathway from atop or on the sides.

The Sensory Garden Project in Staffordshire, England, which Thrive designed for persons with multiple sclerosis and other people with disabilities, emphasizes the use of all senses to experience gardens and landscapes. The subtle sounds of feet on pavement or mulch, rustling leaves on weeping trees, moving water and fountains, chimes and school or church bells, small animals, birdsong and birdplay, buzzing bees and other beneficial insects are all auditory cues to help gardeners and visitors orient themselves and enjoy the landscape.

After visual and auditory enjoyment, people probably most appreciate the scents of flowers and plants. These are the perfumes and other aromas of pollinating and flowering flora, of dry and damp landscapes, of flowering blooms, or of zests and oils released on one's fingers or feet when brushing or crushing a leaf. Scents also come from streetscapes, and the more pleasant, interesting, and life-affirming ones come from streetscapes in walkable and mixed-use neighborhoods and downtowns. People seek to retire to places such as these not only for the sights, but also for the smells.

Gardening in itself provides many personal benefits, including exercise, social connectedness, home-grown and possibly organic produce, personal fulfillment, and an opportunity to educate the next generation. Participating in community gardens provides many quality-of-life benefits to people (Wallczek et al., 1996). Research conducted for the Garden Writers Association Foundation found that 71% of U.S. households report having some form of lawn or garden. And of these individual households, over half plan to use their gardens for relaxation or as a spiritual retreat, and 40% use the garden as a social or entertaining space (Garden Writers Association Foundation, 2006). Gardening is especially suited for older adults, as it offers a range of low- to moderate-exercise intensities (Park, 2006). Additional information about the therapeutic benefits of gardening and horticulture can be found at the American Horticultural Therapy Association's Web site (see http://www.ahta.org), as well as at the Web site of the Healthcare and Therapeutic Design Professional Practice Network of the American Society of Landscape Architects (see http://host.asla.org/groups/tgdpigroup).

## PEDESTRIAN REALM

The importance of exercise, walking, and walkability in senior-friendly outdoor environments cannot be overstated. Pedestrian circulation design issues involve six main elements: paved walkways and sidewalks, crosswalks, grade changes (curb cuts and ramps), clearways, seating, and lighting. Walkways generally refer to paths through a landscape. Sidewalks are walkways that run parallel to vehicular routes. Crosswalks are dedicated walkways within the vehicular realm. Easily navigable sidewalks are essential to the pedestrian feel of a community. If people feel they can travel safely as pedestrians, then they will use sidewalks more frequently and become less dependent on their cars. Local governments and property owners must continually maintain their paved walkways to ensure public safety and to foster the public perception of safety. If people do not perceive that the sidewalks are clean and well maintained and cleared of leaves, snow, and litter, they will avoid walking on them.

The construction of walkways, sidewalks, and outdoor pedestrian plazas varies depending on the materials used to construct them. A smooth, nonslip, nonglare paved surface with sufficient grading and drainage is important. Materials such as broom-finished concrete, exposed aggregate, and colored concrete are common choices, as are black and colored asphalt. Cobblestone, brick, slate, and marble paving are discouraged, as they become slippery and glary when wet and tend to become uneven over time with roots, thermal expansion, and uneven wear. Concrete pavers are acceptable, if they are level and installed with no spacing. Responsible parties must repair uneven surfaces, cracks, or other obstructions. Cracks, joints, or other openings between pavers can be a tripping hazard or perceived as a hole by a person with diminished visual acuity. Some communities, such as Long Beach, San Francisco, and Santa Monica, California, are testing recycled modular rubber panels for pavements (*Bay City News*, 2005). The panels would create a softer walking surface and could possibly help reduce injuries due to falls. There should not be any grates or openings within the pedestrian pathway of a sidewalk. The scoring and construction joints of a concrete sidewalk or patterns in stamped concrete or asphalt should be uniform and not be confusing to a person. Expansion joints should be made of a plastic filler material. The walkway itself should be a continuous common surface without steps.

The width of the sidewalk, however, may vary. Community designers recommend that the sidewalk be a minimum of 5-feet wide in residential areas (think of two people walking side by side) and 10-feet wide in commercial areas. Portland, Oregon, identified as one of America's most pedestrian-friendly communities, has established guidelines for pedestrian safety throughout the city. One of the city's primary goals is to install safe sidewalks on both sides of the road, thereby reducing the width of roads to accommodate better sidewalks, if necessary (*Portland Pedestrian Design Guide*, 1998).

**Figure 8.7.** Pedestrians use flags when crossing the street in Salt Lake City. (Courtesy of Jack Carman)

Designers should designate the space between the sidewalk and the street curb for all utility corridors, signage, landscaping, and other street furnishings and amenities. The space should be wide enough to accommodate street trees and other landscape plantings. A minimum width of 6 feet is recommended to accommodate street trees, benches, signs, fire hydrants, street light posts, and other street furnishings. Utility corridors, or amenity strips, are the spaces to designate for street vendors, such as food and merchandise carts, as well as for special events, such as art shows, flea markets, and other street life. Designers may increase the width of the utility corridor, depending on adjacent vehicle speeds, to create a stronger physical and psychological buffer between vehicles and pedestrians. Whenever possible, the width of the sidewalk should be wider than the utility corridor.

Crosswalks and street crossings should be well marked and signed to alert motorists and to facilitate safe pedestrian pathways, especially for an older adult with diminished visual acuity. There needs to be a shift in precedence of the car over the pedestrian (i.e., that the car intrudes on the pedestrian right-of-way, instead of vice versa). Street departments sometimes use brightly painted neon yellow stripes, pre-cast pavers in distinctly

**Figure 8.8.** An example of a wide, safe, and well-marked street crossing. (Courtesy of Jack Carman)

contrasting colors, or other alternative paving materials to alert both the pedestrian and the driver that the crosswalk exists. A different textured surface, such as one that pedestrians and motorists can see, feel, and hear, is always advisable. The National Institute of Traffic Engineers provides state and local governments with technical guidance on crosswalk design in high-pedestrian areas, as well as other "traffic calming" speed-control measures, such as raised crosswalks, speed humps, roundabouts, traffic islands, narrowed cartways, and "neckdowns" (curb extensions at intersections that reduce roadway width curb-to-curb).

Universal crosswalk standards are not yet available; each state and local government has its own preference, which tends to confuse motorists unfamiliar with local conditions. The Federal Highway Administration and the American Association of State Highway and Transportation Officials, however, are working with state departments of transportation on "context sensitive design" solutions that would allow for general consistency in highway and crosswalk design while maintaining sufficient flexibility for local conditions.

Pedestrian-safe crosswalks should connect sidewalks into parking lots to reduce walking distances across travel lanes, aisles, and parking bays.

**Figure 8.9.** Landscaping can be used to separate sidewalks from automobile traffic. (Courtesy of Jack Carman)

Island planters, if the roadway widths permit, should allow seniors time to rest, if necessary, while crossing a street. Standard crosswalk crossing signal timing, which is an average of 2.8 feet/second (215 feet per minute), is based on the crossing time for a young, healthy individual. Transportation agencies must extend crossing times for older adults to accommodate a walking speed of 1.4 feet/second (Federal Highway Administration and U.S. Department of Transportation, 1998). The use of microwave technology can detect a person in the crosswalk and extend the allowed crossing time (Voorhees Transportation Policy Institute, 2003). The incorporation of auditory signals for visually impaired individuals is essential, as is sufficient, nonglare lighting for people with diminished visual acuity.

If communities are to be designed or redesigned with the pedestrian in mind, curb cuts that favor vehicular access should be minimized. Pedestrian-oriented curb cuts are paired flared ramps that are offset to define corners with nonslip surfaces. The ADA allows a maximum grade of 1:12 (8.333%); however, designs should provide a gradual slope whenever possible. This is important for people in wheelchairs and walkers, as they cannot access grades that exceed slopes greater than 2% or 3% without assistance. Curb cuts and ramp areas should be clear of all obstructions, both visual and

**Figure 8.10.** Crosswalks in shopping centers should be well marked and incorporate landscaping. (Courtesy of Jack Carman)

physical, that would impede a person's ability to distinguish safe and clear passage across an intersection. There should not be any obstructions within 25 feet of the curb line of a street intersection (*Portland Pedestrian Design Guide*, 1998). The pavement surface of all crosswalks and ramps must be a textured surface that allows a person to feel a change in pavements. This is important for people with reduced visual acuity. Designers have used broom-finished concrete, rough-textured pre-cast pavers, contrasting-colored materials, and shallow pedestrian "stubble paving" to help make people more aware of the location of street intersections.

According to ADA requirements, ramps and slopes may not exceed 8% and can be no greater than 2.5% at building entries. This is very limiting for a person in a wheelchair or other assisted-mobility device. In actuality, the slope on sidewalks should be no greater than 2% whenever possible and also have a cross-slope no greater than 2%. There should be a 5-foot-long landing graded at 1% away from doors and with no steps. If there are slopes greater than 2%, designers should incorporate handrails that are compatible with the typical style of street furnishings or building architecture. There should be handrails on both sides of a ramp at a height of between 26 and 32 inches, which includes extension of the handrail at each end.

It is critical to provide clear access, free of obstructions, for people who are either on foot or in wheelchairs or other assisted devices. The width of the walk leading up to a building should be a minimum of 4 feet to allow a person to navigate easily, especially if using an assisted-mobility device. Be sure that the path is free of protrusions and overhanging branches (*Portland Pedestrian Design Guide*, 1998). The height of tree branches should not obstruct passage on a sidewalk. Clear passage should allow a person using an umbrella in the rain, for instance. In Portland, recommended clearance heights are 7.5 feet on average under trees (*Portland Pedestrian Design Guide*, 1998). However, sidewalks should be continuously shaded whenever and wherever possible. Direct sunlight and glare are two factors that may limit use of sidewalks by older adults whose eyes take longer to adjust to bright conditions than those of younger people. Designers recommend shade trees that provide more even shading; interruptions in shade patterns on a sidewalk can confuse a walker with diminished visual acuity and cause him or her to interrupt his or her stride and possibly trip. Appropriate shade trees include those with a solid canopy. Trees that shed fruit or nuts over walkways should not be used. If they are, maintenance staff should regularly clean and maintain the walkways underneath existing female trees. There should be plenty of room to plant such trees in other parts of the outdoor environment.

Sufficient resting areas are needed along all pedestrian corridors. Chairs, benches, rocking chairs, seat walls, and other spontaneous seats should be located at designated intervals. A comfortable walking distance varies with each person's physical abilities; however, experts recommend spacing some form of seating at 100-foot intervals. The seat should be between 18 to 19 inches in height and its depth should be a minimum of 15 inches. An armrest is important to assist a person in rising up off the seat. If individual furniture is used, it should be sturdy and not prone to tipping. Wood, metal, or composite material furniture is typically sturdier than plastic furniture. Concrete furniture is too often cold and appears uninviting. Slightly pitched seating sheds water and allows for quicker drying. There should be room for wheelchairs alongside permanent furniture. Moreover, the chairs and benches should be movable whenever possible to allow a person to arrange a comfortable seating position. The sitting areas should be in both shade and sun locations to accommodate personal preferences in seating positions as well as seasonal variations. Surfaces should be nonglare to reduce visual discomfort for older adults whose eyes adjust more slowly to outside lighting.

Lighting is a critical senior-pedestrian issue, because it extends use of outdoor environments after sunset and makes these places more safe and secure for people with physical and cognitive impairments. People want to participate in activities and be able to socialize within their communities. Outdoor environments should be designed to allow people to move about comfortably and securely after sunset. If older adults want to participate in nighttime activities, light levels must be adjusted so that they feel safe and are secure venturing out at night. Ground-level lighting illuminates pathways while creating a certain nighttime ambience and visually accenting landscape and building features. Other considerations include motion and sunset sensors, lighting levels for stores and parking lots, and illuminated directional signs. Signs should be either internally illuminated or reflective paints should be used to allow a person to visibly understand the message of the sign. It is important for drivers to see the road and be aware of all conditions. It is equally important for pedestrians to be able to see traffic and walk safely within a community. Environmental conditions, such as light pollution, solar energy, and renewable energy alternatives, are also considerations in illuminating outdoor environments.

Senior-friendly outdoor environments require lighting along walking paths and at intersections as well as grade changes, transit stops, rest areas, building entrances, and so forth to increase safety. The Illuminating Engineering Society (IES) has established light-level guidelines for a variety of situations for older adults. IES released a practice recommendation titled "Lighting and the Visual Environment for Senior Living" that calls for a minimum of 5.0 foot-candles (equal to the amount of light generated by one candle at a distance of one foot) to be distributed uniformly along exterior walkways and 10 foot-candles at exterior entrances to buildings (Illuminating Engineering Society, 1998). IES recommends street lamp spacing at a 1:4 or 1:5 ratio (height of lamp to distance between lamps) to reduce glare or hotspots. The foot-candle (fc) level rises for pedestrian security from 0.8 fc for low activity to 4.0 fc for high activity. The light level for an open-air (no roof covering) parking lot, for example, is 0.2 fc for low activity and 0.9 fc for high activity. Considering that a full moon on a clear night is 2.0 fc, the levels indicated may not be adequate (IES, 1998).

## PERSONAL AND MASS TRANSIT

People want to remain independent as long as possible. Because they may not be familiar with other transportation alternatives, many will want to keep using their cars, even if they can no longer drive safely or cannot afford to maintain a vehicle in safe condition. The Federal Highway

Administration is educating highway designers regarding the challenges of older automobile drivers by discussing issues surrounding reduced mobility, vision, attention span, and reaction times as well as medication side effects. Its Web site has several downloadable publications that are oriented to senior-driving issues (see http://safety.fhwa.dot.gov/older_driver/index.htm). The U.S. Department of Health and Human Services and the National Highway Traffic Safety Administration also provide guidance on senior-mobility issues (Burkhardt et al., 1998).

Community planners in successful smart growth communities are taking another approach to making outdoor environments more inviting. They are designing and locating parking lots, garages, and other built structures to be secondary to the pedestrian and mixed-use outdoor environments on main streets by hiding or obscuring them from view, even in residential areas. They are regulating surface parking lots to the sides or rears of building and not to the fronts, where they can infringe on pedestrian areas.

Although some seniors may choose not to own and operate an automobile any longer, they may still desire the feeling of independence provided by personal transit. Baby boomers will demand that the marketplace supply personal transportation options so that they can access local destinations, such as retail centers, health care facilities, or parks, as well as visit family and friends. The use of bicycles and adult tricycles, mopeds, motorized wheelchairs and scooters, golf carts, Segways, or other forms of assisted-mobility devices will increase in coming years. Senior demands for choice and flexibility in personal-transit alternatives will exceed those of other generations, thereby helping to reduce automobile dependency and promote smart-growth lifestyles. Wherever possible, "places of public accommodation" that provide nonautomotive personal-transit parking spaces will be required. There also may be a need for special transportation lanes, just as there are bike lanes along side roads or designated bike paths adjacent to sidewalks.

Although many senior citizens are regular users of public transportation (7% of the 9.6 billion yearly transit trips in the United States are made by people over the age 65), most suburban senior baby boomers are not (American Public Transportation Association, 2006). The Linda Bailey Surface Transportation Policy Project's 2004 study *Aging Americans: Stranded Without Options* documents the problems of senior mobility. The study found, for example, that 21% of Americans age 65 and older do not drive and that half of all seniors, particularly in rural and small towns, have no public transportation service at all (American Public Transportation Association, 2004).

If baby boomers are to remain active and connected to society, improvements will need to be made to local and regional paratransit and public transportation systems. Modes of mass transit, or public transportation, can be in the form of ride-share vans, light rail systems, buses, or other motorized vehicles. They should connect a wide range of residential and commercial destinations. How one boards and how long one has to wait for a mass-transit vehicle are as important to an individual as the route one chooses to reach a destination. Smart transportation design and advanced technology should be used to enhance a senior rider's transit experience. Geographic positioning system units can allow mass transit vehicles to notify awaiting passengers via cell phone or via a monitor at a "smart stop" when a bus or train will arrive. Transit waiting stations must have proper shelter and lighting, standardized at-grade vehicle boarding areas, and no steps or other safety hazards.

Transit stops should be conveniently and clearly located in safe, welcoming, and convenient locations. Transit operators, in partnership with local governments, commercial property owners, and housing developers, must provide better and expanded information services, such as transit schedule displays and new-rider welcoming programs at kiosks in neighborhood, commercial, and employment centers. Schedules must be designed and written in larger typefaces to be less confusing and easier to read. Transit vouchers should be available for purchase by use of debit or credit cards and for printing via home computer, by wireless payment via cell phone, or by any other prepaid ticketing system. Boarding assistance, escort, and concierge services that are focused on senior needs also will enhance the senior baby boomer transit experience. Boomers and other age groups will use and support transit systems that meet their needs, such as comfort, security, affordability, schedule reliability and frequency, service hours, inter-modal connections, and destination choice.

Helpguide.org, a joint effort of the Rotary Club of Santa Monica and Center for Healthy Aging, publishes a senior citizen Web page dedicated to senior-driving and transportation issues and resources (see http:// www.helpguide.org/elder/senior_citizen_driving.htm). The organization stresses the five As of senior-friendly transportation:

1. *Availability*: Transportation exists and is available when needed (e.g., transportation is at hand evenings and/or weekends).
2. *Accessibility*: Transportation can be reached and used (e.g., bus stairs can be negotiated; seats are high enough; bus stop is reachable).

3. *Acceptability:* Deals with standards relating to conditions such as cleanliness (e.g., the bus is not dirty), safety (e.g., bus stops are in safe areas), and user-friendliness (e.g., transit operators are courteous and helpful).

4. *Affordability:* Deals with costs (e.g., fees are affordable, fees are comparable to or less than driving a car; vouchers/coupons help defray out-of-pocket expenses).

5. *Adaptability:* Transportation can be modified or adjusted to meet special needs (e.g., wheelchair can be accommodated or trip chaining is possible).

## A NEW BEGINNING— NOT NECESSARILY A CONCLUSION

One thing is certain—baby boomers will reinvent their golden years, just as they have done with every other stage of their lives. They are not content to accept the status quo of how retirement has been experienced by previous generations. As a result, the concept of the traditional nursing home is fading and the ideas of continuing care retirement communities, cohousing and shared-housing arrangements, NORCs, and other senior-housing models are taking shape. Essential elements in the development of these new communities are that boomers will want to have opportunities to maintain and improve their health and well-being and will need to feel safe and secure as they move about a community. Boomers also want the feeling of community and of being part of a community. They are looking for neighborhoods that offer a sense of stability and traditional values through architecture and community design. The front porch, the community park, and park benches may be symbols of a previous generation, but they may also be the language of the landscape for the coming age wave.

Many boomers have led good and active lives and will want to continue to participate in all that life has to offer throughout the "second half of life." Communities should be representative of aspects of their past. Knowing what seniors have experienced throughout their lives and incorporating various elements from their pasts can only serve to heighten their enjoyment of and participation in the community. These elements do not have to be fake storefronts; they can be functional architectural and natural features that can help to accentuate the living experience.

People who are aging today are in better physical health, are more active, and have more disposable income. They will have the time to shop, exercise, and participate in community events. They are a force to take seriously and will play active roles in defining the culture of a community. "Boomers focus not so much on age as on lifestyle. To them, growing old is not simply a matter of just getting by, it's about being vital and enjoying the lifestyle they choose" (Novelli, 2002). Boomers have begun to formalize this stage of their lives, which will be a component of the later stage of their lives as well. They have the disposable income, time, and desire to make it happen. The role of housing and community developers is to bring that desire to fruition.

## CASE ILLUSTRATIONS

### Case Study 1: Therapeutic Gardens in Public Outdoor Environments

Public gardens can be designed to accommodate the needs of individuals with specific needs and can offer benefits to all users. In 1999, eight gardens were developed as part of a community outreach project jointly sponsored by the Alzheimer's Association and the American Society of Landscape Architects. Three of the eight gardens were created in public settings. One of the three public gardens, the Portland Memory Garden, is a public park located in a residential neighborhood in northwest Portland, Oregon. The second garden, the Monroe Community Hospital Alzheimer's Garden, is located on the campus of the Rochester, New York, health care facility. The third garden is the Alzheimer's Garden and is located in Macon, Georgia. The goal in developing the gardens was to raise awareness for the need for safe outdoor environments in which people with dementia could safely visit with a caregiver. Current statistics indicate that up to 70% of people with AD are living at home at any one time. The success of these gardens exemplifies the need to continue to promote and develop similar gardens in communities throughout the United States. The following are common characteristics of the public gardens:

- *Visibility:* Into and from within the garden
- *Size:* Easy to see most areas of the garden; not too large (i.e., less than 0.5 acre)
- *Convenience:* Easy to access, by foot or vehicle
- *Wayfinding:* Easy to navigate one's way throughout the garden; no dead ends; clearly defined paths

- *Restroom facilities:* Modern toilets and places to wash up
- *Visual interest:* Familiar garden elements such as wind chimes, herbs, vegetables, sculptures, plants and feeders to attract birds, and so forth
- *Sensory plant materials:* Herbs, perennials, and other plants that provide stimulating colors, scents, and textures
- *Path surfaces:* Level, smooth, nonglare, and minimally sloped
- *Furniture:* Sturdy, comfortable, and movable
- *Enclosure:* A fence, hedge, or other means to prevent elopement (wandering unsupervised outside of a safe environment).

## Case Study 2: Alliance for Cardiovascular Health, Utah Health Department

Jane Lambert, Physical Activities Director at the Utah Health Department, has been actively promoting walkable communities and active-community environments. As a cardiovascular health professional, Jane understands the need to get people to walk. Walking is one of the easiest and most universally available forms of exercise and is a very social form of activity. The Alliance for Cardiovascular Health began through the involvement of the various departments of health in Utah. The Alliance began to expand by incorporating the interests and concerns of various community groups regarding the health of Utah residents. The overall mission of the Alliance has been to create communities that encourage active lifestyles that have a positive effect on the senior segment as well as on the overall state population.

The Alliance has promoted activities that include the Utah Walks program and the Summer Games. Family and community involvement are encouraged as part of the Summer Games. Local families in a section of a community participate as a group to compete against other groups. In this way, people get to know each other and can support each other. Seniors are not left to compete against younger individuals, but are part of a group of friends and family members who are also there to support them.

The alliance includes:

- Nutrition professionals
- Medical professionals
- Local AARP (offers financial aid [e.g., through the Baby, Boomers & Beyond Program)

- Department of Transportation (provides enhancement funding)
- City planning (as part of the overall master plan, prepares discussion of development of trails, sidewalks, paths, etc.)
- Department of Air Quality (encourages people to get out of their cars)
- Light rail system (increases use as an alternative to the car)
- Parks and Recreation.

Improvements that have been advanced by the Alliance for people of all ages, but especially for seniors, include changes to the physical environment, such as the installation of new sidewalks or the replacement of existing sidewalks. There is a grass or landscaped area between the road and sidewalk to offer physical and visual separation for pedestrians. Shade over the sidewalks and pedestrian areas is created by trees and overhead structures. There are benches for people to sit and rest or just to socialize while out walking. And there are drinking fountains or other sources of water for people.

The Alliance believes that walking should be an integral part of a person's lifestyle. People should walk to the store, church, and to their neighbor's house. People who walk their dogs get regular exercise, whether they admit or recognize that they are exercising.

The programs promoted by the Alliance have spread throughout the various counties in and around Salt Lake City. Davis County Commission Chairman Dannie McConkie expressed the feelings of the local government officials by stating that "In our county, we are looking at the next 10 years when our elderly population will surpass our current school enrollment. So, if people take some initiative to get active, it may end up saving us money down the road, in terms of aging services."

## CASE STUDY 3: SENIOR NEIGHBORS OF CHATTANOOGA, INC.

A Chattanooga, Tennessee, community garden project uses a team of self-directed older people to help a school in their local neighborhood—a reviving, socioeconomically diverse neighborhood—build a community garden as a living testament to the role of senior volunteers in the community. Through training and working in the gardens, the older volunteers will become specialists in the varying aspects of building and maintaining a garden. Some will offer expertise on herbs, others on vegetables and flowers, and others on soil and container gardening. It is hoped that the garden will become an intergenerational gathering place for the various cultural and ethnic groups in the community, that generations will learn from each other as they share the fruits of their labors, and that this will become a cottage industry for the community (e.g., several locally owned restaurants have promised to consider purchasing produce from this community garden).

## REFERENCES

Active Living Research. (2005). Designing for active living. Retrieved March 2006, from http://www.activelivingresearch.org.

American Association of Retired Persons. (2005). *Livable communities: An evaluation guide.* Washington, DC: AARP Public Policy Institute.

American Public Transportation Association. (2004). Aging Americans: Stranded without options. Retrieved January 2008, from http://www.apta.com/research/info/online/aging_stranded.cfm.

American Public Transportation Association. (2006). Public transportation fact book. Retrieved December 2006, from http://www.apta.com/research/stats/factbook/documents/passengers.pdf.

Armstrong, E. (2004). *America's 100 best places to retire: The only guide you need to today's top retirement towns* (3rd ed.). Houston, TX: Vacation Publications.

Ball, K., Baumen, A., Leslie, E., & Owen, N. (2001). Perceived environmental aesthetics and convenience and company are associated with walking for exercise among Australian adults. *Preventive Medicine, 33,* 434–440.

Ball, M. S. (2004). Aging in place: A toolkit for local governments. Retrieved May 2008, from http://www.atlantaregional.com/documents/Aging-In-Place_Tool.pdf.

*Bay City News.* (2005, January). Rubber sidewalks make debut in San Francisco. Retrieved December 2006, from http://www.ktvu.com/news/4077618/detail.html.

Bland, W. R. (2005). Retire in style: 60 outstanding places across the USA and Canada. Chester, NJ: Next Decade, Inc.

Burkhardt, J., Berger, A., Creedon, M., & McGavock, A. (1998). Mobility and independence: Changes and challenges for older drivers. Washington, DC: U.S. Department of Health and Human Services and National Highway Traffic Safety Administration.

Evanson, K. R., Rosamond, W., Cai, J., Diez-Roux, A. V., & Brancati, F. L. (2002). Influence of retirement on leisure-time physical activity. *American Journal of Epidemiology, 155,* 692–699.

Ewing, R. (1999). *Traffic calming state of the practice* (Publication No. IR-098). Washington DC: Institute of Transportation Engineers.

Federal Highway Administration and the U.S. Department of Transportation. (1998). *Older driver highway design handbook* (Publication No. FHWA-RD-97-135). Retrieved February 2008, from http://www.tfhrc.gov/safety/pubs/97135/index.htm.

Garden Writers Association Foundation. (2006, June). *Garden Trends* (Summer Survey), pp. 6–16.

He, W., Sengupta, M., Velkoff, V. A., & DeBarros, K. A. (2005). *Current population reports: Special studies: 65+ in the United States.* Washington, DC: U.S. Census Bureau. Available at http://www.census.gov/prod/2006pubs/p23-209.pdf.

Howe, D. A., Chapman, N. J., & Baggett, S. A. (1994, April). *Planning for an aging society* (Planning Advisory Service Report No. 451). Washington, DC: American Planning Association.

Illuminating Engineering Society. (1998). *Lighting and the visual environment for senior living* (Recommended Practice No. RP-28-98). New York: Illuminating Engineering Society of North America.

International Federation on Aging. (1990). Declaration of rights and responsibilities. Retrieved January 2008, from www.ifa-fiv.org/docs/IFA Declaration of Rights and Responsibilities.doc.

Jeffrey, C. R. (1971). *Crime prevention through environmental design.* Beverly Hills, CA: Sage Publications.

Jenum, A. K., Anderssen, S. A., Birkeland, K. I., Holme, I., Graff-Iversen, S., Lorentzen, C., Ommundsen, Y., Raastad, T., Ødegaard, A. K., & Bahr, R. (2006). Promoting physical activity in a low-income multi-ethnic district: Effects of a community intervention study to reduce risk factors for type 2 diabetes and cardiovascular disease. *Diabetes Care, 29* (July), 1605.

Kuo, F. E., Sullivan, W. C., Coley, R. L., & Brunson, L. (2002). *Nice to see you—How trees build a neighborhood.* Urbana, IL: University of Illinois at Urbana-Champaign.

McCann, B. (2005, February). Designing for active recreation. *Active Living Research*, p. 2.

Ministry of Municipal Affairs and Housing. (2005). Planning for barrier-free municipalities. Retrieved January 2008, from http://www.mah.gov.on.ca/Page 1290.aspx.

*Money Magazine.* (2005). Best places to retire. Retrieved February 2008, from http://money.cnn.com/magazines/moneymag/bpretire/2005/index.html.

National Center for Health Statistics. (2002). Summary health statistics for the U.S. adults: National health interview survey. *Vital and Health Statistics, 10*(209), 121.

Newman, O. (1972). *Defensible space: Crime prevention through urban design.* New York: Macmillan.

Newman, O. (1975). *Design guidelines for creating defensible space.* Washington, DC: National Institute of Law Enforcement and Criminal Justice, Law Enforcement Assistance Administration, U.S. Department of Justice.

Newman, O. (1996). *Creating defensible space.* Washington, DC: U.S. Department of Housing and Urban Development, Office of Policy Development and Research.

Novelli, W. D. (2002). How aging boomers will impact American business. Lecture presented at the Harvard Club, New York, February 21.

Nozzi, D. (2006). Model urban design regulations. Retrieved January 2008, from http://www.walkablestreets.com/model.htm.

Park, S.-A. (2006). Older adults reap benefits of gardening. Retrieved January 2007, from http://www.acsm.org/AM/Template.cfm?Section=Home& TEMPLATE=/CM/ContentDisplay.cfm&CONTENTID=5375.

*Portland Pedestrian Design Guide.* (1998, June). Portland, OR: City of Portland Office of Transportation Engineering and Development, Pedestrian Transportation Program. Available at http://www.portlandonline.com/shared/cfm/image .cfm?id=84048.

Sandhu, J. S. (2001). An integrated approach to universal design: Toward the inclusion of all ages, cultures, and diversity. In W. Preiser & E. Ostroff (Eds.), *Universal Design Handbook* (pp. 3.1–3.13). New York: McGraw-Hill.

Saranow, J. (2005). Bill signals safer roads for seniors. Retrieved January 2007, from http://online.wsj.com/public/article_print/SB112553491024228583.html.

Savageau, D. (2004). *The retirement places rated: What you need to know to plan the retirement you deserve* (6th ed.). Hoboken, NJ: Wiley.

Schneider, J. K., Mercer, G. T., Herning, M., Smith, C. A., & Prysak, M. D. (2004). Promoting exercise behavior in older adults: Using a cognitive behavioral intervention. *Journal of Gerontological Nursing, 30*(4), 45–53.

Southworth, M. (2005, December). Designing the walkable city. *Journal of Urban Planning and Development,* 248.

Sullivan, W., Kuo, F. E., & DePooter, S. F. (2004). The fruit of urban nature: Vital neighborhood spaces. *Environment and Behavior, 36*(5), 678–700.

U.S. Department of Housing and Urban Development. (2005). American housing survey for the United States: 2005. Retrieved January 2007, from www.census .gov/prod/2006pubs/h150-05.pdf.

U.S. Department of Justice. (1994). *Americans with Disabilities Act standards for accessible design* (28 CFR Part 36, revised July 1, 1994, Appendix A). Retrieved December 2006, from http://www.usdoj.gov/crt/ada/stdspdf.htm.

U.S. General Services Administration. (2007). Sustainable design program. Retrieved January 2008, from http://www.gsa.gov/Portal/gsa/ep/channelView .do?pageTypeId=8195&channelPage=%2Fep%2Fchannel%2FgsaOverview .jsp&channelId=-12894.

Van der Bij, A. K., Laurant, M. G. H., & Wensing, M. (2002). Effectiveness of physical activity interventions for older adults. *American Journal of Preventative Medicine, 22*(2), 120–133.

Visser, M., Pluijm, S. M. F., Stel, V. S., Bosscher, R. J., & Deeg, D. J. H. (2002). Physical activity as a determinant of change in mobility performance: The longitudinal aging study Amsterdam. *Journal of the American Geriatrics Society, 50*(11), 1774–1781.

Voorhees Transportation Policy Institute. (2003, September). Living longer, walking stronger: The design needs of senior pedestrians. *NJ Walks and Bikes,* 1–3.

Wallczek, T. M., Mattson, R. H., & Zajicek, J. M. (1996). Benefits of community on quality-of-life issues. *Journal of Environmental Horticulture, 14*(4), 204–209.

Weuve, J., Kang, J. H., Manson, J. E., Breteler, M. M. B., Ware, J. H., & Grodstein, F. (2004). Physical activity, including walking and cognitive function in older women. *Journal of the American Medical Association, 292*(12), 1454–1461.

Wheeler, D. (2005). The customer-driven community: A recipe for success. Retrieved February 2008, from http://www.huntersville.org/article_0.html.

Young, L. C., & Pace, R. J. (2001). The next generation universal home. Retrieved February 2008, from http://www.architectureweek.com/2001/0620/building_1-1.html.

9
_____

# TECHNOLOGY AND AGING

## Adapting Homes and Shopping Environments with Assistive Technologies

*Emi Kiyota*

SUPPORTING AND MAINTAINING INDEPENDENT LIVING for elderly residents in a community requires innovative approaches to overcome various obstacles. New technologies are gaining enormous interest as promising solutions for the future. Various technologies are currently being developed to assist older adults in living independently in their own homes, which may ultimately enhance their quality of life. This chapter focuses particularly on enhancements to the shopping experience because it is an important activity for independent living and because it has received little attention within the field of assistive technology and therefore reveals ample opportunities for improvement.

Research has shown that aging in place is beneficial for and preferred by older adults. As a result, researchers and practitioners have focused on enabling older adults to continue to live in their own homes. However, remaining in one's home does not necessarily equate to living independently, which requires that individuals be able to perform certain tasks, such as shopping. Being able to shop in one's own neighborhood helps a resident to purchase basic necessities and also provides opportunities to meet and socialize with other residents. The small, local grocery stores of past years, however, have been slowly replaced by large-scale grocery stores and warehouse shopping centers primarily located in suburban areas. Consequently, shopping is heavily dependent on personal transportation and is becoming increasingly problematic for older adults who are no longer able to drive.

If older adults cannot take care of such tasks as shopping on their own, the tasks will need to be performed for them and necessary services will need to be delivered to them at home. While such options can help older adults remain in their homes, they may not be economically viable for some. Moreover, because aging in place can result in social isolation for older adults, they may have no one to assist in performing certain tasks. Living independently is a challenge for these individuals. Aging in place must be revisited within a broader context, therefore, from the residential to the neighborhood scale.

This chapter explores how technology can support independent living and also maintain the community socialization of older adults who choose to remain in their own homes. The role of technology is examined in relation to the task of shopping because it is an essential function for people to be able to live independently in their homes.

## BACKGROUND

In considering technological innovations within community-living environments, there are a number of critical issues that require careful examination: the development of age-related modifications, elder-friendly technology design, the impact of technology on human relationships, feasibility, and so forth. As people age, individuals tend to develop age-related physical, sensory, and cognitive impairments. As these changes occur, homes and neighborhoods can become challenging and even ill-suited environments for a person to live in safely and independently. In many instances, age-related impairments can be alleviated and improved through technological interventions. Technologies can be used to maintain and enhance the abilities of older adults in order for them to live independently for as long as possible (Christensen et al., 2000). When technology is used to enable older adults to maintain social contacts, it can improve their lives.

### BOOSTING COMPETENCE

As a result of age-related declines in physical, sensory, and cognitive abilities, the competence level of older adults decreases. Competence is defined as biological health, sensory-motor functioning, cognitive skills, and ego strength (Lawton & Nahemow, 1973). When an older adult's competence level diminishes, he or she becomes more susceptible to the demands of the surrounding environment, both at home and within the community. In other words, the surrounding environment affects the challenges presented by particular activities. Initially described by psychologists M. Powell Lawton and Lucille Nahemow, this concept is referred to as *environmental press*. The degree to which an environment presents challenges will affect the environmental press. Reducing environmental press can make an activity easier to accomplish.

Technological interventions should afford each individual the opportunity to successfully function within his or her competence level and environmental press. Using the Lawton and Nahemow environmental press theoretical model, my research identified two types of technological interventions to achieve this objective: (1) assistive technologies, or devices that can increase one's competence level, and (2) technologies that minimize the demands of the physical environment. Although assistive technologies can minimize physical barriers and may maximize an older adult's functional abilities, they cannot fully compensate for all of an individual's needs related to daily living. These limitations can be enhanced only through help from family members, neighbors, and community social services. These elements of social support are critical when considering the use of technological interventions.

## RANGE OF OPTIONS

Technologies that compensate for age-related impairments are evolving at a rapid pace, and more sophisticated products are emerging every day. Some are low-tech, such as walkers or lever-style door handles, while others are high-tech computer-operated systems, such as screen readers or digitally programmed hearing aids.

Little empirical research is available regarding the technological, physical, and social interventions that can be used to assist older adults with disabilities with the task of shopping. The limited number of discussions related to retail shopping and electronic commerce (or e-commerce), such as shopping cart designs or Web site designs, are primarily found in consumer magazines, newspaper articles, and Web sites. Recommendations for improving the shopping experience for older adults, such as modifying the physical environment or providing assistive devices, are fragmented and have been examined within different disciplines, such as occupational therapy, psychology, architecture, and sociology. More research using a multidisciplinary approach is needed to understand the challenges that older adults face when shopping, as well as the impacts of technology on their everyday lives.

Researchers have nevertheless identified the following useful technologies: mobility aids; daily living aids (personal care, housework, cooking, leisure); environmental control systems; communication systems; security devices (wearable safety alarm, wander guard for a person with dementia); the Internet; and reminder aids (Barlow & Venables, 2004; Cash, 2003; Dewsbury et al., 2001; Hammel et al., 2002; Louise-Bender Pape et al., 2002; Marquie et al., 2002; Marshall, 1999; Steultjens et al., 2004). Other technologies recommended in the literature include the "smart home" (an electronic and computer-controlled integration of many of the devices found within a home), and telecare/telemedicine (technologies that allow health care to be delivered from a distance or remotely, including transmitting images for investigation, making available community nursing, and advising patients via live teleconferencing) (Dewsbury, 2001; Dewsbury et al., 2003; Lansley et al., 2004). Researchers have also identified technological intervention issues related to feasibility, design, reliability, acceptance, and training and education (Dahlin-Ivanoff & Sonn, 2004; Dewsbury et al., 2001; Hammel et al., 2002; Steultjens et al., 2004).

## POTENTIAL DRAWBACKS

A major concern for older adults regarding technological interventions is financial feasibility. In order to alleviate the financial burden, mass production of an assistive technology is necessary. In addition, subsidies and financial contributions from the public sector should be legislated to support low-income elderly individuals who are in need of assistive technologies to maintain independent living (Stickel et al., 2002).

Design issues are another consideration that can affect how receptive older adults are to using assistive technologies. Common concerns expressed by older adults are that technological devices are too complex for their abilities (Cash, 2003), that they are not user-friendly, that they lack a human response, and that training and instructions are not tailored to older learners (Demiris et al., 2004). Simple and intuitively designed devices with appropriate instructions for older adult users may ease the resistance to use of assistive technologies (Cash, 2003). Many older adults are also reluctant to use assistive devices due to the stigma associated with them. They are afraid of using or wearing the devices because they do not want to be perceived as being disabled. In order to be accepted by older adult users, the design of these technologies should be unobtrusive, easy to use, and reliable (Cash, 2003).

## BENEFITS FROM ON-LINE SERVICES

Before the Internet age, people commonly went to grocery stores, warehouse shopping centers, and malls to shop. Many consumers are now purchasing a variety of goods through the Internet by simply using their home computers. The rapid development and wide use of computer technologies have expanded the options for shopping. Many households have access to the Internet. On-line shopping affords easy access to a wide variety of items, regardless of their geographical locations. For people with mobility challenges, on-line shopping is a viable and valuable alternative for purchasing daily necessities without having to leave the home. While many older adults are taking advantage of on-line shopping, purchasing products via the Internet can be challenging for some older adults with limited knowledge about computers and Web searches. More user-friendly features, such as easy font-size adjustment, color contrast, simple and intuitive Web site design, screen reader, voice activation, and a simple and safe checkout process, must be developed to meet the needs and abilities of older adults.

On the highest end of electronic assistance, on-line shopping can be integrated into smart home technologies to enable people with cognitive impairments to live in their own homes for a longer period of time. If the home automation and communication systems are connected to a service provider, an Internet order can be made without using a personal computer. For example, a refrigerator can monitor the stock of food, automatically generate a food list, send the information to a grocery store, and request delivery.

## IMPROVEMENTS TO TRADITIONAL OUTLETS

Despite the convenience of shopping on-line, many older adults prefer the option of shopping at retail stores, in part as a way to maintain physical and mental health. Retail shopping provides opportunities for both physical exercise and socialization. Few communities, however, offer retail stores within walking distance anymore. In many suburbs, shopping depends heavily on mobility and personal transportation and is becoming increasingly problematic for many older adults. Technological interventions therefore need to focus on increasing accessibility to a store as well as lessening the sometimes challenging experience of shopping in a store. Interventions may involve developing modifications to the surrounding neighborhood, the retail store, or the transportation system.

Today's stores have become very large and are often filled with multiple visual, auditory, olfactory, and tactile stimulations that can be disorienting for an individual. A store's indoor environment can consist of many corridors, aisles, and elevators; multiple levels of display shelves; and unfamiliar categorizations. For the public, generally, a store environment can be busy and confusing for customers negotiating their purchase choices. For older adults with physical, sensory, and/or cognitive impairments, shopping in a store can become an even more confusing and challenging task.

Because of the American's with Disabilities Act, people who use a wheelchair are able to safely maneuver their way within most stores; however, finding and reaching products remains a challenge. Appropriate display strategies need to allow people with physical and sensory impairments to shop with greater ease. Legible signage with large fonts, recognizable symbols, and clear color contrast helps older customers find items as well as orient themselves to a store's layout. Older adults may benefit from using memory aids, such as simple lists and message devices to stay on task and to help avoid confusion and anxiety. A more sophisticated memory-aid device may be smart cart technologies, which are being tested in some U.S. grocery stores. For example, when a customer swipes his or her membership card through a computer mounted on a cart, the cart generates a shopping list based on the customer's purchasing history and can direct him or her to the items, with flashing ads and coupon offers along the way. Such a cart would help older individuals with cognitive impairments orient themselves as well as remind them of the more common items they need.

At the cashier counter, existing credit card readers have small touch keys with poor color-contrasted display screens. Large touch keys with braille and enlarged display screens with adequate and clear color contrast are needed to accommodate customers with vision loss. Combining multiple communication methods, such as integrating visual, auditory, olfactory, and tactile stimulations as well as using high-tech systems (e.g., smart phones), is another way to enhance the shopping experience of elderly individuals who have various sensory and physical impairments.

After purchasing products, the final challenge older individuals have to manage is taking their purchases home using their own car or public transportation. Store delivery service options would allow older customers to make the trip back home with greater safety and ease.

## MODIFICATIONS TO THE BUILT ENVIRONMENT

Modifying built environments to meet the needs of older adults will enable them to shop independently at stores. Beginning with the home, modifications such as installing ramps, eliminating steps, or providing adequate lighting help prevent older residents from falling when entering and leaving. Once outside the home, safe sidewalks are needed for elderly residents to walk to a store or to access public transportation. For example, eliminating steps and gaps on sidewalks accommodates individuals who use a walking device and prevents them from falling. Seating areas adjacent to sidewalks offer a resting place for those who have reduced stamina. Crosswalks with a longer crossing-time duration allow elderly pedestrians to safely cross streets at their own pace. Some city crosswalks assist people with visual and auditory impairments by incorporating sounds that signal when the traffic light is green and numerically displaying the time remaining to cross before the light changes. Legible signage systems with recognizable symbols help to orient older adults with cognitive impairments.

The use of a wheelchair is a basic intervention for an individual with mobility problems. While wheelchairs help people to move around, they still require significant upper-body strength. Power-operated wheelchairs assist users with diminished strength. Adjustable-height wheelchairs allow users to easily view objects within the landscape and provide opportunities for the user to communicate comfortably with others at the same eye level. Intelligent wheelchairs that automatically avoid obstacles, however, are under-developed (Levine et al., 1999; Yanco, 2001).

Simple assistive devices, such as eyeglasses, hearing aids, and walking and blind sensing canes, assist elderly residents in safely accessing a store and with shopping. Some devices are being developed with computer sensors to enhance safety and reliability on the street, such as a smart cane or walker that can detect obstacles along a path, record and retrace a user's steps along a path, and monitor the user's heart rate (Haoyong et al., 2003; Wasson et al., 2001). A computerized road-crossing aid measures the width of a road and the color of a traffic light, thereby assisting a person with visual impairment (Knight, 2004). The Seeing Eye Glove helps a visually impaired person to "sense" his or her surroundings by providing tactile and auditory feedback and by safely orienting the person by way of integrated technologies such as speech recognition and satellite and position technology (Stephen, 2004).

## TRANSPORTATION ALTERNATIVES

Many older adults still drive to the store. Driving may, however, become a more challenging task for them as they develop age-related disabilities. Assistive devices for a car, such as a lift, wheelchair carrier, power seats, or a joy stick, can enable older drivers to travel safely. Other more technological devices include remote engine start, keyless entry, and back up sensors as well as in-vehicle security, communications, and diagnostics systems (e.g., OnStar®). Geographical orientation devices, or Global Positioning Systems (GPS), assist drivers in navigating through a community by way of voice-guided directions and maps that can be viewed via a screen that is either dash mounted or set within the dashboard. The directions need to be precise and audible to reduce confusion and avoid hazardous situations when driving (Nancy, 2004). Geographic information systems (GIS) can monitor the location of an older adult driver, giving family members a sense of security by knowing where their loved one is.

At stores, designated parking spaces can be assigned for older drivers, which could help them to avoid crossing vehicular traffic to access the entrance of a store. Wide automatic entrance doors can accommodate people with mobility and visual impairment.

For those older adults who can no longer drive or who do not have use of a car, access to public transportation services with senior-friendly design features is crucial. Buses and trains can provide step-free access by means of accurate docking at raised curbs. They can also communicate better with people with various disabilities through multiple cues, such as sounds, flashing lights, and legible signage and symbols, including braille. Sophisticated devices such as cell phones with GPS technology that can track the arrival of a bus or train and pre-paid swipe cards that allow riders to pay and board more easily can also enhance the experience of using public transportation.

Even if an older adult is able to access a store and purchase a product, he or she must then take the product back home. A participant in a study that examined older adults' experience of using public transportation expressed concern that "the bus stop is far away. . . . I am not able to walk on those days when I have something to carry" (Carlsson, 2004). Public modes of transportation should accommodate for decreased functional abilities by providing such customized services as a dial-a-ride system, which is successfully used in major U.S. cities as well as in Europe (Alexander, 2005), bus route deviation service for registered users, and reduced taxi rates for older adults.

## ISSUES RELATED TO TECHNOLOGY AND AGING

Technology offers useful interventions that enable older adults to live at home independently, to shop from home, and to communicate from home with family members or friends. In addition, smart house technologies lessen the burden of family members or neighbors who may provide formal or informal help to an older adult (e.g., reminding an individual to take a medication; monitoring the use of hazardous equipment, such as a kitchen stove; contacting outside help if needed; and monitoring behaviors to assess whether a person is distressed [Orpwood et al., 2001]). Technological interventions, however, may result in social isolation by reducing the opportunities for older adults to have incidental encounters with others within their community. On-line shopping may be a convenient method for older adults to purchase necessary goods without leaving their homes; however, it also prevents them from socializing one on one with people in their community. The balance between convenience and assistance and the opportunities for socialization should be carefully considered. For example, if an older adult has difficulty shopping in stores, a family member, neighbor, or volunteer can provide the needed assistance, thereby encouraging socialization.

Another important issue related to on-line shopping is virtual security. Virtual crimes in the form of credit card fraud or identity theft are risks associated with shopping on-line. Older adults can easily become victims of these crimes, especially those with cognitive impairments. Reliable and effective security systems need to be developed and maintained to protect older adults from these crimes.

Potential issues also exist with respect to the physical or built environment. Accessibility to retail stores can be improved by developing an age-friendly environment where technological interventions are integrated into the community. Supporting small neighborhood stores to stay in business, providing easy access to public transportation, and creating safe pedestrian corridors will allow older adults to continue to access retail stores. Supportive outdoor environments will encourage elders to go outside, thereby increasing the opportunity to socialize and to engage in physical activities.

A balance must also be considered with respect to convenience and assistance and the functionality and user-friendliness of technologies that allow older residents to live independently. Too many technological devices may very well impede an individual from maintaining his or her abilities. Technological interventions that are designed to aid an older adult with impaired abilities should be useful and easy to use.

## CONCLUSION

Technology alone cannot achieve the objective of helping older adults to age in place. In developing technological interventions, important factors such as creating and supporting elder-friendly physical and social environments cannot be overlooked in maintaining the autonomy and freedom of older adults. Also, technology should never replace or stand in the way of the care and support of family, friends, and neighbors. Although the development of socially responsible assistive technologies is strongly encouraged to meet the needs of a growing aging population, human interactions and active engagement in neighborhood life should be continually valued, encouraged, and supported.

## REFERENCES

Alexander, K. J. (2005). Getting there: A personal perspective from two coasts. *Physical & Occupational Therapy in Geriatrics, 24*(2), 63–69.

Barlow, J., & Venables, T. (2004). Will technological innovation create the true lifetime home? *Housing Studies, 19*(5), 795–810.

Carlsson, G. (2004). Traveling by urban public transport: Exploration of usability problems in a travel chain perspective. *Scandinavian Journal of Occupational Therapy, 11*(2), 78–89.

Cash, M. (2003). Assistive technology and people with dementia. *Reviews in Clinical Gerontology, 13*, 313–319.

Christensen, K., McGue, M., Yashin, A., Iachine, I., Holm, N. V., & Vaupel, J. W. (2000). Genetic and environmental influences on functional abilities in Danish twins aged 75 years and older. *Journals of Gerontology Series A: Biological and Medical Sciences, 55*(8), 446–452.

Dahlin-Ivanoff, S., & Sonn, U. (2004). Use of assistive devices in daily activities among 85-year-olds living at home focusing especially on the visually impaired. *Disability & Rehabilitation, 26*(24), 1423–1430.

Demiris, G., Rantz, M. J., Aud, M. A., Marek, K. D., Tyrer, H. W., & Skubic, M. (2004). Older adults' attitudes towards and perceptions of "smart home" technologies: A pilot study. *Medical Informatics & the Internet in Medicine, 29*(2), 87–94.

Dewsbury, G. (2001). The social and psychological aspects of smart home technology within the care sector. *New Technology in Human Services, 14*(1–2), 9–18.

Dewsbury, G., Clarke, K., Hughes, J., Rouncefield, M., & Sommerville, I. (2003, March). Growing older digitally: Designing technology for older people. Paper presented at the Inclusive Design for Society and Business conference, London, England.

Dewsbury, G., Taylor, B., & Edge, M. (2001, September). The process of designing appropriate smart homes: Including the user in the design. Paper presented at the EQUATOR Workshop on Ubiquitous Computing in Domestic Environments, Nottingham University.

Hammel, J., Lai, J.-S., & Heller, T. (2002). The impact of assistive technology and environmental interventions on function and living situation status with people who are ageing with developmental disabilities. *Disability & Rehabilitation, 24*(1–3), 93–105.

Haoyong, Y., Matthew, S., & Steven, D. (2003). An adaptive shared control system for an intelligent mobility aid for the elderly. *Autonomous Robots, 15*(1), 53–66.

Knight, W. (2004). Electronic eye helps blind across the road. Retrieved November 2004, from http://www.newscientist.com/article.ns?id=dn6693.

Lansley, P., McCreadie, C., & Tinker, A. (2004). Can adapting the homes of older people and providing assistive technology pay its way? *Age & Ageing, 33*(6), 571–576.

Lawton, M. P., & Nahemow, L. (1973). Ecology and the aging process. In D. Eisdorfer & M. P. Lawton (Eds.), *Psychology of Adult Development and Aging.* Washington, DC: American Psychological Association Press.

Lawton, M. P., & Simon, B. B. (1968). The ecology of social relationships in housing for the elderly. *The Gerontologist, 8,* 108–115.

Levine, S. P., Bell, D. A., Jaros, L. A., Simpson, R. C., Koren, Y., & Borenstein, J. (1999). The NavChair assistive wheelchair navigation system. *IEEE Transactions of Rehabilitation Engineering, 7*(4), 443–451.

Louise-Bender Pape, T., Kim, J., & Weiner, B. (2002). The shaping of individual meanings assigned to assistive technology: A review of personal factors. *Disability & Rehabilitation, 24*(1–3), 5–20.

Marquie, J. C., Jourdan-Boddaert, L., & Huet, N. (2002). Do older adults underestimate their actual computer knowledge? *Behaviour & Information Technology, 21*(4), 273–280.

Marshall, M. (1999). Technology to help people with dementia remain in their own homes. *Generations, 23*(3), 85–88.

Nancy, F. (2004). GPS tells elderly motorist to do u-turn on expressway . . . so he does. Retrieved November 2004, from http://www.spacedaily.com/news/gps-04zzzzm.html.

Orpwood, R., Adlam, T., Gibbs, C., & Hagan, S. (2001). User-centered design of support devices for people with dementia for use in a smart house. In C. E. A. Marincek (Ed.), *Assistive Technology*. Neatherlands: IOS Press.

Stephen, S. (2004). Perfecting the "seeing-eye glove." Retrieved September 2002, from http://geoffandwen.com/Blind/newsarticle.asp?u_id=563.

Steultjens, E. M. J., Dekker, J., Bouter, L. M., Jellema, S., Bakker, E. B., & Van Den Ende, C. H. M. (2004). Occupational therapy for community dwelling elderly people: A systematic review. *Age & Ageing, 33*(5), 453–460.

Stickel, M. S., Ryan, S., Rigby, P. J., & Jutai, J. W. (2002). Toward a comprehensive evaluation of the impact of electronic aids to daily living: Evaluation of consumer satisfaction. *Disability & Rehabilitation, 24*(1–3), 115–125.

Wasson, G., Gunderson, J., Graves, S., & Felder, R. (2001). An assistive robotic agent for pedestrian mobility. *Proceedings of the Fifth International Conference on Autonomous Agents, Canada*, 169–173.

Yanco, H. A. (2001). Development and testing of a robotic wheelchair system for outdoor navigation. *Proceedings of the 2001 Conference on Rehabilitation Engineering and Assistive Technology Society of North America, 21*(1), 145–147.

# Preparing for the Near and Distant Futures

THE GROWING NEEDS OF 72 MILLION AGING BOOMERS are a call for moving away from the practice of compartmentalizing knowledge and practical responsibilities across various fields. Toward this end in Chapter 10, Collaboration as the Key to the Successful Future of Aging, Bob Scarfo argues for building diverse collaborative teams that span areas of knowledge and that reduce the amount of time needed to develop practical applications of that knowledge for the benefit of the aging cohort. The types of social networking, interdependence, social programs, and modifications to the natural and built environments that contribute to healthy aging and healthy communities must be examined collaboratively across areas of research, education, and practice to bridge theory and practice.

Such collaborations are occurring among forward-thinking planners and in specific communities, but greater momentum and responsiveness is needed in the face of the population pressures that are already building today. The goal of this book is to initiate increased dialogue and awareness among all the professionals who can play a role in re-creating our neighborhoods for the successful aging of today's and tomorrow's older adults.

10
_____

# COLLABORATION AS THE KEY TO THE SUCCESSFUL FUTURE OF AGING

*Bob Scarfo*

THIS CHAPTER IS AN INTELLECTUAL ARGUMENT for building greater collaboration among and between diverse professional groups and the greater public. The development of this argument is an outgrowth of two years of workshops, seminars, and discussions as well as six years of design studio projects at Washington State University Spokane's Interdisciplinary Design Institute that included health care, public health, and medical practitioners alongside architects, landscape architects, urban designers, city and rural planners, and members of the general public. Each of the events focused on building collaborative problem-solving environments. The common ground used to call people together was each profession's mandate or layperson's wish to foster and sustain the public's health, safety, and welfare in the face of trends related to aging, health, and energy. The outcomes sought were guided by the common wish to find ways to effectively combine participants' knowledge and skills in the planning and design of built environments and social programs that support healthy and active aging in energy-efficient, more sustainable neighborhoods and communities.

In efforts to orchestrate effective collaborative activities, the following models of interaction were explored and will be discussed below: social capital building; action research; multi-, inter-, and transdisciplinary research and practice; community-based research; future search techniques; and asset building.

## SOCIAL CAPITAL BUILDING IN COLLABORATION

Seventy-eight million baby boomers are approaching retirement at the same time that the United States faces an obesity epidemic and an energy crisis. The aging of America can no longer be considered in isolation of these two other significant challenges. One reason to consider the three trends together is that each benefits from a similar kind of built environment—one that is high density, pedestrian friendly, mixed use, and multigenerational. A second reason is that joining together the specialized areas of research, education, and practice for each trend provides a more comprehensive approach to knowledge generation, learning and practice, and knowledge application for the benefit of the public and the environment. A third reason is the immediacy of the aging, health, and energy trends, which calls for the trends to be dealt with by collaborative groups of diverse professionals and public organizations. The first of the boomers began turning 60 in 2006, two thirds of Americans are currently overweight or obese, and petroleum is rapidly becoming a scarce commodity. Society can no longer afford the delays built into a "trickle down" of knowledge through education to practice and into the community (Windley & Weisman, 2004). Although inclusive models of interaction do exist and are practiced, there is still a need for a more generally practiced form of interaction that enables diverse groups of researchers, educators, and practitioners to recognize people's needs and to work with them. The model with the most promise for success is *social capital building,* primarily because it is a relatively common practice across public, professional, academic, and research populations.

Social capital refers to social networks and norms of reciprocity and trustworthiness that arise from connections among individuals and is closely related to what some have called "civic virtue" (Putnam, 2000). The difference between social capital and civic virtue is that

> Social capital calls attention to the fact that civic virtue is most powerful when embedded in a sense network of reciprocal social relations. A society of many virtuous but isolated individuals is not necessarily rich in social capital. (Putnam, 2000, p. 19)

Social capital consists of the stock of active connections among people: the trust, mutual understanding, and shared values and behaviors that bind the members of human networks and communities and that make cooperative action possible (Cohen & Prusak, 2001). In 1959, Jane Jacobs witnessed the heart of social capital, or what she referred to as a "ubiquitous principle," in cities fostering an "intricate and close-grained diversity of uses that give each other constant mutual support, both economically and socially" (1961, p. 14). In cities across the United States and Canada, she observed that social and economic well-being went hand in hand with a built environment that increased the potential and probability of people making social connections as they carried out their daily routines. Jacobs's "sidewalk environments" foster trust. In 1995, Daniel Kemmis, political activist and former mayor of Missoula, Montana, observed a trust-building environment in a community farmers' market. He described the market's social character of civility as being related to the character of the built environment in which it was found. These qualities of public collaboration— Putnam's social capital, Jacobs's ubiquitous principle, and Kemmis's civility—can be capitalized on to foster and support healthy aging, improved health, and energy conservation within a community.

As a basic framework with which to prepare for the challenges of aging, health, and energy, social capital building is by no means a cure-all. People willing to build and sustain cohesive, trusting social environments are found more in some built environments than others, "making possible the achievement of certain ends that in its [social capital] absence would not be possible" (Coleman, 1988, p. S98). There are also questions as to the ability of social capital to grow in "poorly maintained built environments" (Araya et al., 2006, p. 3074). Still, there are sufficient examples where despite the quality of the physical setting, the basic spatial character of the place enables residents to interact in ways that contribute to a higher quality of personal and group life. What had once been a Boston slum shunned by local planners, a Missoula community lacking in fresh produce and social cohesiveness, and an East St. Louis neighborhood all but destroyed are now three places renewed (Jacobs, 1961; Kemmis, 1995; Reardon, 2003). The key in each case was one of proximity; people, to a great extent, interacted with each other on a regular basis and openly shared their wishes for something better. The physical closeness of people talking with each other is a critical component in collaboration. Another component is a return to a more commonly shared language, which is discussed in more detail below in Approaches to Collaboration. Each of the three communities ultimately benefitted from combining the specialized knowledge and skills of professionals with the understanding and involvement of the general public.

## INTERDISCIPLINARY COLLABORATION

In the late 1800s, Frederick Law Olmsted, the founder of landscape architecture, believed that people's individual and community social health was interrelated with the quality and character of the landscapes in which they lived (McLaughlin & Beveridge, 1977; Rybczynski, 1999). His work, however, was based more on observations derived from his experiences as the head of the U.S. Sanitary Commission during the Civil War than on any scientific studies. Dr. Richard Jackson, former director of the Centers for Disease Control and former director of public health for California, has been among the main advocates for greater research into the links between public health and the built environments (Frumkin et al., 2004; Jackson & Kochtitzky, 2006):

> I think that planners, builders, architects, and zoning agencies need to realize that they are also public health officials. . . . They influence the health of the community in profound ways, perhaps more than the doctor who's giving out pills. (Jackson, 2003, p. A03)

Primarily prompted by what is termed the *obesity epidemic*, Dr. Jackson and an array of health care, medical, exercise physiology, nutrition, gerontological research, transportation, and land planning specialists have begun to generate a growing body of health–built environment literature, including *Urban Sprawl and Public Health* (Frumkin et al., 2004), *Health and Community Design* (Frank et al., 2003), *Neighborhoods and Health* (Kawachi & Berkman, 2003), and *Society and Health* (Amick et al., 1995). The compendium of published research in journals related to public health, preventive medicine, gerontology, and gerontological nursing is growing daily. Still, given the immediacy of the baby boomers coming of age, collaboration across the health and built environment disciplines and professions remains slim.

One difficulty in creating health–built environment collaborations is the historical development of professions into increasingly specialized areas of research, education, and practice. Disciplines are now comprised of so many subordinate specialty areas that the term *interdisciplinary* is equally applied to a collection of medical researchers or a gathering of environmental designers. *Successful Aging* by Rowe and Kahn (1998) summarizes 10 years of McArthur Foundation–supported research aimed at establishing an "authentic interdisciplinary science" that moves "beyond the limited view of chronological age" (1998, xii–xiii). Well prepared and easily read, even by a novice in the world of gerontology such as myself, a landscape architect, *Successful Aging* is an example of why interdisciplinary collaboration needs to be more broadly defined in practice. The MacArthur Foundation's 16-member interdisciplinary team only included medical and social science specialists. A broadening of the health–built environment collaboration would create more comprehensive and immediately practical outcomes. Slightly more inclusive, the collected works found in *Productive Aging* (Morrow-Howell et al., 2001) and *Achieving a Productive Aging Society* (Bass et al., 1993) bring together the viewpoints of historians, economists, policy analysts, and spiritualists. Still, absent are the spatial thinkers and practitioners who deal with transportation and land planning (Frank et al., 2003; Frumkin et al., 2004), architecture and landscape architecture (Wahl et al., 2003), and the geographic perspective Graham Rowles brings to *Prisoners of Space?* (1978).

Without the involvement of spatial thinkers in the research and analyses of successful, productive, and healthy aging, the questions will go unasked or unanswered about the elder cohort's proximity to goods and services, residential density and diversity, travel time spent fulfilling daily needs, and outdoor active-living environments related to places of paid employment, volunteer activities, and various forms of social capital building. One example is seen in a major survey of older adults' participation in physical activity programs (Hughes et al., 2005). The survey did not consider how those living in "walkable" neighborhoods, which provide the opportunity for daily exercise, would feel little need to join a local health club. Also, the study made no mention of how the built environment may have prevented a portion of the cohort from getting to and from an organized activity program.

One reason that spatial thinking has not been incorporated is how gerontologists and health care professionals define words such as *availability* and *access*. For many health-related professionals, the two terms refer to whether or not a health care delivery system exists in a given locale. Not typically considered is its location, the distance from an end user's home, pedestrian access, or proximity to mass transit. In a like manner, *environment* is considered in relation to social, economic, familial, and political situations, but not in relation to the spatial character of physical environments. For many spatial thinkers, such as urban designers and landscape planners, *access* and *availability* refer to such factors as proximity to where an end user lives, one's ability to climb stairs in and around a built environment, and the physical movement in and out of courtyards, building entrances, and the like. Topography, building materials, and a person's ability to read the spatial organization of a place and to find his or her way all play a role in healthy aging and active living.

Many authors recognize the need to develop an interdisciplinary research agenda and call for the creation of more theoretical and conceptual work through interdisciplinary inquiry and practical application (Morrow-Howell et al., 2001). To date, however, the various interdisciplinary teams have remained narrow in their diversity. As a result, absent in major national surveys are the spatial concerns of the design and planning professions: form, mass, sequence of flow, and traffic stream (Simonds, 1984); legibility, imageability, and the structural features of paths, edges, districts, nodes, and landmarks (Lynch, 1960); and spatial dialog, spatial metaphors, and placemaking (Schneekloth & Shibley, 1995).

Another reason why interdisciplinary collaboration would gain from greater inclusiveness is so the work can be more quickly interpreted into practical policies and practices that can be readily applied in neighborhoods and communities (Lipsey, 2005; Rosenfield, 1992; Windley & Weisman, 2003). Time is of the essence. More so than ever, the rate at which structural lag can be minimized and institutions can adapt to growing trends is critical. The social, economic, and business pressures associated with 78 million baby boomers approaching retirement are already making news. In May 2004 National Public Radio noted that from 2004 to 2009, 50% of all public utility employees would be eligible for retirement. The anticipated shortfall in teachers for 2010 is 200,000 (Freedman, 1999), and for 2020 there is an anticipated shortage of 800,000 nurses (Zimmerman, 2006). The 2000 census shows that 51% of farm operators are between 45 and 64 years of age. The average age of a registered nurse working in a hospital is about 52. The impetus for the creation of the NASA Explorer Schools was the impending shortfall of scientists and engineers. While the full impact of boomers reaching retirement will not occur until 2030, at which time 24% of the U.S. population will be 65 years of age and older, the window of opportunity to prepare is in the years leading up to 2012. Given the need to overcome the inertia of structural lag, institutional and financial obstacles, and discipline-specific turf boundaries, the small window of opportunity calls for changes to be in the works now (Garner, 1995; Riley et al., 1994; Rosenfield, 1992; Schon, 1983).

## COLLABORATION AND TRENDS
## IN AGING, ENERGY, AND HEALTH

As previously noted, two other trends are converging with the onslaught of aging baby boomers: a growing energy crisis (Heinberg, 2005; Kunstler, 2005; Shuman, 2000), and the deteriorating health of Americans due to obesity, type 2 diabetes, and their comorbidities (Dannenberg et al., 2003; Ewing et al., 2003; Yancy et al., 2002). The window of opportunity associated with these two trends is nearly closed.

In August 2002, BBC News reported that a jump in oil prices to $29 per barrel was a threat to the world's economy. At that time in the United States, gasoline cost about $1.60 per gallen. In May 2008, oil had soared to $125 a barrel and gasoline cost over $3.50 per gallon. Gone are the days of cheap oil. Half of the oil in the ground has been harvested, and that was the inexpensive, easy-to-harvest half. Oil has become increasingly more difficult and costly to mine and refine, which has been compounded by the fact that the countries with the most oil are politically unstable.

Also in 2002, few people outside of the scientific and medical communities were aware of the deteriorating health of Americans. In 2007, 66% of Americans were overweight. An obesity epidemic is influencing airlines' gas consumption, has resulted in $117 billion in annual health care costs, and is contributing to children developing diseases that were only considered adult illnesses 20 years ago.

The convergence of this perfect storm of aging, energy, and health challenges calls for a more inclusive and comprehensive examination and interpretation of these issues as well as an understanding of their influences on health and the built environment. Each of the three trends is occurring for the first time. Each is global as well as national, local, and personal. And each trend's uniqueness is compounded by the three trends' concurrent growth and overlap into people's daily lives as well as by their influence on the greater community. The issues and implications of successful and productive aging, energy conservation, and healthy living are not independent of each other. Each is linked to the built environment. Sprawling, homogeneous, automobile-dependent landscapes require more energy to sustain than do denser, mixed-use, pedestrian-friendly environments. Environments that require people to use an automobile for even simple chores contribute to weight gain (Ewing et al., 2003; Transportation Research Board, 2005), type 2 diabetes, and asthma (Jackson & Kochtitzky, 2006), and influence people's social well-being (Beem, 1999; Glaeser et al., 2003; Putnam, 2000). While in need of more detailed study, the indications are that the kinds of built environments that limit social interactions also lessen the potential for successful and productive aging.

The overlapping implications of aging, energy costs, and healthy living as they influence and are influenced by the built environment illuminate the array of partners to be called upon to collaborate. By no means complete, the list includes gerontologists, health care and public health professionals, nutritionists, and physical therapists alongside architects, landscape architects, urban designers, urban and rural land planners, geographers, and geographic information specialists as well as the general public. Linked in their goals, such collaborative teams would present a stronger coalition when arguing for change and would reduce the time between knowledge generation and its interpretation through practice into policies, programs, and built forms. Building such collaborations requires a form of communication that would allow knowledge to be shared across disciplines and professions, a democratization of the processes employed that includes the general public, and a practicality in the research conducted that is evidenced in the policies applied to and products left with the public. Bringing people together is one matter; employing a model that enables and empowers their interaction is another. Identifying such a model, given a rather limited time frame, requires a move beyond the discrete forms of multi- and interdisciplinary collaborations to a more transdisciplinary approach to research, education, and practical applications models that will allow communities, regions, and the country to prepare for the converging trends.

## COLLABORATION THAT REDUCES BARRIERS

Thinking on new or renewed models that aim to combine research, education, practice, and community involvement is driven by the fact that aging does not occur in isolation. The same understanding should be applied to developing ways that people can work to build a world that is supportive of healthy aging. The historical development of many academic and research disciplines and professions and the character of suburban communities, however, have become characterized by separation and homogeneity. The Association of American Geographers has 56 "specialty and affinity groups" (see http://www.aag.org/sg/sg_display.cfm); The American Society of Landscape Architects has 17 "professional practice network groups" (see http://www.asla.org/members/ppn/home.htm); and the Gerontologi-

cal Society of America has 5 "sections" (see http://www.geron.org/sections
.htm), while its more professional counterpart, the American Society on
Aging, has 8 "constituent groups" (see http://www.asaging.org/members/
brochure/page6custo.cfm).

Throughout modern history, increased specialization has played a
major role in distinguishing areas of knowledge (Baum, 1983; Howe,
1994; Larson, 1977), academic programs, professions and their particular
realms of practice (Blakely & Snyder, 1997; Duany et al., 2000; Jacobs,
1961; Putnam, 2000). The efforts of discipline-specific professionals and
their practitioner counterparts to gain public recognition and support have
led to a high level of autonomy within and between researchers, academics,
and practitioners as well as to a separation from the general public (Lawson,
1997). The subcategories of professional specialties further separate and
distance disciplines and professions:

> Theoretical distinction tends to overshadow practical talent *at the same
> time* that it tends to become more esoteric, granted to specialists by spe-
> cialists, and fully meaningful only in their circles. . . . Thus at the level of
> theoretical production, colleague sanction of individual talents becomes
> more legitimate *at the same time* that it becomes narrower and less accessi-
> ble to the general view. (Larson, 1977, p. 45)

To a great extent education remains hierarchical, with teachers separated
into departments and "with high degrees of role differentiation and specialization" (Garner, 1995, p. 3). The scope of professional practices has
become increasing refined and specialized in their values, philosophies, and
skills (Baum, 1983; Larson, 1977). Strict certification and licensing procedures restrict entry into specialized practices that link knowledge through
practice to the built environment and to the benefit of the general public.
Economic and social diversity are also increasingly absent in neighborhoods, which are distinguished by homogeneous land uses, narrowed socioeconomic populations, and a growing number of gated communities
patrolled by private security forces (Holz Kay, 1997; Duany et al., 2000).
The all-too-often physical and intellectual separation and segregation of
research areas, academic programs, professions, and land-use makeup of
communities is further reinforced by a time lag between the generation
of new knowledge and its interpretation into practice and application
(Riley et al., 1994):

> While the 20th century has experienced a revolution in human develop-
> ment and aging, there has been no comparable revolution in the role

structures of society to keep pace with the changes in the ways people grow up and grow old. The lag involves not only institutional and organizational arrangement, but also the many aspects of culture that, in addition to being internalized by people, are built into role expectations and societal mores and laws. (Riley & Riley, 1994, p. 16)

For myriad reasons, U.S. culture to a great extent has become characterized by separation. Researchers separate themselves along lines of specialization:

Combining research concepts and approaches is not sufficient, "there is a need for a different approach to social–natural science interaction" [Bennett, 1980], where instead of arguing for disciplinary ownership, there is an assimilation of concepts and approaches. (Rosenfield, 1992, p. 1345)

Even when researchers tout the "interdisciplinary" nature of their work, when attempting to build a sense of inclusiveness, often the participants are a sample of a relatively small community. The separation of university departments into separate buildings or floors within buildings often impedes faculty and student access to and exchange of knowledge (Keyfitz, 1991). Education more often than not is characterized by individual curricula housed in separate buildings. One example from the 1980s was seen along the mall at the University of Maryland. Housed in two adjacent buildings were the departments of Human Ecology and Natural Ecology. Like many professional associations, they had their own jargon, journals, and numerous professional subsections.

The individualizing of knowledge contributes to what can be argued to be incomplete knowledge. In turn, incomplete research, studies so well defined in an effort to do good research, can easily become counterproductive. Likewise, the work of practitioners who rely on incomplete or outdated knowledge can become equally counterproductive. Of particular importance is a need for greater collaboration along the progression from researcher to end user, and specifically, joining knowledge and practice among those who research, teach, and practice in the areas of health and the built environment. A quick review of existing approaches to collaboration provides a foundation from which to outline collaborative sharing.

## APPROACHES TO COLLABORATION

To recommend that new models of collaboration be developed is a bit misleading. Excellent multi- and interdisciplinary research, educational, and

professional practice models exist in various forms. Their existence, however, too often remains unknown to professionals and practitioners outside
their respective disciplines. The new, or newer, model calls into play a
heightened degree of collaboration, or social connectivity and interaction,
that respects diversity and difference; builds on the assets of people and
communities; and links end users, producers, educators, students, and
researchers. People's differences should be recognized as resources at the
same time that collaborators become more comfortable with those differences. A more generally accepted rather than discipline-specific language
plays a major role in building collaborations across disciplinary and professional boundaries as well as across the spectrum linking research with end
user. The ability of health care, public health, and environmental design
and land planning professionals to expedite changes that are supportive of
healthy aging calls for:

1. Research that responds to the needs recognized by the community of users
2. Timely interpretation of research findings into practical forms of
   application
3. Education of the next generation of professionals to be sensitive
   to and capable of contributing to the "greater-than-the-sum-of-
   the-parts" values derived from transdisciplinary collaboration.

Meeting these three goals calls for a smooth, coordinated flow of discussion
among researchers, educators, professionals, and community members.
This dialectic calls for a form of collaboration within and across the realms
of knowledge generation, interpretation, translation, application, and use
(e.g., inclusive of opportunities for feedback). The typical barriers to meeting the three goals include professional language and the time lag between
research and application, data interpretation into policy and strategic
plans, and community-based research agendas. These barriers need to be
dissolved, and the models that aim to do this include:

- Action research
- Multi-, inter-, and transdisciplinary research/practice
- Community-based research
- Future search techniques
- Asset building.

Each of these approaches draws strength from increasing degrees of interaction among more and more diverse participants. At the more passive end of

the spectrum, specialists within discipline-specific areas of knowledge, research, education, and practice work alone or to some extent pull in specialists from other subsets of the same or closely related areas of discipline or practice. In an effort to define boundaries and provide for a focused methodology, their view to the world remains narrowly defined. The outcomes are expected to trickle down to the practitioners:

> Reflecting the traditions of logical positivism, particularly in the natural sciences, far too many researchers still view issues of application to be outside their purview. They see their role limited to the generation of knowledge, with others picking up and utilizing this knowledge as they see fit. (Windley & Weisman, 2003, p. 337 [from Weisman, 1983])

Action research is defined as the "collaborative knowledge building that involves clients, practitioners, consultants, and researchers whose collective aim is to produce practical knowledge useful to the everyday lives of people" (Windley & Weisman, 2003, p. 341 [from Senge & Scharmer, 2001]). Wallerstein and Duran observed that 60 years after Kurt Lewin coined the term *action research*, "only relatively recently have researchers begun to question if the reality of participation reflects the ideal" (2003, p. 32). Questions have also arisen regarding who represents the community (Jewkes & Murcott, 1998), what the time limitations are for building a trusting relationship (Israel et al., 2001), and whether or not researchers' agendas are those of the community members (Fine, 1994; Huberman, 1991).

Action research can be considered an umbrella under which *multi-*, *inter-*, and *transdisciplinary research* approaches are located (Dyer, 2003; Rosenfield, 1992). In each approach, specialists with increasingly divergent knowledge and worldviews are brought together. Knowledge is shared in multi- and interdisciplinary approaches. The interdisciplinary approach, more than the multidisciplinary, encourages sharing whereby researchers and practitioners learn about each other's approaches and practices. Still, the outcomes to a great extent remain separate. A transdisciplinary team approach aims to produce new conceptual frameworks in which the sum total of the diverse areas of knowledge bases and skills is greater than the parts (Dyer, 2003). Outcomes are combined into more comprehensive products:

> Representatives of different disciplines are encouraged to transcend their separate conceptual, theoretical, and methodological orientations in order to develop a shared approach to the research, building on a common conceptual framework. (Rosenfield, 1992, p. 1351)

Through open, active involvement of community members, teams work to build new frameworks of understanding, and they work in combination with the end users. Together researchers, educators, practitioners, and end users share information, views, and values. Community-based research of this nature moves toward a level of mutual understanding and eventually combines outlooks and knowledge into newer, higher-level constructs. Research becomes situated in the larger context of daily life, and end users become vested in the processes that give rise to the products with which they come to live. Through a transdisciplinary approach, "a new type of research should emerge that enables the analysis of a particular problem to be located in the transdisciplinary conceptual framework, and . . . [r]ecommendations for action deriving from such an analysis . . . should be more readily implemented and more likely to achieve lasting results" (Rosenfield, 1992, p. 1352).

The call for a larger conceptual framework appears in different areas. Howard Frumkin calls for public health practitioners to rediscover the importance of place and to join in active, positive collaboration with a diversity of professions: "As health professionals, urban planners and architects, transportation engineers and real estate developers, environmental psychologists and geographers learn the vocabularies and perspectives of each other's fields and pursue active collaborations, . . . healthier, more sustainable human environments will be envisioned, planned, and built" (2003, p. 1454). Frumkin's call is echoed by Windley and Weisman (2003), who maintain that progress has been gained at the cost of social connectivity and who note that environmental gerontology, in focusing on the "individual as the primary unit of analysis," limits the ability to understand "the neighborhood and community scale" (2003, p. 355). They also call for a reduction in the time lag between gerontological research and the practical application of its findings to the built environment. Work in this direction would be helped by the sense of community research done by community psychologists (Glynn, 1981; McMillian, 1976; McMillian & Chavis, 1986).

Rosenfield stated that a "respect for the contributions that other disciplines can make to solving the common problem needs to be inculcated from the earliest stages of graduate training" (1992, p. 1354). The next generation of researchers and professional practitioners, those students who are currently involved in health care, public health, environmental design, and land planning programs, needs to be drawn under this banner of inclusion. People working with people, trusting each other, building a mutual understanding, and producing shared conceptual bases for action plans can be brought into the realm of theory, education, and practice in a way that works to reduce structural lag.

Improved collaboration is the key to reducing the time lag between needs recognition, research aimed at quantifying and qualifying needs, the translation of the research data into policies and strategies, and the interpretation of policies and strategies into built form and social programs that sustain and are sustained by the built outcomes (Schneekloth, 1987; Seidel, 1985; Windley & Weisman, 2003). Given the immediacy of the aging, energy, and health trends, research cannot continue to occur apart from the recipients of the results, nor can professional practitioners continue to design programs and communities based on outdated beliefs and information. Windley and Weisman describe the problem as being "rooted in institutionalized separation of research and practice" and propose "some variant of action research" (2003, p. 335). They refer to their strategy for linking research and practice as *research utilization,* or minimizing the delay between researchers generating new knowledge and its communication to professional practitioners and use by potential end users (Sommer, 1997).

Windley and Weisman frequently note the need for an action research approach that includes the end users and that is a part of the educational process of current and future land planners and architectural designers and gerontologists. Such an approach can be used to build more complete and interactive collaborations and should involve the triad of multi-, inter-, and transdisciplinary research and practice. Table 10.1 provides a brief overview of the multi-, inter-, and transdisciplinary triad. Simply, there is a shift from knowledge and skills remaining discrete within specific disciplines (multidisciplinary) to a sharing and building of a more holistic conceptual framework and outcome (transdisciplinary). In the multidisciplinary approach, discipline-specific participation and contributions remain distinct and are often seen as separate chapters in a book or a report. Interdisciplinary collaboration involves more shared interaction among participants. Although programming decisions are made by the group, assessment and implementation typically remain discipline-specific (McCormick & Goldman, 1979). The transdisciplinary approach "can provide for a more comprehensive organizing construct" (Rosenfield, 1992, p. 1351). The difficulty faced by participants is in the release of "some functions of one's primary discipline [or viewpoint] to other team members" (Orelove, 1995, p. 33). Another stumbling block in "moving beyond multidisciplinary [to transdisciplinary] research requires supportive academic institutions, sufficient funding, and satisfying career opportunities" (Rosenfield, 1992, p. 1355). In that change is often regrettably slow, especially in academia, one solution has been to "just do it." A common-ground approach has been used that addresses similar goals as a means to bring diverse groups of professionals, students, and community people together. Discussion in such gatherings often begins with participants questioning the potential of success. However, the workshops and design studios at Washington State University Spokane's Interdisciplinary Design Institute have shown that once people start talking, hesitation quickly turns to involvement.

Since 2002, workshops around the United States and interdisciplinary design studios at Washington State University's Interdisciplinary Design Institute in Spokane have specifically aimed to build cross-disciplinary collaborations. Architecture, landscape architecture, interior design, and urban planning professionals and students were brought together with their nursing, public health, gerontology, nutrition, and physiology counterparts. In each event the goals were to (1) introduce people to the ease with which they can work together; (2) expand understanding that can be realized through shared knowledge and experience; (3) see ways to improve health delivery systems, built environments, and the policies that drive the two; and (4) generate ideas as to how the growing baby boom population might be employed to the benefit of the greater community. Workshops and design studios typically began with a brief presentation on the common goals of public health, safety, and welfare among the various professional and academic programs. Then, in discipline- or profession-specific groups, the participants were asked to define such terms as *access*, *available*, and *environment*. Participants in interdisciplinary teams usually found that their definitions were divided between spatial and built-environment descriptions as well as between public health and health care issues and delivery systems. Through cross-disciplinary discussions and conceptual diagrams of the ideas presented, participants began to realize certain benefits to seeing the world through the others' lenses. Designers became more familiar with a defined cohort and began to realize their own outdated and often "anecdotal" understanding of older adults and aging. Health-oriented participants became increasingly sensitive to the spatial aspects of life in a community, such as proximity to family, friends, and food; residential density and diversity; available modes of travel; and time spent traveling to fulfill daily needs.

After six years of workshops, talks, and design studios that involved students, professionals, and Spokane's neighborhood residents, people's long-standing beliefs and habits are showing signs of opening up to shared views and a willingness to move from a multidisciplinary to a transdisciplinary approach to collaboration. Researchers are beginning to meet with public health practitioners and neighborhood activists in an effort to

**Table 10.1.** Overview of multidisciplinary, interdisciplinary, and transdisciplinary approaches to research

| Approach | Form of Collaboration | Team Composition | Organizational Structure | Outcomes |
|---|---|---|---|---|
| **Multidisciplinary** ". . . most common approach to collaborative research." (Rosenfield, 1992, 1351). | • Single individual, discipline-specific gatekeeper decides which disciplines participate.<br>• Shared vs. collaborative communication.<br>• Independent decision making vs. coordination of information (Dyer, 2003).<br>• Concepts and perspectives remain discipline specific. | • Team composition determined by self-selected team leader.<br>• Members remain independent and discipline specific.<br>• Work independently. | • Independent and separate assessments, planning, and provision of services with little coordination.<br>• Independent rather than coordinated decision making (Dyer, 2003).<br>• Set unique, discipline-specific goals.<br>• Blending of outcomes takes form of sequential involvement. | • Submission of separately prepared findings and recommendations.<br>• Usually published as separate chapters of report.<br>• Discipline-specific goals, work within discipline-specific parameters to achieve goals independently.<br>• Method and service plan communicated to rest of group. |

"Not usually conceptually pathbreaking, but has shed light on different aspects of a particular problem, leading to immediate, but possibly short-lived solutions." (Rosenfield, 1992, p. 1351).

| Approach | Form of Collaboration | Team Composition | Organizational Structure | Outcomes |
|---|---|---|---|---|
| **Interdisciplinary** Require[s] organizational infrastructure that promotes interdependence, self-management, individual responsibility to group performance, and student outcomes (Dyer, 2003, p. 186). | • Collaborative vs. shared communication.<br>• Collaboratively developed team goals and service plan.<br>• "Team members are involved in problem solving beyond the confines of their disciplines." (Dyer, 2003, p. 186). | • Team composition determined by perceived needs of target group.<br>• Knowledge and skill shared but individuals remain anchored in own discipline, office, or organization. | • Collaboratively establish team goals and service plan.<br>• Infrastructure promotes inter-dependent work, self-management with responsibility to team's performance and outcomes.<br>• Coordinated communication between and within team and target group. | • Determined by perceived needs with involvement of the target group.<br>• Combined description of procedures to be carried out and descriptors of results sought.<br>• Interpretation of service plan remains each discipline's representative. |

"Knowledge usually remains "reported in a partial, discipline-by-discipline sequence. These serious projects are contributing new knowledge, but it is knowledge partitioned off from other relevant elements. It is only by removing the partitions which form the disciplinary boundaries . . . that more profound insights will [come] to underpin analyses and interpretation of findings, and importantly, recommendation for actions by individuals." Rosenfield, 1992, p. 1351).

| **Transdisciplinary**<br>"A devaluing of turf issues and a trusting relationship among team members is essential for successful group dynamics." (Dyer, 2003, p. 187).<br><br>". . . promotes efficiency in the delivery of educational or health care services." (Dyer, 2003, pp. 186–187). | • Leader selected relative to dominant issues.<br>• Frequent collaborative communication.<br>• Cross-disciplinary appreciation for others' knowledge and views.<br>• Transcends separate conceptual, theoretical, and methodological orientations to build a common conceptual framework.<br>• Transdisciplinary nature of more holistic knowledge, skills, and outcomes carried through to practical application.<br>• End users involved in process, promoting and understanding of the whole person. | • Ongoing sharing of knowledge, skills, and responsibilities across traditional disciplinary boundaries in problem definition, assessment, and service planning. | • Requires supportive institutional structure that overcomes turf boundaries and contributes to new career paths.<br>• Builds trusting relationship regarding others' abilities and commitment to process and products.<br>• Members' information communicated through leader.<br>• Individuals competent, professional, and secure enough to believe in process and give up habitual roles and skills for new ones. | • Frequent communication leads to efficient promotion and sharing of outcomes in form of services.<br>• Definitions and analyses of research problem and development of new approaches more appropriate to "historical and present-day reality" in which the problem is situated. (Rosenfield, 1992, p. 1351)<br>• ". . . there is an intergenerational transfer of this experience through extensive involvement of students." (Rosenfield, 1992, p. 1351) |
|---|---|---|---|---|

Go beyond target population or issue to also provide recommendations for institutional and social compositional modifications that are "more readily implemented and more likely to achieve lasting results."

identify research programs that contribute to practical outcomes. City planners are asking how zoning and comprehensive city and county plans can better support healthy aging and active living. Also, the business community is beginning to recognize that "retirement industry" can mean so much more than those businesses that sell goods and services to older people. *Retirement industry* can mean seeing older Americans as a human resource that can be employed in building the social and economic vitality of a community.

Literature and case studies on multi-, inter-, and transdisciplinary approaches typically describe or call for the involvement of community members. Still, their involvement often appears to be more that of a recipient of the outcomes. In efforts to minimize structural lag through inclusion, the *future search* and *asset building* approaches give greater emphasis to the end users' involvement in the problem-solving processes and products. Future search, however, is more a process-management technique, while asset building identifies the capacities, skills, and strengths everyone can bring to an endeavor. In asset building, "the key to neighborhood regeneration . . . is to locate all the available local assets, to begin connecting them with one another in ways that multiply their power and effectiveness, and to begin harnessing those local institutions that are not available for local development purposes" (Kretzmann & McKnight, 1993, p. 5). A major characteristic is "moving from experts solving problems for people toward everybody, experts included, and improving whole systems" (Weisbord, 1992, p. xi). Weisbord and others see this as a means of building stronger communities. If the populations of researchers, academics, students, practitioners, and local residents are seen as communities that make up a larger population, then the value of "building stronger communities" to initiate collaboration across the discipline–end-user spectrum becomes all the more apparent.

Kretzmann's call for serious community builders "to return to basics, to the communities themselves to rediscover and mobilize the strengths, capabilities, and assets within those communities" (National Housing Institute, 2006) is a call for (1) a practical approach to building a community; (2) a closer integration of diverse kinds of knowledge and skills; and (3) a positive, constructive approach, rather than seeing the end users as deficient and needy. Seeing individuals (young and old, able and disabled) as well as associations and institutions as resources and energy is critical to knowing what resources exist and where they are when the goal is to mobilize a neighborhood, community, or cohort. For these reasons, asset building starts with mapping a group's personal and institutional resources. The mapping process recognizes local resources, garners investment, and sees people and institutions as interdependent. Again, the aim is a practicality of interaction, not of separation; an ongoing involvement, not cursory participation; and a product that, in its developmental process, builds cohesion that continues beyond the end of the initial project's time frame. The multiplying of strengths of people and institutions boosts their energy and potential. By building trust and a positive form of sharing, the collaborators' relationships work to reverse the inertia of the distinctiveness and separation seen in many professions, academic programs, research specialties, and community neighborhoods.

## HOW WE GOT HERE

Each of the five approaches to collaboration discussed in this chapter aims to minimize the separation of researchers, academics and their students, practitioners, and the end users. Generally, the goal of the Washington State University workshops and design studios has been to integrate the capabilities, skills, and resources of each group in ways that foster and sustain their interaction. This is the foundation and the function of social capital building, the outcomes of which "are most powerful when embedded in a dense network of reciprocal social relations" (Putnam, 2000, p. 19). "The trust, mutual understanding, and shared values and behaviors that bind the members of human networks and communities and make cooperative action possible" (Cohen & Prusak, 2001, p. 4) are recognized by the World Bank "as the glue that holds them together" (World Bank, 1999).

That glue is the essential quality of people socializing in ways that build trust and understanding across gender, age, and economic lines as well as across professional and disciplinary specialties. The social bonding that comes from knowing each other cements the potential energy in people who are willing and capable of working together, sharing leadership when appropriate, and conversing in a manner that validates the other as an equally important asset and contributor to a holistic approach to research, teaching, practice, implementation, and use. While there are numerous examples of social bonding in the workshops and studios, two events help to illustrate the potentials embedded in seemingly diverse professional groups. As they joined architecture and landscape architecture students in a design studio, nursing students wondered, "What are we doing here?" What both groups of students knew about Spokane's elderly residents had been acquired through personal, nontechnical narrative encounters. The nursing students' practicum had required interviewing clients in their homes. The design students had interviewed people on the sidewalks and in shops in the community. Within minutes of coming together, both groups of students realized that they had complementary understandings of the elderly population's feelings regarding their surrounding environments. The students' hesitation was quickly dispelled by talking about common issues related to their respective viewpoints, which contributed to their recognition of shared understandings.

The second event occurred at the conclusion of a four-hour workshop with a group of public health employees in Boston. Even though the public health practitioners felt that "We don't know how to talk to architects and urban planners," that had not stopped them from identifying land use issues that are critical to healthy aging and active living. They, along with other workshop, seminar, and studio project participants, brought to light a less exclusionary form of collaborative interaction that retains the benefits of the collaborative approaches noted above. Even with successful collaborative, cross-disciplinary meetings, however, there are still the issues of structural lag (Riley et al., 1994), institutional and financial obstacles (Rosenfield, 1992), and discipline-specific turf boundaries (Dyer, 2003) to be overcome. Despite this, experience has shown that the more common the shared language, the less discipline- and profession-specific the languages used, and the greater the head start to dissolving barriers. Most people have experienced social capital building in the grocery store, at the water cooler, along a sidewalk, and in a coffee shop. The practice of community building identified with social capital is just as readily accessible and employable across widely diverse groups of people.

The process by which people invest themselves in social capital building relies on four expectations: Jurgen Habermas's four validity claims as they are guided by his four rules of discourse (Habermas,1970a; 1970b; 1979; 1981). Interestingly enough, people who want a strong and vibrant community already hold those expectations and practice the rules of discourse. Even when coming from different professional backgrounds, workshop and studio participants expect to be able to *comprehend* each other. When they speak, they do so with the expectation that they will be listened to and understood. Participants also expect that what is discussed is *appropriate* to the situation at hand. If individuals did not expect this, then much of the knowledge, skills, and views would be meaningless. People's third expectation is that the other speaks the *truth*; that what a person expresses is not a lie or is not being said to mislead. The fourth expectation is that people be *sincere* in what they say and what they aim to accomplish.

Without this expectation, "we'd never trust anyone we listened to, or even trust that we could check with someone else to see what was really meant" (Forester, 1985, p. 209).

Violation of these presupposed validity claims contributes to a social environment characterized by confusion, mistrust, anger, disbelief, and a lack of cooperation. A social environment that builds trust and cooperation endeavors to at least arrive at an agreement, if not a consensus. However, even when people express themselves in ways that are comprehensible and that are truthful, appropriate, and sincere, there is often still the need for clarification. Habermas's rules of discourse, which many of us regularly employ, help to clarify discussions among individuals and can be used as a means to arrive at a level of mutual understanding. His four rules assume that:

1. "No speaker ought to be hindered by compulsion . . . all are provided a reciprocal openness [to express] their true intentions and motives and an equal chance to express their attitudes, wishes, and needs" (White, 1988, p. 56).

2. Those involved may freely introduce any proposal into the discourse, with the assurance that the dialogue will continue until each participant agrees they both understand, ideally through reiteration.

3. Each participant may question any validity claim, and (a) consider a question settled when a satisfactory answer has been provided (the question is not dropped prior to that), or (b) let an assertion drop when it turns out to be false.

4. Each person will follow his or her own advice should he or she find him- or herself in the same situation as the listener (McCarthy, 1978).

Practiced to close the gap between what some know and what others wish to learn, "the rules here are not restrictions; they enable us to know what one another means" (Forester, 1985, p. 208). As is often found when neighborhood residents, city leaders and staff, academics, and students come together, to mutually understand what is being discussed does not necessitate agreement regarding the knowledge being applied, the proposed action, or the appropriateness of the conclusion. People can agree to disagree and still strive for mutual understanding. In so doing, the resultant form of interaction contributes to an explicit expression of viewpoints between two or more people who may then work toward consensus, or a clarification of the realm of knowledge being applied to solving a problem and an eventual agreement on the appropriate cognitive and behavioral skills to be exercised. In this way structural lag is reduced between research, implementation, and use for the benefit of the public.

Habermas's thinking speaks to how people interact and how their interactions contribute to and are an outgrowth of their larger communities. He also speaks to the dynamics that enable people to draw together diverse backgrounds as well as people's sincere wish to draw on each other's assets in the building of stronger social networks that contribute to stronger communities. Habermas's thinking is echoed in Robert Putnam's work on social capital. The common belief in the interplay of the built environment and aging, the built environment and health, and the built environment and energy is what prompts neighborhood people and academics in environmental design, city- and county-elected officials, and gerontology and health care professionals to come together. When brought together through workshops and design studio projects, participants quickly realize, despite obvious differences, that they are able to contribute their knowledge and experiences to issues related to the built environment. When participants apply Habermas's rules of interaction, they "resolve collective problems more easily"; build trust through "repeated interactions" that enable them to "advance smoothly"; interact through questions that widen their awareness of "the many ways in which [their] fates are linked"; and build networks "that serve as conduits for the flow of helpful information that facilitates achieving [their] goals" (Putnam, 2000, pp. 288–290). The latter point is important to workshop and design studio outcomes becoming realities.

Social energy binds participants as they realize that others are working toward similar goals. The sharing of knowledge through seemingly common language is the true value of workshops and design studio projects. By beginning to build the social networks that Putnam sees as breaking down in America, participants are also beginning to work toward developing more holistic solutions to aging in healthy built environments. What must also be noted is that the use of workshops and design studios as a means to build the social capital of a community is strengthened by the subsequent application of asset building and a transdisciplinary approach to moving the workshop's results in three directions. With diverse social groups formed, ideas can be contributed to develop research programs based up a community's needs and wishes. The group's ideas can be reformulated into curricula that can be used to educate the next generation of designers and health care professionals. And in continuing to work together, the breadth of the groups' expertise becomes a stronger body when speaking—as a group—to city and county councils, elected officials, and their staffs.

Over the years that the workshops, seminars, discussions, and design studio projects were conducted, two outcomes helped to clarify efforts to orchestrate collaborative activities. The first outcome was reflected in many of the participants as they observed and realized the diversity of backgrounds in the room. Within minutes of sharing their respective approaches to working with older populations, participants usually became involved in and comfortable with sharing what they knew about older people's ability to participate in neighborhood life. The second outcome was observed in building an understanding of forms of collaboration that reduced the time lag between knowledge generation and its practical application. The same difficulties that tended to separate disciplines were experienced. Differences in words used and how they are defined were also seen. Words such as *accessible*, *available*, and even *environment* were common across the various professions. For this reason, after personal introductions the workshops began with participants sharing their definitions of commonly used words. By sharing each other's definitions and applications of common concepts, as applied through practice, workshop participants came to realize the value of collaborating as their ability (and willingness) to converse became easier. Once language became a shared medium, it was key to building a more diverse community of people with diverse backgrounds and skills but with similar goals.

## CONCLUSION

Time is of the essence. Considering the immediacy of the trends in aging, health, and energy, knowledge regarding how to address these challenges must rapidly be shared, interpreted, and put to use. From 2005 to 2008, oil prices per barrel almost tripled, thousands of older adults reached retirement age, and life expectancy declined for the first time in almost 100 years (Ezzati et al., 2008).

In order to address successfully the challenges associated with healthy aging, active living, and energy conservation as well as to reduce the time it takes to design research that results in products that are responsive to and immediately useful for end users, transdisciplinary collaboration that is grounded in social capital building is needed. Health care, medical, and built environment professionals will need to work together to support the successful and productive aging of the baby boomer cohort. Looking ahead over the next 30 years, even broader transdisciplinary collaborative efforts will be necessary to address changes in the greater global context that will impact successful aging. The converging trends of climate change, water scarcity, energy depletion, and obesity are modifying the ways people carry out their daily lives as well as the ability of businesses to meet the needs of their customers. If successful aging is interrelated with active living communities, readily available nutritious foods, and high levels of social connectivity, how will these necessities be met when a barrel of oil costs $200, $300, or more? What will active living communities look like when people are more dependent on locally produced foods? How will a multigenerational blend of people solve many work force needs when so many older Americans live in homogeneous, automobile-dependent suburban communities? These are the questions that require diverse groups of professionals to come together to integrate research and practices that can be readily interpreted into practical outcomes and uses.

## REFERENCES

Amick, B., Levine, S., Tarlov, A., & Walsh, D. (Eds.). (1995). *Society and health.* New York: Oxford University Press.

Araya, R., Dunstan, F., Playle, R., Thomas, H., Palmer, S., & Lewis, G. (2006). Perceptions of social capital and the built environment and mental health. *Social Science and Medicine, 62*, 3072–3083.

Bass, S., Caro, F., & Chen, Y. (Eds.). (1993). *Achieving a productive aging society.* Newport, CT: Auburn House.

Baum, H. (1983). *Planners and public expectations.* Cambridge, MA: Schenkman.

Beem, C. (1999). *The necessity of politics: Reclaiming American public life.* Chicago: University of Chicago Press.

Bennett, J. (1980). Social and interdisciplinary sciences in U.S. MAB: Conceptual and theoretical aspects. In E. Zuke (Ed.), *Social sciences, interdsiciplinary research, and the man and the biosphere (MAB) program.* Washington, DC: U.S. Department of State.

Blakely, F., & Snyder, M. (1997). *Fortress America: Gated communities in the United States.* Washington, DC: Brookings Institution.

Cannuscio, C., Block, J., & Kawachi, I. (2003). Social capital and successful aging: The role of senior housing. *Annals of Internal Medicine, 139*(5), 395–399.

Cohen, D., & Prusak, L. (2001). *In good company: How social capital makes organizations work.* Boston: Harvard Business School Press.

Coleman, J. C. (1988). Social capital in the creation of human capital. *American Journal of Sociology, 94*, S95–S120.

Dannenberg, A., Jackson, R., Frumkin, H., Scheiber, R., Pratt, M., Kochtitzky, C., & Tilson, H. (2003). The impact of community design and land-use choices on public health: A scientific research agenda. *American Journal of Public Health, 93*(9), 1500–1508.

Duany, A., Plater-Zyberk, E., and Speck, J. (2000). *Suburban nation: The rise of sprawl and the decline of the American dream.* New York: North Point.

Dyer, J. (2003). Multidisciplinary, interdisciplinary, and transdisciplinary educational models and nursing education. *Nursing Education Perspectives, 24*(4), 186–188.

Ewing, R., Schmid, T., Killingsworth, R., Zlot, A., & Raudenbush, S. (2003). Relationship between urban sprawl and physical activity, obesity, and morbidity. *American Journal of Health Promotion, 18*(10), 47–57.

Fine, M. (1994). Working the hyphens. In N. K. Denzin & Y. S. Lincoln (Eds.), *Handbook of Qualitative Research* (2nd ed., pp. 107–132). Thousand Oaks, CA: Sage.

Forester, J. (Ed.). (1985). *Critical theory and public life.* Cambridge, MA: MIT Press.

Frank, L., Engelke, P., & Schmidt, T. (2003). *Health and community design: The impact of the built environment on physical activity.* Washington, DC: Island Press.

Freedman, M. (1999). *Prime time: How baby boomers will revolutionize retirement and transform the world.* New York: Public Affairs.

Frumkin, H. (2003). Healthy places: Exploring the evidence. *American Journal of Public Health, 93*(9), 1451–1455.

Frumkin, H., Frank, L., & Jackson, R. (2004). *Urban sprawl and public health: Designing, planning, and building for healthy communities.* Washington, DC: Island Press.

Garner, H. (1995). *Teamwork models and experience in education.* Boston: Allyn & Bacon.

Glaeser, E., Liabson, D., Scheinkman, J., & Soutter, C. (2003). Measuring trust. *Quarterly Journal of Economics, 115*(3), 811–846.

Glynn, T. (1981). Psychological sense of community: Measurement and application. *Journal of Human Resources, 34*(7), 789–818.

Habermas, J. (1970a). On systematically distorted communication. *Inquiry, 13,* 205–218.

Habermas, J. (1970b). Toward a theory of communicative competence. *Inquiry, 13,* 360–375.

Habermas, J. (1979). *Communication and the evolution of society* (T. McCarthy, Trans.). Boston: Beacon.

Habermas, J. (1981). *The theory of communicative action: Reason and the rationalization of society* (Vol. 1) (T. McCarthy, Trans.). Boston: Beacon.

Heinberg, R. (2005). *The party's over: Oil, war, and the fate of industrial societies.* Gabriola Island, British Columbia: New Society.

Howe, E. (1994). *Acting on ethics in city planning.* New Brunswick, NJ: Center for Urban Policy Research.

Huberman, M. (1991). Linkage between researchers and practitioners: A qualitative study. *American Educational Research Journal, 27*, 363–391.

Hughes, S., Williams, B., Molina, L., Bayles, C., Bryant, L., Harris, J., Hunter, R., Ivey, S., & Watkins, K. (2005). Characteristics of physical activity programs for older adults: Results of a multisite survey. *The Gerontologist, 45*(5), 667–675.

Israel, B., Lichtenstein, R., Lantz, P., & McGranaghan, R. (2001). The Detroit Community-Academic Urban Research Center: Development, implementation, and evaluation. *Journal of Public Health Management and Practice, 7*(5), 1–19.

Jackson, R. (2003, August 29). Suburbia USA: Fat of the land? Report links sprawl, weight gain. *Washington Post*, p. A03.

Jackson, R., & Kochtitzky, C. (2006). *Creating a healthy environment: The impact of the built environment on public health.* Washington, DC: Sprawl Watch Clearinghouse, Monograph Series. Available at http://www.cdc.gov/healthyplaces/ articles/Creating%20A%20Healthy%20Environment.pdf.

Jacobs, J. (1961). *The death and life of great American cities.* New York: Vintage.

Jewkes, R., & Murcott, A. (1998). Community representatives: Representing the "community"? *Social Science Medicine, 46*(7), 843–858.

Kawachi, I., & Berkman, L. (Eds.). (2003). *Neighborhoods and health.* New York: Oxford University Press.

Kemmis, D. (1995). *The good city and the good life: Renewing the sense of community.* New York: Houghton Mifflin.

Keyfitz, N. (1991). Interdisciplinary analysis in four fields. *Options* (June), 4–11.

Kretzmann, J. P., & McKnight, J. L. (1993). *Building communities from the inside out: A path toward finding and mobilizing a community's assets.* Evanston, IL: Center for Urban Affairs and Policy Research, Northwestern University.

Kunstler, J. (2005). *The long emergency: Surviving the converging catastrophes of the twenty-first century.* New York: Atlantic Monthly.

Larson, M. (1977). *The rise of professionalism: A sociological analysis.* Berkeley: University of California Press.

Lipsey, M. (2005). The challenges of interpreting research for use by practitioners. *American Journal of Preventative Medicine, 28*(2S1), 1–3.

Lynch, K. (1960). *The image of the city.* Cambridge, MA: MIT Press.

McCarthy, T. (1978). *Critical theory of Jurgen Habermas.* Cambridge, MA: MIT Press.

McCormick, L., & Goldman, R. (1979). The transdisciplinary model: Implications for service delivery and personnel preparation for the severely and profoundly handicapped. *AAESPH Review, 4*(2), 152–161.

McLaughlin, C., & Beveridge, C. (Eds.). (1977). *The papers of Frederick Law Olmsted: The formative years, 1822–1852 (Vol. 1).* Baltimore: Johns Hopkins University Press.

McMillian, D. (1976). Sense of community: An attempt at definition. Unpublished manuscript. Nashville, TN: George Peabody College for Teachers.

McMillian, D., & Chavis, D. (1986). Sense of community: A definition and theory. *Journal of Community Psychology, 14*, 6–23.

Minkler, M., & Wallerstein, N. (2003). *Community-based participatory research for health*. San Francisco: Jossey-Bass.

Morrow-Howell, N., Hinterlong, J., & Sherrand, M. (Eds.). (2001). *Productive aging: Concepts and challenges*. Baltimore: Johns Hopkins University Press.

National Housing Institute. (2006). Building communities from the inside out. Retrieved August 2006, from http://www.nhi.org/online/issues/83/buildcomm.html.

Orelove, F. (1995). The transdisciplinary model in education programs for students with severe disabilities. In H. Garner (Ed.), *Teamwork models and experiences in education*. Boston: Allyn & Bacon.

Putnam, R. (2000). *Bowling alone: The collapse and revival of American community*. New York: Simon & Schuster.

Reardon, K. (2003). Ceola's vision, our blessing: The story of an evolving community-university partnership in East St. Louis, Illinois. In B. Eckstein & J. Throgmorton (Eds.), *Story and sustainability: Planning, practice, and possibility for American cities*. Cambridge, MA: MIT Press.

Reason, P., & Bradbury, H. (2001). Inquiry and participation in search of a world worthy of human aspiration. In P. Reason and H. Bradbury (Eds.), *Handbook of action research: Participative inquiry and practice* (pp. 1–14). London: Sage.

Riley, M., Kahn, R., & Foner, A. (1994). *Age and structural lag: Society's failure to provide meaningful opportunities in work, family, and leisure*. New York: Wiley.

Riley, M., & Riley, J. (1994). Structural lag: Past and future. In M. Riley, R. Kahn, & A. Foner (Eds.), *Age and structural lag: Society's failure to provide meaningful opportunities in work, family, and leisure* (pp. 15–36). New York: Wiley.

Rosenfield, P. L. (1992). The potential of transdisciplinary research for sustaining and extending linkages between the health and social sciences. *Social Science and Medicine, 35*, 1343–1357.

Rowe, J., & Kahn, R. (1998). *Successful aging*. New York: Dell.

Rowles, G. (1978). *Prisoners of space? Exploring the geographical experience of older people*. Boulder, CO: Westview.

Rybczynski, W. (1999). *A Clearing in the distance: Frederick Law Olmsted and America in the 19th century*. New York: Scribner.

Schneekloth, L. (1987). Advances in practice in environment, behavior, and design. In E. Zube & G. Moore (Eds.), *Advances in environment, behavior, and design* (Vol. 1) (pp. 307–334). New York: Plenum.

Schneekloth, L., & Shibley, R. (1995). *Placemaking: The art and practice of building communities*. New York: Wiley.

Schon, D. (1983). *The reflective practitioner: How professionals think in action*. New York: Basic Books.

Seidel, A. (1985). What is success in environment and behavior research utilization? *Environment and Behavior, 17*(1), 47–70.

Shuman, M. (2000). *Going local: Creating self-reliant communities in a global age*. New York: Routledge.

Simonds, J. (1984). *Landscape architecture*. New York: McGraw-Hill.

Sommer, R. (1997). Utilization issues in environment–behavior research. In G. Moore and R. Marans (Eds.), *Advances in environment, behavior, and design: Toward the integration of theory, methods, research, and utilization* (Vol. 4) (pp. 347–368). New York: Plenum.

Thompson, J., & Goldin, G. (1975). *The hospital: A social and architectural history.* Forge Village, MA: Murry Printing.

Transportation Research Board. (2005). Does the built environment influence physical activity? *Transportation Research Board Special Report 282.*

Wahl, H.-W., Scheidt, R., & Windley, P. (Eds.). (2003). Aging in context: Socio-physical environments. *Annual Review of Gerontology and Geriatrics, 23.*

Wallerstein, N., & Duran, B. (2003). The conceptual, historical, and practice roots of community-based participatory research and related participatory traditions. In M. Minkler & N. Wallerstein (Eds.), *Community-based participatory research in health* (pp. 27–52). San Francisco: Jossey-Bass.

Weisbord, M. (1992). *Discovering common ground.* San Francisco: Berrett-Koehler.

White, S. K. (1988). *The recent work of Jürgen Habermas.* Cambridge, UK: Cambridge University Press.

Windley, P., & Weisman, G. (2003). Environmental gerontology research and practice: The challenge of application. *Annual Review of Gerontology and Geriatrics, 23,* 334–365.

World Bank. (1999). What is social capital? Retrieved August 2007, from http://povlibrary.worldbank.org/library/view/12049/.

Yancy, W., Olsen, M., Westman, E., Bosworth, H., & Edelman, D. (2002). Relationship between obesity and health-related quality of life in men. *Obesity Research, 10*(10), 1057–1064.

Zimmerman, E. (2006). For lack of teachers, students are turned away from nursing. Retrieved January 2008, from http://www.nytimes.com/2006/08/13/jobs/13jmar.html?ex=1313121600&en=2c9b18fc8bb3b1db&ei=5088&partner=rssnyt&emc=rss.

# INDEX